MW00893368

This book is dedicated to my children, James and Amelia,

and to my Lord and Savior, Christ Jesus.

"Don't let anyone think less of you because you are young. Be an

example to all believers in what you say, in the way you live, in your

love, your faith, and your purity." 1 Timothy 4:12

Scripture quotations are taken from the *Holy Bible*, New Living Translation, copyright © 1996, 2004, 2007 by Tyndale House Foundation. Used by permission of Tyndale House Publishers, Inc., Carol Stream, Illinois 60188. All rights reserved.

Many thanks to my wife, Indra Edmonds for her continuous encouragement in the writing of this book, and to my proof reader, Cyndi Buck!

The Adventures of Pete and Rob!

A Year in the Life of Two Boys and an Eternal God

By

Thomas Lee Edmonds

Table of Contents

Introduction

Introduction

You are about to embark on an amazing adventure!

The story I'm about to tell you is an adventure tale about two boys and their encounters with the eternal, living God of the universe over the course of a year. So let's get started! Please allow me to introduce you to the main characters of this story:

Peter Johnson is ten years old. Pete is a Christian, and he does well in school. He seems to have the perfect life and the perfect family, but not everything is as perfect as it seems! One *huge* problem that Pete has been facing lately is that, despite the fact he knows his Bible well and faithfully attends Church each Sunday, Pete has been ignoring God's presence and direction in his life. As a result, he has gradually become a miserable, cranky Christian who has difficulty seeing how his present action of slighting God's company is negatively influencing his thoughts and actions.

Robert T. McGwyn is eleven years old. Unlike Pete, Rob does not practice following any religion at all; he knows very little about God. He lives alone with his mother in one side of a rundown duplex.

He has never seen his father. Rob tends to be a loner and is constantly getting into trouble in and out of school due to such actions as fighting, stealing, and cheating among many other devious activities. The only close friend Rob seems to have at all is Pete. Despite his social drawbacks, Rob's greatest goal in life is to somehow stop being a 'loser' and, instead, become a very popular and famous person.

God, unlike the boys (and the rest of us human types for that matter), is eternal and is therefore everywhere at every time. God has a wonderful family in heaven and wants both Pete and Rob to be part of it in spite of their current troubles. Through various adventures, such as the investigation of a "haunted" house, a daring, deep woods rescue during a camping trip, and a snowball fight involving yellow snow (That's right - frozen dog pee!), God consistently shows up in the lives of Pete and Rob in order to accomplish his goal within a year's time. If you are interested in finding out how these remarkable — and sometimes odd — situations bring Pete and Rob closer to God and each other, then keep reading! I can't wait to tell you the whole story!

*　　　　　*　　　　　*

Some years ago, I was a club leader for our church's Wednesday night boys' club. I found it very difficult at that time to find Bible-based short stories for boys in the nine to thirteen year age range which our group of boys would find interesting, challenging and relevant to their own lives. So I decided to write a collection of my own short stories for our boys' club designed to help those kids gain a better understanding about the basic concepts of the Christian faith in an entertaining format in which they could easily relate. The result was this book.

The greatest benefit that this book will offer you as a young reader, parent, or Christian educator will be to provide entertaining material intended to strengthen your understanding about what it means to be a true follower of Jesus Christ, and demonstrate how the basic Christian principles discussed in each chapter may be applied to your own, real-life adventures in today's world. Additionally, you will find a reference and questions section at the end of each chapter. The Bible verse references relate to the subject matter of that chapter, and many of the questions that are presented at the end of each chapter are self-reflective; they are intended to start conversations between adults and kids regarding the main points in the story, and how they may relate to their own lives.

As I read these stories during club night, my group of rowdy, high energy boys would settle down quickly and focus solely on the stories without making a sound — even for stories that could take up to fifteen minutes to read! At the end of each story, I usually found that many of them had insightful questions and observations that they wanted to discuss relating to what they just heard. The boys were usually disappointed when I didn't have a "Pete and Rob" story ready to read to them during club nights. To this day, these former boys — now young men — still fondly remember the Pete and Rob adventures. Recently, I have been reading these stories to my Sunday school class of both boys and girls, and I have discovered that the girls enjoy these stories just as much as the boys!

The collection of stories presented in this book has proven to nicely fit the educational and entertainment needs for the various groups of tweenagers I have been teaching over the years, and I am hopeful that they will prove to be helpful, pertinent and enjoyable for you today. Thank you for reading this book. Enjoy!

In Christ's love,

Thomas Lee Edmonds

Chapter 1

Ever have the Feeling you're being Watched?

"Ever have the feeling you're being watched?"

Peter Johnson (or "Pete" as most people called him) glanced away from the baseball cards he was thumbing through to look toward the source of the whispering voice emanating over his left shoulder.

"It's kind of weird," the voice continued, "but that boy over there is staring at you for some reason."

The whispering voice had come from Pete's father who was presently stooping low behind Pete while extending a pointed finger in the direction of the curious onlooker.

Pete turned in the direction his father indicated and observed a slender boy with light brown hair and gray eyes staring curiously back at him from a few feet away. This boy appeared to be rifling through a pile of baseball cards as well. Pete rolled his eyes with embarrassment and smirked after he recognized that he was looking at his own reflection in a large, antique mirror standing a short distance from him.

"Nice one, dad," Pete snickered. "Pretty tricky. You almost got me with that one!"

"Actually, I *did* get you on that one. It looked to me like you were 'beside yourself' with embarrassment. Get it? It's a play on words. You were '*beside* yourself'," Pete's father said with a chuckle as he made his way over to the mirror. "Anyway, I hope that my little practical joke doesn't '*reflect*' badly on me as your parent!"

"Okay, okay, dad!" Pete said with a wry grin. "You can stop with the bad mirror puns anytime now, alright?"

"You know," Mr. Johnson said as he closely examined the mirror's frame, "I think this might be something that your mother would actually be interested in. Maybe I should get it for her birthday."

Pete continued to look through the basket of baseball cards he had found on top of an old dresser among the numerous items laid out in the neighborhood yard sale. Pete loved collecting old baseball cards as a hobby. His grandfather had given Pete his own baseball card collection several years ago, and Pete had been adding to his grandfather's old cards ever since.

"Hey dad!" Pete said enthusiastically as he approached his father with the basketful of cards in his hands. "Look at this! There must be over a hundred baseball cards in here, and the sticker on the basket says that it costs just one dollar for all of them!"

"Very nice," his father said automatically without looking away from the antique mirror.

"I didn't really see anything too valuable in the pile," Pete continued, "but I'd still like to buy them…if it's okay with you." His father didn't seem to hear him.

Pete grabbed onto his dad's arm and gently tugged it. "Hey, dad? Can I get them? I really think that grandpa would want me to have these to add to his collection."

"Did you say that they're a dollar for the whole collection?" his father asked as he briefly turned his attention away from the mirror to glance at his son.

Pete nodded. "Yep! Just one, little ol' dollar!"

"Okay," his father replied. "It's fine with me. Go for it." He turned his attention back to the mirror, but noticed that Pete was still hovering next to him. He looked at his son once more with an inquisitive expression.

"Uh…dad?" Pete began timidly.

His father smiled. "No money, huh?" he guessed.

"Yeah," Pete nodded shyly. "I'm a little short on cash right now."

Pete's father laughed softly and withdrew a dollar bill from his wallet. "Here," he said. "Take this and pay me back when you become a rich philanthropist some day, okay?" he said jokingly.

Pete grinned as he took the money from his father.
"Thanks!"

Pete patiently waited in line to pay for the cards. The man in charge of the yard sale was making change for the woman ahead of him. Both were immersed in an intense conversation regarding the joys of living in northern New England where the many yard sale offerings seemed to frequently reveal truly valuable treasures at "rock bottom" prices.

After the woman left, Pete quickly set the basket of cards down on top of the table in front of the man. As he did this, several of the cards slipped off the top of the pile and onto the ground.

"Oh man!" Pete groaned. "I didn't want to lose any of these or get them dirty," he complained as he bent down to retrieve the cards.

"Oh!" said the man with a smile. "I'm glad to see that these cards are going to someone who wants to keep them in good condition! That's the collection I used to have when I was about your age, and they're still in great shape. I've got just the thing right here that will help you get all of them home safely." The man grabbed a cardboard box that was on the table next to him and dumped the cards gently into it. He handed the box to Pete. "There you go," the man said. "That should be easier for you to carry home. I hope you enjoy them as much as I did!"

When Pete returned home with his dad, he ran directly upstairs to his bedroom and dumped the contents of the box onto the top of his desk. As he fanned out the cards, he noticed something in the pile that looked out of place. It seemed that a greenish-white piece of paper had gotten mixed up in his baseball card collection. As he slowly pulled the paper out from the pile of cards, his eye's opened wide with surprise.

"Wow!" He whispered to himself. "A five dollar bill!"

But that couldn't be right. Pete blinked his eyes a couple of times and looked at the money again. He saw his mistake.

"Wait a minute...It's not a five dollar bill. That's Ulysses S. Grant on the front! It's a *fifty* dollar bill! Fifty dollars!" he shouted. "I can't believe this!"

"What's that, Pete?" his mom yelled from downstairs.

"I just found something so cool in my baseball card collection!" Pete exclaimed with delight.

"A rare find?" his mother asked.

"Definitely!" Pete replied.

"Do you think it's valuable?"

"You bet it is!"

"How much do you think it's worth?"

"Oh...about fifty dollars."

"Really?" His mother sounded very impressed. "I'd love to see it. I'll be right up in a second."

"Sure...ahh...wait! No!"

Pete's expression of placid elation suddenly turned to that of frantic terror. He quickly shoved the fifty dollar bill into the pocket of his pants. "What I mean, mom, is that it's...uh...not really *that* important to see it right *now*! Maybe I can show it to you later."

"Well, just tell me then...what's the name of the player?" his mother called from the bottom of the stairs.

"Uh...well...it's a guy named Grant," Pete replied nervously.

"Grant? What team did he play for?"

"Um...the Blue Coats," Pete's voice cracked tensely. "They're an old team from way back. Y'know...from the sixties? Anyway, it was before your time!"

5

"The Blue Coats?" Pete's mom repeated with a hint of confusion. A brief moment of silence passed before she replied. "Never heard of them."

"Well, that's what's makes it so special," Pete quickly stated. "It's real rare to find something like this in your typical baseball card collection these days."

"Well, you're the baseball expert around here," his mother said casually. "I guess you never know what kinds of valuable things you might find in a yard sale, huh? I'll leave you alone with your collection then, and I'll take a look at it later, alright?"

"Sure thing, mom!"

Pete breathed a long sigh of relief as he quickly closed his bedroom door. He pulled the fifty dollar bill from his pocket and looked at it longingly.

"Why didn't I just tell her I found a fifty dollar bill mixed in with my card collection," he mumbled to himself. "I kind of feel…bad or something. Like I did something wrong. But it's not like I really lied to my mom or anything." He looked at the bearded face of the eighteenth President of the United States on the front of the bill. "I mean, his name is Grant after all. And he did fight with a bunch of guys wearing blue coats in the Civil War back in the sixties. Well…the 1860's that is, but still…it wasn't like I was lying or anything."

Pete began to pace restlessly back and forth across his bedroom floor while continuing to stare at the money in his hands.

"And it's not like I stole this money," he continued to mutter to himself. "I'm no thief. Besides, I paid for *everything* that was in the collection. *Everything*! That includes this money. And isn't it really the responsibility of the man at the yard sale to know exactly what he was giving me anyway? Of course it is! So he must have wanted me to have this money, or else he would have taken it out of the box before he gave it to me, right?" A confident grin spread across his face. "Hey! I guess I really don't have anything to worry about then. I didn't do anything wrong. The fifty dollars is now officially and legally mine!"

Pete heard a slight "clicking" noise behind him from the direction of his bedroom door. Despite his new-found assurance that he was innocent of any wrongdoing, he quickly hid the money inside his pocket again and spun around as if he was expecting to see someone standing in the doorway. He made a sigh of relief when he discovered that the noise had come from his cat, Charley, who was playing with a marble near the door. Pete noticed that his heart was pounding loudly in his chest as small beads of sweat began to form upon his worried brow.

"Wow!" he said as he wiped his forehead. "What's wrong with me? It feels like someone is standing behind me and watching me even though there's actually nobody around! It's creepy!"

He removed the crumpled bill from his pocket and stared at it.

"I know what I got to do to make this creepy feeling go away. And the sooner I do it the better! I gotta spend this money fast! When the money is all spent and gone, I won't have to worry about it anymore! Problem solved!"

He stuffed the bill into his pocket and asked his parents if he could walk down to the local shopping plaza. After his parents said "yes", Pete ran out of the house and quickly made his way downtown.

As he was running down the street, he heard a voice call to him from behind: "Hey, stop! Johnson! Stop!"

Pete's heart jumped and he spun around quickly with a terrified look on his face as if he expected to see a policeman chasing after him ready to make an arrest. Pete breathed a sigh of relief when he saw instead a thin boy with messy, pitch black hair, blue eyes, pale skin and shabby clothes running toward him waving a partially eaten chocolate bar in the air. This boy was one of Pete's friends from school named Rob.

Rob's real name was Robert T. McGwyn, but most everyone called him Rob or Robby. Rob was eleven years old and lived only with his mother. He was always getting in trouble wherever he went. He often had to remain after school in the afternoons to serve detention for constantly breaking the school rules. Rob was even held back a grade level two years ago due to his poor school performance. When that happened, Rob was placed into Pete's class the following year, and that was when the two boys first met.

"What's wrong?" Rob asked. "It looks like you've seen a ghost!"

"You scared me to death, Rob!"

"Why? What's up?"

"Nothing," Pete said trying to appear calm.

"Are you sure?" Rob asked as he studied Pete's face. "Your cheeks and ears are, like, real red!"

"Like I said," Pete replied hastily, "nothing is going on! I have nothing to hide!"

"Alright, alright!" Rob said trying to calm his friend. "Take it easy, Johnson! You just kinda seem spooked about somethin', that's all." After a brief pause, Rob held his chocolate bar in front of Pete face. "Want half?"

"You didn't steal it or anything," Pete asked suspiciously. "I know you steal things sometimes, and I don't want to take something that was stolen!"

"Do ya want half or not?" Rob responded with annoyance. He slowly waved the candy below Pete's nose. Pete made a resigned sigh.

"Yeah, sure. I'll take half."

Rob broke the bar and gave part of the chocolate to Pete.

"Eww! It's gooey!" Pete complained.

"What do you want?" Rob replied with an irritated tone. "It's the middle of August, and it's like ninety degrees in the shade today! Chocolate is gonna get a little melty!"

The two boys walked down the street as they talked about the various activities they had done during summer break.

"I had a birthday last month," Rob said glumly.

"Why do you sound so bummed-out about it?" Pete asked. "Birthdays are usually a good thing."

"I'm bummed-out 'cause I got nothin'," Rob said. "My mom can't afford to buy presents right now. We can just barely afford to pay the electric bill! I wish that someday we would win the lottery or somethin' so we wouldn't have to worry about money all the time."

Pete looked cautiously up and down the street. "You wanna see something really cool?" he asked Rob quietly.

"Yeah, sure," Rob said with a curious stare.

"You promise to keep it a secret?" Pete asked.

"Yeah, you know me," said Rob.

"Yeah, I do know you! That's why I want you to promise! Don't tell anybody. Okay?"

"All right already! I promise! I'll keep it a secret!" Rob replied restlessly.

"Okay, then. Here...hold this for a second." Pete handed Rob the uneaten portion of his chocolate bar, and then fished the fifty dollar bill out of his pocket. He quickly flashed it in front of Rob's eyes, and then quickly stuffed back into his pocket.

"Wow!" Rob shouted excitedly. "Fifty dollars! Hey, where'd you get a fifty dollar bill?"

"Rob!" Pete whispered angrily. "You just promised not to tell anybody! Don't yell it out for the whole world to hear!"

"Let me see it! I want to hold it!"

"No, it's mine!" Pete said defensively.

"Where did you get it?"

"Well, I...uh...found it!"

"I wish I found fifty dollars!" Rob said. "You know what I'd do with fifty dollars? I'd buy all the new video games I could get my hands on." Rob paused and looked at Pete thoughtfully. "Hey, wait a minute! I know what we can do! We can go right down to the video store and buy the new Super Truck II game that just came out. You just said the other day that you really wanted it! Then we can play it together at your house!"

Pete's eyes grew large with excitement.

"Yeah! That's an awesome idea! Let's do it!"

At the Video store, the two boys found the Super Truck II video game and were about to pay for it when Pete fearfully raised his head and stared up at the ceiling. He started to shake with fear. He broke out of the checkout line and quickly

10

returned the game to it original location on the shelf. Rob followed him with a confused expression upon his face.

"What are you doing?" Rob asked. "Why are you putting it back?"

"I just remembered something," Pete said. "A friend in my Sunday school class told me something important, and I just remembered it. I think I just saved myself from making a really bad mistake!"

"Oh, great!" Rob said sarcastically. "So, what did this churchy kid have to say? That if you buy a video game and have fun playin' it, then it's gotta be bad for you, because religious people aren't supposed to have any fun? You're afraid you're gonna get kicked out of your church, aren't you?"

"No," Pete said with a serious tone. "It's even worse than that! My friend from Sunday school said that no matter where we go or what we do, we are always being watched! And when I was standing in the checkout line just now, I could really feel that I was being watched—just like he said!"

"Are you for real?" Rob asked with a cynical laugh. "Do you really believe that?"

"Yeah, I do," Pete said nodding his head soberly. "I'm glad I finally figured it out before I paid for anything. I mean, besides feeling like we're were being watched, it also felt like someone was trying to tell me not to buy the game in the first place."

"So, Bible-boy," Rob said as he crossed his arms over his chest in a judgmental manner, "*who* do you think is watching us from up above then — as if I couldn't guess?"

"The Video Police, of course!" Pete whispered earnestly. Rob's eyebrows shot up with surprise.

"Video Police? What the heck are Video Police?"

"Shh!" Pete hissed as he put his index finger to his lips to silence Rob. "Listen, Rob!" he whispered. "My friend told me that the Video Police are always watching you here. If they see you doing something wrong, they'll record it on a video camera and show it to your parents. Then you'll have to go to jail for the rest of your life!"

"Get out!" Rob said with disbelief. "You *can't* be serious!"

"My friend from Sunday school wouldn't lie to me, Rob!" Pete retorted. "He's a Christian, just like I am! And besides, his own brother used to work here, and that's what his brother told him to tell all of his friends like me! His own brother should know!"

Rob shook his head in disbelief.

"That's, like, so dumb!" Rob said. "He just made that up! There's no such thing as Video Police!"

"Oh yeah?" Pete asked as he pointed at the ceiling over the checkout area. "Then why don't you tell me what *that* thing's for?"

Rob looked up and saw one of the store's video security cameras looking directly down at the person at the head of the checkout line.

"Take it from me, Johnson...I can tell you from *my* own personal experience that you only have to worry about that camera if you're gonna be stealin' stuff. We're not stealing! You got the money to pay for this!"

"But, let's just say that they *think* I stole it or something," Pete suggested. "Like, what if by mistake they think that the money that I found belongs to someone else? I mean, whoever heard of an ordinary ten year old kid walking around with a fifty dollar bill in his pocket anyway! Wouldn't you be suspicious? Wouldn't you, like, maybe call the police or FBI or something like that?"

"First of all, Johnson," Rob began, "I personally try to stay as far away from the police as I possibly can. Secondly, why do you always worry about stupid stuff like getting busted for paying for a video game with a fifty dollar bill? Would you feel better if you paid for it in tens and twenties? Sometimes you can be such a dork! If it was me, I'd just shut up and buy the video game with the fifty. I wouldn't even care if the money *was* stolen or if anyone *did* see me!"

"That's because you're so used to getting in trouble that no one trusts you anyways! Everyone already knows that you're a thief and a liar! What do *you* got to lose?"

"Hey!" Rob said with an offended tone.

"I'm not buying the game! Period!" Pete stated confidently.

"Let me buy it then!" Rob pleaded. "Give me the money, and I'll do it for you, you big chicken!"

"Uh-uh! No way!" Pete replied.

"Well, if you're not gonna buy anything," Rob said hotly, "I guess there's no point in hangin' out with you anymore! You're not very much fun to be around anyway. For some reason, you're real crabby today, and you're acting real weird! Fifty dollars or not, I'm outta here!"

On the way back home, Pete acted extremely uneasy. He continued to look over his shoulder from time to time as if he

13

believed someone were following him and watching his every move.

"Why do I feel so guilty?" he muttered to himself. "I didn't do anything wrong. And why does that commandment from the Bible about how bad it is to steal keep popping up in my head? 'You must not steal! You must not steal!' That's been going on since I left my house to go downtown. It's starting to get real annoying! I'm not a thief! I didn't actually steal this money, right? I just have to keep reminding myself of that, and everything will be okay."

Pete hid himself behind a large maple tree near his house. He removed the fifty dollar bill from his pocket and slowly unfolded it.

"Oh no!" he said to himself with despair as he looked closely at the front of the bill. "I made a chocolate thumbprint right next to President Grant's face when I showed this to Rob! What do I do now?" Pete tried vigorously to erase the thumbprint with his shirt, but the print remained unchanged. It had become a permanent part of the bill.

"Oh great!" Pete said sadly. "It won't go away! If I try to spend this now with my thumb print on it, then the FBI or police can trace the money back to me! And if I keep it, then I'll spend the rest of my life looking over my shoulder to see if someone's coming to arrest me or something!" Pete abruptly stopped his musing and squeezed his eyes shut as if he we're trying to block out the true situation in which he found himself. "What am I saying? Don't you remember, Pete? You didn't actually steal this money! You're not a thief!"

Pete wearily opened his eyes again, shoved the money back into his pocket, and slowly slumped down next to the tree with his head between his knees. He sighed heavily.

"Lord?" he prayed out loud. "What am I doing to myself here? I'm starting to feel sick to my stomach! I think I gotta get some help or something." he groaned.

When he arrived home, Pete slowly entered the living room with his head bent low, eyes to the ground. He bumped into something hard near the middle of the room which startled him. He looked up and yelped in terror at what he saw. The antique mirror that his father had bought at the yard sale that morning was standing before him, but what had scared Pete was the sight his own miserable reflection glowering back at him. It was an image revealing elements of anger, fear, sadness, hopelessness and misery traced out in the sullen furrows which ran round his face. Pete was so disgusted by his own pathetic image that he turned quickly away from the mirror. His eyes focused instead at the far corner of the room where he saw his dad reading a book on the couch. Pete tried to appear at ease in front of his father.

"Oh! Uh… hi, Dad. What's up?"

"Sorry about that, Pete," Mr. Johnson said as he looked up at his son. "I meant to move that thing upstairs but I haven't got to it yet. I heard you bump into it."

"I wasn't looking where I was going," Pete said. "It kinda scared me, that's all."

"Yeah, it scares me too. Every time I look into that mirror I see this old guy who needs to lose weight staring back at me. That's not how I prefer to think of myself most of the time, but

15

the mirror doesn't lie. When the truth stares you right in the face it can be hard to accept sometimes, can't it?"

"What are you reading?" Pete asked, quickly changing the subject.

"I'm doing a Bible study for my men's group at church. I'm reading a passage from the book of Job."

"What's it about?"

"It's about this man named Elihu who is telling another man, named Job, what God is like."

"What's he say God's like?"

"Well, he says, 'God watches how people live; He sees everything they do. No darkness is thick enough to hide the wicked from his eyes.'"

Pete gulped.

"Is that true, Dad?"

"Of course! God's eternal. He knows everything and is everywhere all at once."

Pete looked down at the floor glumly.

"Oh brother! That explains everything! God's been watching me!"

"What's that?" Mr. Johnson asked.

Pete shook his head sadly. "Dad, I have something I need to tell you...and God. I think it will kinda disappoint both of you." Pete pulled the money out of his pocket and showed it to his father. "I found this in the box with the baseball cards and didn't tell anyone. I was going to keep it and spend it on something for me, even though...it really doesn't belong to me." Pete's expression looked like he might start crying at any moment. "I feel terrible about it, dad. I did something I knew was wrong.

16

I've been dealing with this all day! I'm so sorry. I just hope that you and God will forgive me."

Mr. Johnson placed his Bible on the table and looked intently at his son. "So why did you keep the money so long when you knew it was wrong?"

"I don't know. I notice that I get this way when I'm around money for some reason. Maybe I have some kind of problem with greed. Maybe I'm addicted to it or something."

"Well, that's an issue we can work on together," Mr. Johnson said.

"Really?" Pete said enthusiastically.

"Yes," Mr. Johnson smiled, "I'd be happy to help you with your money problem. Count on it."

Pete looked very relieved.

"Thanks, dad!" Pete's smile turned into a worried frown. "Are you disappointed with me?"

"Pete, I'm not disappointed in you. I love you, and I'm proud of you. Let me tell you why." Mr. Johnson had Pete sit down beside him on the couch. "Okay Pete, let's face the facts. You did something that you knew was wrong. In other words, you sinned. In the book of James, the Bible says, 'Remember, it is sin to know what you ought to do and then not do it'. So not only did God know that you were sinning, but deep down inside, you knew it too. But it really seems to me that you are truly sorry about what you did. You appear to be pretty ashamed of yourself. You really regret what you did, don't you?" Pete nodded in agreement. "The reason I'm proud of you, Pete, has to do with the way you finally handled the situation you found yourself in after you sinned. You confessed to me and God about what you did wrong, and then you turned back to God by asking him to forgive you. I certainly forgive you, but more importantly, so does God. Being truly sorry for sinning and asking God to forgive you is called repentance, and God loves a humble and repentant heart."

"But how can I be sure that God forgives me?" Pete asked.

"Well, it says in the book of First John 'If we claim we have no sin, we are only fooling ourselves and not living in the truth. But if we confess our sins to him, he is faithful and just to forgive our sins and to cleanse us from all wickedness'. That's how I know." Pete's discouraged expression quickly faded away. "Now that you have been forgiven," Pete's father continued, "God expects that you'll really try to avoid repeating the same sin again."

"That's where you come in!" Pete said cheerfully. "With you helping me with my money problem, that should be no problem, right?"

Pete's father nodded with a smile. "But we still have this fifty dollar bill that we have to deal with. So what do you think we should do about that?"

"I know what to do," Pete stated confidently. "It's what I should have done from the very beginning when I found the money in the first place. I'm going to take the money back to the man that sold us the baseball cards — I have a feeling that it belongs to him."

Pete and his dad brought the money back to the man who sold them the cards. The man was indeed very happy. He said he thought he had lost the money outdoors while he was making change. He figured that he must have put the money in the

18

cardboard box to keep it safe while he made change for the person in line just before Pete. Afterward, he had forgotten the money was still inside the box when he filled it with Pete's baseball cards. The man thanked Pete for being so honest and shook his hand.

When Pete arrived home, he walked past the large antique mirror once more. He stopped to look at himself and smiled. His body seemed relaxed and his face appeared tranquil, in a state of complete peace. He reflected on the way he felt just an hour earlier when he was almost sick to his stomach due to the stress of living a lie and from trying to ignore both God and the truth. It seemed that Pete was truly starting to realize how sin can wear you down and turn you into a totally miserable person.

"I still feel that you're watching me, God," Pete said softly as he turned away from the mirror. "But this time I feel really good about it!"

Questions:

1) What would you have done if you were in Pete's situation in finding something very valuable that you really wanted to keep but knew that it belonged to someone else? When you thought about what you would do in this case, did you consider the possibly of simply keeping the valuable item for yourself without trying to return it to its rightful owner? How do you think that would make you feel? Like Pete, would you constantly worry about getting caught and being punished?

2) What is sin?

3) What is repentance?

4) Why do you think Pete felt so relaxed and peaceful after he confessed his sin to his father and to God? Do you think that Pete truly felt sorry for what he did? Do you think that Pete felt encouraged knowing that God would forgive him after he repented?

Bible References relating to the Story:

Job 34:21-22

Psalm 11:4

Hebrews 4:13

James 4:17

1 John 1:8-9

Psalm 32:3-5

Chapter 2

Here's the Good News!

The Good News Gazette

Anyone who calls on the name of the Lord
WILL BE SAVED!

SAVED
by FAITH in JESUS CHRIST!
By Paul

GOD is LOVE!
By John
Heaven ans Earth

GOD IS LOVE

Sacrificial Love saves the day...
and us too!

During a beautiful September afternoon, Robert T. McGwyn was in the process of serving a school detention after he was caught trying to steal a full carton of half-and-half from the teachers' lounge earlier that day. Unfortunately for Rob, Mr. Moressy, the fifth grade English teacher, had hurried into the lounge at the same time that Rob tried to hurry out, and the two literally ran into each other. The quart of coffee creamer, which Rob had hidden under his jacket, slipped from his grasp and landed on Mr. Moressy's foot. Greatly surprised by this event,

Mr. Moressy jumped back into Mrs. Stein who had followed him into the lounge. To make the situation worse, Mrs. Stein happened to be holding a cup of hot coffee which she spilled down the front of her white pantsuit when Mr. Moressy collided into her. At that point, Rob couldn't be sure if the steam he saw rising from around Mrs. Stein's head was due to the hot coffee she had spilled on her clothes, or if it were due to some type of naturally occurring steam which could radiate from a livid human face fuming with anger. Oh, poor, poor Rob!

Finally, at four O'clock, Rob was released from school. Pete had waited for Rob outside the main entrance of the school so that they could walk home together.

"Wow!" Pete exclaimed as Rob exited the school. "It's only been a couple of weeks since school started, and you've already been in detention three times so far this year. This must be a new record for you!" Rob cast a nasty look at Pete. "I heard that you stole some coffee creamer or something from the teacher's lounge. Is that true?"

"Yep."

"But why? Didn't you think you might get caught? Didn't you think you'd get in trouble?"

"Of course I knew I might get in trouble!" Rob said with an irritated tone. "I'm not stupid! We ran out of milk at home, and the school has plenty. It's a public school, right? And I'm part of the public so I'm just takin' what's really mine anyway."

"Give me a break!" Pete responded. "You know as well as I do that it was still wrong to try to sneak off with it. Why didn't you just ask a teacher if you could take it instead?" Rob simply snickered at Pete's suggestion with contempt. "It's too bad that you just can't change who you are and start acting like a good person for once," Pete lectured his friend sternly. "Then I wouldn't have to waste my time waiting for you after school's out."

"Hey, if you don't want to wait, then don't," Rob said coolly. "I can walk home by myself. I'm a big boy."

Pete frowned. "I won't be able to wait for you tomorrow anyways," he said. "I have Meagan's birthday party to go to. It's right after school."

"I never get invitations to parties," Rob said with a solemn sigh. "Nobody likes me."

"Well, maybe if you didn't get into trouble so much, people would have more respect for you. Then maybe you would get invited to some parties."

"Yeah, right!" Rob replied sarcastically. "Like that's gonna happen! Nobody invites me anywhere."

"I do!" Pete smiled. "You're one of the best video game players in the entire school. I love playing against you — you're really hard to beat!" Rob smiled slightly with a hint of pride. "And since we just brought up the topic of video games and getting invited places, I'd like to invite you to come over to my house right now so we can race monster trucks together. Do you think it will be okay with your mom?"

"My mom don't care where I go or what I do," Rob replied. "With her it's like an automatic 'yes' to these kind of things. I think she actually likes it when I'm not around. So, yeah. I'll come over for a little bit."

"Sweet!" Pete said happily.

Both boys headed toward Pete's house.

When they arrived Mrs. Johnson told Pete that he would have to bag the garbage upstairs and downstairs and bring it to the end of the driveway. She asked Rob to wait in the living room while Pete finished his chores. Rob slowly ambled into the living room and saw Pete's dad working at the computer.

"Hi Mr. Johnson. What's up?"

"Hi Robby! I'm just about to send an email to an old friend of mine. I'm inviting him to go to church services with us two weeks from now. He's interested in going back to church again, and we would love to take him."

"Why do people go to church anyways?" Rob asked. "What's it like?"

"You don't go to church, Robby?"

"No."

"Would you like to visit our church sometime? That's the best way to see what happens. We can call your mom to make sure it's alright with her."

"You're inviting me?"

"Well, yes. If it's alright with your mother."

Rob thought for a moment. "I don't know. Is it going to be boring?"

"Maybe," Mr. Johnson shrugged. "But you won't know unless you give it a try. If you wanted to try it out sometime, you could go to Sunday school with Pete."

"What's Sunday school like?" Rob asked.

"It has a band that plays fun music, and they usually play some games too."

"Is Sunday school just for kids?" Rob asked excitedly.

"Yes, it is," Mr. Johnson answered.

"Do they have detention?"

"Uh…no," Pete's dad said slowly with a slightly concerned look upon his face.

"Well, that's good," Rob commented. "What else do they got?"

"They got Jesus!" Mr. Johnson said with a smile.

"Huh?" Rob said with a blank stare. "I've heard of Jesus, but didn't he die a long time ago? I don't really know much about him."

"If you like, I can tell you more about Jesus right now."

Rob shrugged. "Okay."

Mr. Johnson invited Rob to sit down on the couch across from him.

"Well first, let's begin with some very good news for you and me and everyone else in the world," Mr. Johnson started. "God loves people."

"What's that got to do with that Jesus guy we were just talkin' about?" Rob asked.

"We'll get there," Mr. Johnson nodded. "But first, there are a few things you should know about God. God created the entire universe and everything in it — including you and me. The Bible says that God *is* love. God wants to have a loving relationship with each of us, and God even wants the people he created to have a loving relationship with each other. That's why God created us in the first place. Loving relationships really please God."

"Loving relationships?" Rob repeated with a frown. "You mean like a lovey-dovey, kissy, kissy kind of love?"

"No, not that kind of love!" Mr. Johnson laughed. "The kind of love I'm talking about has to do with respect and treating each other the way we would want to be treated ourselves. It's a love that is patient and kind. It's not jealous, boastful, proud or rude."

"Oh," Rob said nodding his head. "Well, I show *that* kind of love all the time!"

"Hmmm. Is that right?" Mr. Johnson asked with a hint of skepticism.

"Oh, yeah," Rob said nodding. "All the time. I know that a lot of people think I'm bad and stuff, but if you really get to know me, like inside, then you'd see that I'm really a good guy."

"Well maybe from your own point of view you are. But from God's point of view, do you think you are truly a perfectly 'good guy'?" Mr. Johnson asked.

"Huh?" Rob responded with a quizzical stare. "What do ya mean?"

"Well," Mr. Johnson began, "when God created the universe, he declared that everything in it was good – very good, in fact! Everything was good, but nothing in creation was exactly perfect the way that God is perfect. Since people aren't perfect, we don't always show perfect love to either God or to each other. So God put together a list of commands, called God's law, that were designed to guide us in living the way God desires us to live each day. God's law tells us how to respect God and each other even during those times when we just don't feel like loving or respecting anyone. God wants us to continuously follow his law without fail. Our problem is that we don't. So by God's standard, none of us are perfectly good."

"Speak for yourself, Mr. Johnson," Rob stated boldly. "Like I said, I'm a good guy when you get to know me. In fact, I'd say I'm pretty much as close to perfect as you could get! I think this God of yours would definitely be cool with me. I'm sure we could be like best buds!"

"So, let me ask you then Robby...have you ever become so mad or upset at someone else that you had unkind thoughts about that person?"

"Never!" Rob stated proudly.

"Really," Mr. Johnson said doubtfully. "So, you never have had unkind thoughts about your mom, or your teachers, or any of the kids you go to school with? Never? Now be honest."

"Well, okay," Rob began after a short pause. "I guess if you're gonna mention all *those* people, then I guess I do have thoughts like that sometimes... actually a lot of the time now that I think about it. There's some people that I know that really tick me off, and I feel like I just want to knock 'em into tomorrow."

"Well," Mr. Johnson continued, "by just even having those kinds of thoughts, you're not following God's command to love others. Those kinds of thoughts don't have anything to do with respect or treating another person the way you would want to be treated, right? Would you like someone else to think those kinds of awful things about you?"

"No," Rob replied. "But how am I breaking God's commands if I'm just thinking about doing something rotten to someone, but I don't actually do it? The other person can't, like, just read my mind, y'know."

"That's true," Mr. Johnson agreed. "But *you* know that what you were thinking was wrong...and so does God. God knows what's going on inside everyone's head and heart. He always knows when you're breaking his law."

"That's kinda creepy to think that this God of yours can read my mind like that," Rob said with a worried expression on his face.

"It's worse than creepy," Mr. Johnson added. "It's scary too. When we break God's commands, God gets very upset with us. That's something to be really scared about. You see, a long time ago, God made a promise that he would have to punish anyone who breaks his law, and God has to keep his promises no matter what – even God can't break his own promises. So what that means is that every person on earth who chooses to break God's law has earned God's promise of punishment. And being punished by God is worse than all of the punishments you can possibly think of."

"Well, that's not very good news," Rob stated loudly in an apprehensive tone. "That sounds like really bad news to me!"

"Yeah, you're right. That's terrible news," Mr. Johnson agreed.

"So, what can we do?" Rob asked. "How do we make it right with God so we can save ourselves from havin' to get punished if we break his commands?"

"We can't," Mr. Johnson replied, shaking his head in despair. "We simply can't save ourselves. This isn't something we can fix on our own."

"What?" Rob blurted out. "So you're sayin' that we're all gonna get punished by God then?"

"Well, we all deserve his punishment," Mr. Johnson replied gravely. "After all, God is our creator and he makes the rules. He's in charge, not us. He's been telling people for thousands and thousands of years that we must love him and to love others; he told us that bad things would happen if we didn't."

"But that's not fair!" Rob replied angrily. "Why would God punish us when he made us imperfect in the first place? That's, like, so totally…cruel!"

"Hang on, Robby," Mr. Johnson said calmly. "You haven't heard everything yet. Remember the Good News we talked about at the beginning of this conversation? God loves us! He doesn't want anyone to be punished. God loves us so much that he gave *all* of us a way to have peace with him. But in order to make this happen, God couldn't break the promise he made long ago — the punishment we deserve still had to be given. But, fortunately for us, God had made a remarkable and wonderful and somewhat mysterious plan to rescue us!" Rob leaned in a little closer to Mr. Johnson, obviously very interested in what he was going to say next. "You see," Mr. Johnson continued, "God had also promised long ago that he would send someone to save us since we couldn't save ourselves no matter how hard we tried. Our rescuer was to be someone very special — someone who would follow God absolutely perfectly."

"But Mr. Johnson, you just said a minute ago that no one could follow God's commands perfectly," Rob stated in an authoritative tone.

"Well," Mr. Johnson began, "there was someone in history that did."

"Really?" Rob asked as he sat on the edge of his seat listening intently to each word. "Who?"

"This is where Jesus comes in," Mr. Johnson replied. "Jesus is very special to God; he's God's own Son. Jesus was with God at the beginning of all creation. In fact, everything that God created was created through his Son, Jesus. And it's through Jesus that God gives life to everything in the universe."

"I thought Jesus was just a regular man that died a long time ago," Rob said.

"Well," Mr. Johnson replied, "over two thousand years ago, God sent Jesus to live on earth in a human body. For about thirty years or so, Jesus lived a life as a human being. But there was something very special and different about Jesus. Unlike us, Jesus perfectly followed God's law and did everything that God asked him to do no matter how hard it was. This included taking the all punishment we deserved for breaking God's law. Jesus sacrificed himself to save all of us."

"What?" Rob asked with a shocked expression on his face. "You mean God kept his promise by punishing his own son instead of us?"

"Yes," Mr. Johnson said with a serious tone. "Jesus perfectly obeyed God's plan – even when it meant his own suffering and death. Jesus was made fun of, spit on, slapped, whipped, beaten with sticks, and nailed to a wooden cross. Jesus was tortured and killed in order to save us from God's punishment, and he died to bring us into a relationship of peace and love with God."

"But that still isn't fair!" Rob protested passionately. "How could God let that happen to his own son? That's still cruel!"

"Hold on Robby," Mr. Johnson said gently. "There's still more. You see, God's love is extremely powerful, and God loves his own son more than anything else in all of creation. Because of that love, God brought Jesus back to life three days after he died! And if that wasn't good enough, God also brought Jesus into God's own Kingdom and gave him authority to rule over everything everywhere in the entire universe. Jesus Christ is now the King over all kings and Lord over all lords. That's the best honor and reward that anyone could ever receive."

"Well," Rob said after a brief period of consideration, "I guess that isn't so bad then." Mr. Johnson smiled.

"So," Rob began with a hopeful look in his eyes, "are you saying that since Jesus took God's punishment for everyone, then *I'll* be saved from God's punishment, too?"

Mr. Johnson pulled his chair a little closer to Rob as if he were going to tell him a secret. "Listen to this: If you confess with your mouth that Jesus is Lord and believe in your heart that God raised him from the dead, you will be saved. That, Robby, is the message of the Good News of Jesus Christ."

"What? That's all there is to it?" Rob said with disbelief.

"Of course not!" Mr. Johnson shouted with joyful excitement. Startled by Mr. Johnson's loud reaction, Rob jumped back in his seat. "There's even MORE good news!" As Mr. Johnson continued, his voice became somewhat calmer, but his tone still bubbled over with excitement. "If you truly believe and trust in this Good News, then Jesus, who can never die and gives life to all things, will also give you a new, spiritual body that will last forever. What do you think of that?"

31

"Sounds like good news to me...I guess," Rob replied cautiously. "So are you tellin' me that I won't die if I believe in this...'Good News'?"

"Your human body will still die," Mr. Johnson answered. "But the new, spiritual life that is given to you from God will last forever after."

"So that's all I have to do?" Rob asked. "Just believe and trust in the Good News of Jesus, and then I'll have peace with God and get a new life that will last forever? Don't I have to change the way I act or somethin'?"

"That's a good point!" Mr. Johnson said. "Many people who become Christians will notice that their behavior and actions will change as their faith in Jesus Christ grows."

"Faith?" Rob asked. "What's faith?"

"Oh! Well, having faith in Jesus means that you trust in, believe in, and rely on the promises and guidance of Jesus. Faith in Jesus is a powerful thing; it's actually your *faith* in Jesus' promise of the Good News that saves you and makes you right with God."

"Okay," Rob replied. "Faith can save me, but how's this faith-stuff gonna change me?"

"As you practice living by faith each day, you'll gradually grow in many areas in your life such as your knowledge of God, your self-control, your patience and your goodness. If you continue to mature in your faith, you will eventually grow to have genuine love for everyone around you. You still won't be perfect like God is, but your faith will allow God to work inside of you to give you the *desire* to obey him and the power to do what pleases him each day."

32

Pete finally finished taking care of the trash. He grabbed the video game control unit from his bedroom and raced excitedly into the living room. Pete stopped short of calling for Rob to join him when he realized that Rob was in the middle of a conversation with his father.

"Y'know, Mr. Johnson," Rob said looking at Pete's dad, "I don't know what to think about all this stuff you just told me about God and Jesus. It sounds kinda weird. You actually believe all this stuff yourself?"

"I believe it with my whole heart, Robby," said Mr. Johnson with a reassuring smile.

"Hmmm," Rob replied thoughtfully. "I don't know. It sounds kinda interestin' I guess. I got to think about it some more. But the whole Sunday school thing you told me about before sounds pretty fun. Can I still go with you guys even if I'm not sure about all this Jesus stuff that you just told me?"

"Hey!" Pete blurted out suspiciously. "What's going on here?"

Rob spun around quickly to face his friend.

"Hey, Pete!" Rob said with excitement. "I'm going to Sunday school with you! Your dad invited me!"

"What!" Pete shot an angry and confused look at his dad.

"Well, remember, Robby," Mr. Johnson cautioned, "We still need to make sure it's okay with your mom."

"That's no problem. She don't care where I go or what I do."

"We'll still check with her anyway, okay?"

"Yeah, whatever."

"But dad!" Pete protested with a pleading look upon his face.

"What's wrong Pete?"

"Well... uh ... you promised that you and I would go fishing right after church, remember? So I don't think we have time to..."

Rob's eyes grew large and he sat on the edge of his seat.

"Fishin'? I've never been fishin' before! Can I go too? Please, please, please! Come on, Pete! Come on! Can I go fishin' with you too?"

Pete looked at Rob, then at his dad, and then at the floor.

"It's okay with me," Mr. Johnson said with a nod. "What do you think, Pete?"

Pete hesitated.

"I guess," he finally mumbled.

Rob jumped up off the couch with both arms in the air.

"All right! Yahoo!"

"Give me your mom's number," Mr. Johnson said, "I'll give her a call then."

Questions:

1) What was your reaction when you first heard or read about the Good News of Jesus Christ? (Perhaps the first time you saw the Good News was after reading this story!) Did you believe right away or did you need some time to think about it as Rob did in this story? Do you think the time it takes you to understand and believe the Good News would affect how much God loves you?

2) If you are a Christian, have you ever told someone else about the Good News of Jesus? If 'Yes', how did it go? How did you feel? If 'No', how do you think it would feel to tell a friend or family member about the Good News of Jesus? Why?

3) Do you understand the Good News of Jesus Christ well enough to explain it now to yourself? Try it! Practice it in front of a mirror or in front of your parents.

4) Describe what it means to have faith in Jesus?

Bible References Relating to this Story:

2 Corinthians 5:11-21

Romans 3:21-31

Romans 5:6-11

Romans 10:8-11

Philippians 2:12-13

John 15:9-14

2 Peter 1:5-9

Isaiah 52:7

Romans 10:17

Hebrews 11:1-2

1 Corinthians 13

Chapter 3

The Good, the Bad, and the Judged

After Rob left for the day, Pete entered the kitchen with a lifeless expression upon his face. Pete's mother was also in the kitchen, and she had just emptied the contents of a cat food can into Charley's dish. Charley rushed over and nudged Mrs. Johnson's hand away from the dish and began to eat voraciously. Mrs. Johnson chuckled. She kneeled down and began to gently scratch Charley's head while he ate. She turned to Pete.

"Pete? Would you fill his water dish please?"

Without a word, Pete slowly walked over to the water dish and picked it up.

"I didn't hear anything, mister," Mrs. Johnson said as she eyed her son expectantly.

"Yes," Pete replied glumly. "I'll do it."

Mrs. Johnson stood up.

"What's wrong?" she asked. Pete shook his head with slow frustration.

"I just don't understand," he said. "How could dad do something like that?"

"Do what?"

"Well, he invited a person like Rob to come to our church. He doesn't really know Rob. Neither do you. He's always getting in trouble! He's always breaking the rules at school. He got caught stealing stuff from a store once! He swears a lot when he gets mad. He's been in a bunch of fights with boys *and* girls! The people at church aren't like that. He's bad! He's not like us!"

"Well," Mrs. Johnson began, "if Robby is all that bad, why do you hang out with him? You did say he was your friend, didn't you?"

Pete thought for a moment.

"He stood up for me that one time when I was getting picked on by some bullies at school. He makes me laugh a lot, and he's a great video gamer to play against."

"Okay. So, if I understand this correctly, your dad invited Rob to church, and you have some issues with that. Is that about the gist of it?"

"Yeah!" Pete said with disgust. "And then — to make it worse — Rob invited himself to go on the fishing trip that dad and I planned to go on together after church. Can you believe it? That was supposed to be just dad and me! But then dad said it was okay if Rob wanted to come along too. I'm so frustrated!"

"Well, if you think that your father made a mistake, and it's making you upset, why don't the two of you talk about it then?"

Pete slumped down in a kitchen chair at the table. His mother sat at the table across from him.

"Because," Pete began, "dad spent ten minutes telling Rob all about the Good News of Jesus while I was taking out the trash.

So now both of them — Rob *and* dad — are all excited. Rob's excited to be able get out and have some fun. His mom doesn't even own a car, you know, so he usually doesn't get to go anywhere outside of the neighborhood. And then Dad's excited that maybe Rob will want to follow Jesus because he heard the Good News and will be going to church with us. I guess that I don't want to make either one of them to feel bad about it just because I feel bad."

"That's really thoughtful of you, Pete," Mrs. Johnson said with a soft smile. "And I can certainly understand that you want to spend some one-on-one time with your father. So, I think it would be best if you talked about this whole thing with…"

"Mom," Pete interrupted, "It's alright. Don't worry about it. Probably what will happen is that Rob will go to Sunday school and hate it, and he won't want to come back. Either that, or he'll do something awful in Sunday school, and he'll get kicked out of class. Then he won't be allowed back, and I won't have to worry about it any more. The sooner he leaves or gets kicked out of the church the better it will be for everyone. Trust me, I know. Becoming a Christian just isn't in his future"

Mrs. Johnson looked at Pete with a shocked expression. She leaned closer toward him.

"Pete, we're not God. We don't get to decide who is going to be saved or not. That's between God and each individual person on earth. The responsibility that God gave us human-types is to love each other no matter who that might be. And one of the best ways we can show love to one another is to tell people about the love God shows to *all* people by telling them about the Good News of Jesus Christ. Your father did the right thing just now.

It could help change Robby's life in wonderful ways for an eternity."

Pete remained silent.

"You don't seem convinced," Mrs. Johnson said. She nodded and leaned back comfortably in her chair. "You know, Pete, unlike you, I wasn't raised in a Christian household. When I was your age, I was a terror. Like Robby, I got into several fist-fights with some of the neighborhood kids down the road from me — both girls *and* boys." Pete quickly raised his head and stared at his mother with a surprised look.

"What?" he asked in disbelief. "You?" Pete's mother nodded.

"Here's something else I remember," Mrs. Johnson continued. "My mother used to make me take dance lessons when I was nine. I couldn't stand dance class. We all had to wear these ridiculous looking tutus. Now there was this one girl in class who always tried to bully me. But one day she went too far. We were standing in line waiting for our turn to do our dance routines, and she yanked the back of my tutu really, really hard. She almost pulled me over. I wasn't too upset at her doing that. But the worst part of that whole ordeal was that — as much as I hated that tutu — she had just put a big rip in it. Right down the back. I was furious and embarrassed. So I swore at her."

"You did what?" Pete said in disbelief.

"You heard me right. I swore at her. Then she swore back at me! She called me a very bad name, and that really hurt my pride. I felt like I had to do something about it, so I decided to shove her. I pushed that girl so hard...not only did *she* fall down, but all four girls standing behind her did too — just like dominos. I never had to worry about going to dance class after that. I was kicked out."

Pete fell back limply in his chair with a wide-eyed, awestruck look upon his face. "Whoa!" he exclaimed. "I never would have thought that you would do stuff like that! You're so different from that now!"

"But think about it, Pete. Don't you think it's amazing that God accepted me as one of his children?" Mrs. Johnson asked with a wry smile. "When I started following Christ, both my behavior and the way I thought about people and life all began to change. I became more focused about the things that Jesus would want me to do. And I'm still practicing to improve each day to become more like Christ. It never stops. Remember *my* saying? 'Practice makes improvement?' Well, that's how these changes happen inside us over time. Constant improvements."

"And all these changes started with someone telling me the Good News of Jesus in the first place. When I was thirteen, a schoolmate of mine, named Katie Burrell, invited me to church with her and helped me to understand the Bible. She was so patient, kind and gentle with me. She never judged me either. I could really see the Spirit of God living in her. I thank God for her each day. So Jesus Christ accepted me — a sinner — by working through Katie. She helped to save my life for an eternity."

Pete's wide-eyed, awestruck appearance, which he displayed only moments before, had slowly morphed into a sleepy, uninterested stare which drifted listlessly away from his mother's face and toward the table top.

"Listen to me, Pete," Mrs. Johnson stated in a slightly louder voice, trying to regain her son's attention. "You were raised in a Christian home. Your father and I began teaching you about Jesus from the day we brought you home with us. You've always known about the ways of the Lord. Not everyone has that advantage. People like Robby and I didn't have that advantage." She paused for a brief moment. "So what I'm saying is...I think you have to give Robby a break! Give him an opportunity to discover Jesus Christ just like you have. You say you're his friend. So won't you to try to help him to get to know Jesus better — especially since it sounds to me that he's interested in learning about him right now? Will you do that for me, please?"

"Look mom," Pete said, looking up again at his mother. "I liked your story and all, but I still don't think you get it." Mrs. Johnson raised one of her eyebrows slightly as Pete continued. "Rob's not going to change like you did. I really think that he *can't* change. It's probably genetic or something. If you really knew him, you'd understand. Like you said, Rob *is* my friend, and he's great for some laughs and for playing video games with, but he's just not going to make it as a Christian. I think we should all just try to accept that." Mrs. Johnson remained silent, but her intense gaze made Pete shift nervously in his chair. "I'll prove it to you next Sunday!" Pete offered enthusiastically. "We'll invite Rob to Sunday school just like dad wants. But I guarantee you that if he doesn't get kicked out by the teachers, he won't want to go back again because he'll think the whole singing and praying and Bible reading things that we do are dumb. He'll get bored and go back to his own kind of life. I'll bet you that's what's going to happen, and then you'll see that I was right and that you were...ah...well, that you weren't right!" Pete smiled weakly.

"So...let me ask this just one more time," Pete's mother said sternly as she leaned in closer to her son. "Will you at least *try* to make an effort to work with him to help him learn and understand more about Jesus if he asks?"

Pete stared blankly at the table top and remained silent.

Pete's mother leaned back comfortably in her chair again. "Of course you don't *have* to try if you don't want to," she said in a casual manner.

Pete's expression changed to that of both amazement and relief.

"Really? I don't have to do it if I don't want to?"

"Oh no! Of course not," Mrs. Johnson responded. Her voice sounded calm, but her tone was laced with a generous portion of cynicism. "You don't *have* to do what either I or God are asking you to do. You can certainly play by your *own* set of rules instead. I mean what's a little sin here or there? Actually, I think that you and Robby have more in common than you think — breaking and disregarding God's commands whenever you feel like it. It seems that you know what's best for both you *and* Robby." Mrs. Johnson's tone suddenly shifted from sarcasm to great earnestness: "But quite frankly, Peter Daniel, I would have expected a very different response from someone who claims to have close relationship with Jesus and wants to serve him faithfully."

"Wait! What are you talking about, Mom?" Pete asked with sincere concern. "You just said I'm sinning! How am *I* sinning?"

"By breaking one of God's Ten Commandments, of course. You know...the BIG ten? You're a Bible whiz kid. I'm sure you've memorized them all."

"What?" Pete asked incredulously. "Which one?"

"Which one do you think?"

Pete thought for a brief moment. "It's the Commandment about honoring your parents, isn't it?"

Mrs. Johnson nodded her head in agreement. "I asked you to try to make an effort to talk to Rob about Jesus. If you won't honor my request, then you're certainly not honoring your mother, are you?"

"Aww! Come on, mom! That's a cheap shot! You set me up! Gimme a break!"

"Hmmm," Mrs. Johnson said with a slight smile, "isn't that what I just asked you to do for Robby? To give him a break? To give him a chance to find God's goodness and saving grace just like you and I did?"

Pete cupped his head in his hands and let out a disparaging sigh of defeat. "Okay, okay, mom. When we go fishing next Sunday, I'll try to remember to ask him if he's got any questions about Jesus and the Good News." He paused for a moment before he dolefully mumbled, "Just *please* don't make such a big deal about me breaking a commandment, okay? I mean, I'm sorry for dishonoring you and everything, but it's not like I'm committing the *really* bad sins that Rob does all the time. He

44

and I don't have that in common at all. I'm not anywhere close to being that bad!"

"I know you've memorized many verses out of your Bible, Pete," Mrs. Johnson replied. "Do you remember what the penalty for sin is? It's the same for both you and Robby, isn't it? You and Robby *are* different in many ways, and there are also many kinds of sins that people can commit. But they all have the same punishment, don't they? Different sins, but the same punishment. Remember how very serious God's punishment is? In Hebrews it says it's a terrible thing to fall into the hands of the living God! Is that something you want to happen to someone to whom you refer to as a 'friend'? And remember, Peter Daniel Johnson, none of us are good enough to save ourselves from God's punishment without Jesus, are we? *None* of us — including you!"

"I know that, mom!" Pete said with an exasperated tone. "I was just…well…I was just…"

"Realizing how much you need Jesus Christ to save a sinner like yourself?" Pete's mother interjected. Pete's mouth quickly shut. "If you're really Robby's friend, my darling son, then why don't you let him know that too?"

Questions:

1) In your judgment, do you think that Pete was acting as a good friend to Rob and a good follower of Jesus in this story? Why or why not? How would you have behaved differently than Pete in this situation? If Pete goes to church regularly, knows his Bible so well, and grew up

in a Christian home, why do you think it's so difficult for him to apply what he has learned from these resources in his own life? If you are a Christian, do you act like Pete sometimes?

2) Do you personally know anyone right now who is not a Christian and who you believe is 'not good enough' to join God's family? How do you think that person would react if you were to tell him or her about the Good News of Jesus? Would part of his or her reaction depend on the way that you told them about the Good News?

3) Have you ever thought that you were better than someone else? Do you generally view yourself as a 'good' or 'bad' person, or is it more complicated than this? Do you tend to judge yourself as being a 'good' or 'bad' person by comparing yourself to other people you know or have heard about? How would you judge yourself if you were in God's place, and you had to use God's standard of goodness to make this decision of judgment?

4) If God wants us all to be good and not have to undergo his punishment, why doesn't God just make everyone follow his commands whether they want to or not? What would it mean if God had to force us to be good? What kind of relationship would that suggest? Would this be a relationship necessarily based on love and trust or something else?

Bible References mentioned in the Story:

2 Corinthians 5:11-21

Psalm 75:7

Matthew 7:1-5

Hebrews 10:30-31

Romans 1:16-17

John 15:12-13

Chapter 4

Sunday School

Sunday came and the Johnson family picked up Rob from his house on their way to church. Upon entering the church building, Rob seemed overwhelmed with the many strangers greeting him and offering to shake his hand. Rob refused to shake hands with anyone. He simply mumbled an almost inaudible "hey" and tried his best to avoid eye contact. He nervously hovered close to Pete.

Pete gave Rob a nudge with his elbow. "It's alright to shake hands with these people," he whispered.

"I ain't shaking hands with no strangers!" Rob whispered back.

"It's the polite thing to do," Pete responded sternly.

"I think it's kinda weird, if you ask me," Rob replied. "Besides, some of these people smell like the womens' department at the mall. I don't want to get any of that 'perfumey' smell on me! When do we get to get away from all these adults anyways?"

Pete looked up at the clock on the wall.

"Well, we can go downstairs to the Sunday school classroom a little early if you want."

"Okay," Rob said eagerly. "Anything to get us out of this big crowd!"

As Pete and Rob entered the classroom downstairs, they noticed a young man and young woman hanging a poster on the wall. As soon as the poster was secured in place, the man turned toward the two boys.

"Hey, Pete! What's up? How was your week?"

"Great!" Pete replied.

"I see you brought a friend with you."

"Yep. This is my friend Rob. He's never been to church before. This is his first time."

"Hey, Rob," the man said as he extended his hand toward Rob in greeting. "Nice to meet you. My name is Ben."

Rob looked at Ben suspiciously and remained still. Pete gently shoved his friend from behind in an attempt to encourage him to return Ben's greeting in kind.

"Come on, Rob!" Pete whispered. "Say something!"

Ben quickly retracted his hand. "That's okay, Pete," he said with a smile. "I don't blame you, Rob. I think we all get a little nervous the first time we attend a church."

Ben looked over to the young woman who was still standing next to the poster.

"Rob, this is Jill."

Jill simply smiled and waved to Rob. Rob eyed Jill suspiciously also.

After a brief, awkward silence, Rob finally spoke:

"So...aren't you two a little old to be going to Sunday school with a bunch of kids?"

Both Ben and Jill laughed out loud.

"No, Rob," Ben said with a chuckle, "Jill and I aren't students. We're going to be your teachers!"

"You're teachers?" Rob asked doubtfully. "Well, aren't you both a little too *young* to be teachin' a bunch of kids then?"

Ben and Jill looked at each other with amused expressions.

"Well, I'm twenty," Ben replied. "Is that too young?"

Rob ignored the question and turned his attention toward Jill. "How old is she?" he asked.

"Rob!" Pete said with alarm. "My mom told me you're never supposed to ask a woman her age. It's not polite!"

"Well, I didn't ask *her*, did I?" Rob responded smugly. "I asked him!" he said pointing to Ben.

"I'm nineteen," Jill interrupted.

"You're just a teenager!" Rob cried out in disbelief. "Is it even legal for you to teach kids?"

"I think it's going to be just fine, Rob," Jill said with a reassuring nod.

Rob looked to Pete.

"I don't know if I want no teenager teaching me!" he said.

"Listen, Rob," Ben said loudly with a broad smile, "we're really glad you're here with us today. Why don't you give us a chance and see how we do. What do you think?"

"Well...I guess," Rob muttered.

"Great!" Ben said cheerfully. "Now make yourself useful, big guy, and hang up our jackets in the closet just outside the classroom door please." Ben grabbed his and Jill's jackets from the floor next to his feet and threw them to Rob. "And since you two are early, you can also help us to set up the chairs for the class."

"Wow," Rob whispered to Pete as he stared hesitantly at the two jackets he had just caught. "Maybe this Sunday school thing isn't as good as your dad was making it out to be. These two have already got me doin' their chores for them! They better not ask me to wax their cars next!"

Rob slowly turned around to hang up the jackets as Pete rushed for the stack of chairs.

"He already doesn't like Sunday school, and we haven't even started yet," Pete murmured to himself as he began lifting chairs from the stack. "I just knew he wouldn't fit in!"

Pete already had most of the chairs set up before Rob returned to help him.

"Wow!" Pete exclaimed. "You took forever! How long does it take you to hang up two coats? What were you doing over there anyways?"

Rob shrugged indifferently. "Nothin'," he said casually.

At that moment, the door to the classroom burst open. A man carrying a guitar case and two music stands entered the room. A young girl carrying a bass guitar and a medium sized amplifier followed him. Although Rob didn't recognize the man, he did recognize the slender girl with hazel eyes and dark hair tied neatly into a long ponytail. Her name was Becky Croteau, and she was in some of Rob's classes at school.

Becky looked surprised to see Rob.

"Robby?"

"Hey, Becky."

"Did you come with Pete?"

"Yep."

Becky smiled.

"Well, I'm glad you're here," she said. "The more the merrier! These classes are usually a lot of fun. You'll see."

Pete rushed over to Becky and took the amplifier from her. "Here, let me get that set up for you Becky," he offered.

"Oh, thanks, Pete!"

Pete hurried the amplifier over to the stage at the far corner of the room.

Rob gazed curiously at Becky's bass guitar.

"So, what's that thing you're holdin'?" he asked.

"It's a bass guitar. I play the bass in our little church band." She pointed to the man who had entered the room with her who was presently talking with Ben and Jill. "And that's my dad. He directs the band. We also have an electric guitar player and a keyboard player. We all sing too."

"That sounds cool," Rob said nodding his head with approval.

"Do you play an instrument, Robby?" Becky asked.

Rob laughed.

"Who me? No way! I ain't got a musical bone in my whole body!"

"Well, you never know," Becky said with a friendly wink. "Maybe somewhere deep inside you have a hidden gift for music."

"Yeah, right!" Rob replied sarcastically.

"Well, I have to set up now. I see my dad waving to me. I'll catch up with you in a little bit."

As Becky left, the classroom door swung open again. A slightly chubby, short young boy named Ryan McKenna entered. His short, brown hair was neatly parted at the side, and his large brown eyes looked full of excitement.

"Hi, everybody!" he called out in a loud voice.

Ben came up beside the boy and patted him lightly on the back. "Hey there, Ryan!" he said cheerfully. "Did you memorize your Bible verse for this week?"

Ryan seemed startled. "Oh no!" he cried out. "I forgot to remember my memory verse because I forgot that I had a memory verse to remember!"

"Ryan, we have a memory verse every week," Ben said with a laugh. "Did you forget that too?"

Ryan tapped his lips several times thoughtfully. "I don't remember," he finally admitted.

Pete approached Ben and Ryan.

"Well, maybe you can give Ryan some memory tips, Pete," Ben said as he turned to Pete. "You haven't missed one verse yet." Pete smiled proudly.

Ryan turned toward Rob and stared at him for a moment.

"Who are you?" Ryan shouted.

"My name's Rob!" Rob shouted back with his hands cupped around his mouth to further amplify his voice.

Ryan seemed startled by Rob's loud reply. "Why did you yell at me, Rob?" he asked in a softer voice, a slightly wounded expression upon his face. "I'm not hard of hearing, y'know!"

Rob looked over at Pete with a confused expression, and then stared back at Ryan. "But you yelled at me first!" Rob said. "I just thought..."

"Ryan is loud all of the time," Pete interrupted with a grin, "but he's not deaf or anything. He can hear perfectly fine."

"I'm just loud when I get excited is all!" Ryan trumpeted, his excitement level apparently regaining vigor.

"Just to warn you, Rob," Pete started, "Ryan gets excited a lot! So if you sit next to him, you should get some earplugs or something!"

"Hey, I heard that!" Ryan yelled indignantly.

"Ouch!" Rob replied as he held both hands over his ears in a mocking reaction to Ryan's rather loud response. "Everyone in the whole state just heard *that*!" he said. Pete — and even Ryan — started to laugh as Rob comically shook his head back and forth, pretending to wince in pain.

Five minutes later, the classroom chairs were filled with twelve students. Rob sat between Pete and Ryan. Ben and Jill led everyone in a short prayer. As everyone closed their eyes and bowed their heads in prayer, Rob stared nervously around the room as if he were trying to decide if he should do the same thing.

After the prayer was finished, Mr. Croteau jumped onto the stage and asked everyone to stand.

"Stand? What for?" Rob whispered to Pete.

"For the worship songs," Pete whispered back. "It's a way of showing our respect and thanks to God. Just do what I do."

Mr. Croteau directed the band to play the song *Lord, I lift your name on High*. Two students, Amelia and James, stood on the stage and lead everyone in choreographed hand motions in time with the music as the class sang. Again, Rob looked around the room nervously and remained silent and still.

After leading the students in two more songs, Mr. Croteau stepped off the stage. He turned to Ben and Jill.

"If you need my help, just text me. I'll be upstairs."

"Thanks, but we'll be alright," Ben replied confidently. "Jill and I finished all the training requirements and practice sessions for running this class by ourselves just last week, Mr. Croteau...remember? Besides, we've been doing great a great job leading this class over the past month with very little adult supervision. I don't think there's anything that would come up that Jill and I wouldn't be able to handle on our own. We're ready for anything. You can count on us!"

Mr. Croteau grinned widely. "I'm just a text message away if you need me," he offered again as if he hadn't heard a word that Ben had just said. He gently patted Ben on the back several times in a somewhat sympathetic manner and then disappeared out the classroom door.

"Well! You guys sounded pretty good this morning!" Ben remarked with an enthusiastic smile as he turned to face the class.

"Good job, everyone!" Jill added.

"Alright," Ben began, "before we get started with the lesson today, we should take up the collection. Ryan, would you please grab the collection plate and pass it around?"

"Oh, boy!" Ryan said eagerly as he jumped out of his chair to grab the collection plate. "I love helping!"

"What's a collection?" Rob asked Pete quietly.

"It's when we give money to help out the church and the community," Pete replied softly. "Don't worry about it, Rob. This is your first time here and you're just visiting. Don't feel like you have to give anything."

Ben walked over to Pete and Rob.

"I overhead you guys talking," he said. "Pete is right about the collection, Rob. Please don't feel like you have to give anything. You're our guest today, and we're all just glad you're here."

"I don't mind," Rob said boldly. "I got tons of money."

Pete's eyes shot open with surprise.

"You do?"

"Sure!" Rob replied as he pulled a wallet out of his back pocket. He opened it and removed a ten-dollar bill.

"Whoa!" Pete cried as he jumped out of his seat. "Ten dollars! Can I hold it?"

"Whoa!" Ben said as he placed his hand gently on Pete's shoulder. "Calm down there, Pete! Try to control yourself. It's only money."

"But he's got ten dollars!"

"Yeah, I see," Ben replied calmly. "That's really generous of you to offer ten dollars to God and the church, Rob, but like I just said, you don't have to..."

"It's no problem," Rob interrupted as he fished again inside the wallet and pulled out an additional five dollar bill. "Here. Take five more."

"He's loaded!" Ryan cried out. "All I got is fifty cents!"

"How much money do you have in there?" Pete asked as he quickly grabbed the wallet from Rob and looked eagerly inside.

"Hey!" Rob snapped. "That's mine!"

"Wait a minute," Ben said as he eyed the wallet curiously. "Pete, let me see that, please."

Pete handed the wallet to Ben. Ben looked inside and pulled out his own driver's license.

"Hey! What's going on here?" Ben said crossly. "This is my wallet!" He glared at Rob. "How did you get this?"

"I found it in your coat pocket when I was hangin' it up for you."

"You *found* it?" Ben asked with fury. "Did you take anything else? Did you take anything from Jill's coat?"

"Naw," Rob replied coolly. "She's broke."

"Rob, stealing is wrong!" Ben said sternly.

"I'm sorry. I forgot that you religious types don't like people stealin' stuff from you."

"I don't think religion has much to do with it," Jill interrupted. "I can't think of too many people who like to be robbed, Rob."

There was a low rumble of laughter from the children in response to Jill's witty reply.

"Should we call my dad to come help with this?" Becky quickly suggested.

Ben's angry expression immediately vanished.

"Oh, no, no, no!" Ben said quickly with a hint of panic in his voice. He looked at Jill. "Jill and I are both responsible youth leaders. I think we can handle this situation ourselves, and in our own way, right Jill?"

"I don't know," Jill said with a serious tone. Her eyes focused squarely on Rob. "I think that all depends on what words come out of Rob's mouth next."

"Who, me?" Rob asked pointing to himself. Jill remained silent. She continued to stare intently at Rob. "I said I was sorry." Rob said with a shrug.

"And?" Jill asked.

"Uh…and it was wrong? And I won't do it again?" Rob asked timidly.

"Was that a question or an answer?" Jill demanded.

"An answer?" Rob replied with a hopeful expression. Jill remained silent and folded her arms tightly across her chest. Rob squirmed a little in his chair. "Are you sure you're just nineteen years old?" he asked. "You seem a lot older."

Jill stared at Rob a moment more before she spoke.

"I think we've got everything under control here, Ben," she stated confidently.

"Good!" Ben said relieved.

"Whew! Well, I'm glad that's settled," Rob said as he dropped the money he was holding into the offering plate. "Anyways, there's the fifteen dollars I promised for the church. I hope that helps make up for me stealin' your stuff."

"Wait a minute!" Ben said with a hint of renewed hostility. "That's *my* money! You just can't put *my* money in the offering plate!"

"Technically, it's not really your money," Rob countered somewhat impishly. "It belongs to God…especially now that it's in *his* offering plate. And like you said just a second ago to Pete, 'it's only money'. Of course, if you want to take God's money away from God's church and God's people and keep it for yourself, who am I to stop you?"

For a moment, it looked as if Ben were going to take back the money. He glanced up at the young faces around the room anxiously watching to see what he was going to do next. Ben took a deep breath and exhaled slowly.

"Y'know," he said with forced composure, "we should all give something. That's the right thing to do. So how about if I give...just one dollar instead?"

"That sounds okay with me," said Rob.

"Good," Ben said with relief as he removed the last dollar bill from his wallet.

"But," Rob continued, "I wonder what God will think about you taking all that money back out of his collection plate just to replace it with a measly, little, pitiful, old, stinky, one dollar bill. I guess God's just not worth it then."

"My dad has a Proverb he always says," Ryan interjected. "He says 'riches won't help on the day of judgment, but right living is a safeguard against death.'"

Ben looked at Ryan with a sober expression.

"Of all the verses you had to memorize out of the Bible, that had to be the one, huh?"

Ryan shrugged. "It comes in handy for times just like this!" he replied cheerfully.

After a moment of silence, Jill cleared her throat loudly. Ben glanced over at her. Her arms were still folded over her chest and she raised one eyebrow as if she were silently asking "Ben? Where are you going with this?" Ben turned back to his young, impressionable audience.

"Well," Ben said, sounding somewhat weary this time, "what I actually was thinking I should do in this case is to just add this one dollar bill I have in my hand to the other fifteen already in the plate. I think that's the right thing to do…at this point." He dropped the dollar into the collection plate which Ryan was holding. "Well, that's it. I'm out. That's all I had in there," he said as he examined the inside of his wallet.

"Well, that's *almost* all you had in there," Rob said correcting him. "You also have a driver's license, an insurance card and an old prescription for some acne medicine."

"What's acne?" Ryan asked.

"You really don't know?" Rob replied. "It's what teenagers get, and it's so gross! It's zits and pimples, pus balls and…"

"Okay, then!" Jill interrupted loudly. "Ryan! Keep that plate going around, and let's get onto the rest of the lesson, alright?"

"Right, right!" Ben said as he quickly put his wallet in his back pocket. He looked slightly embarrassed. "Let's stay focused on the lesson here!"

"Is this the kinda thing that always gets you into detention at school?" Pete whispered to Rob.

Rob shrugged.

"Probably."

"So," Ben began, "Who here can tell me last week's memory verse?"

Pete's hand shot quickly into the air.

"Uh…not you Pete," Ben said as eyed the rest of the class. "Let's give someone else a chance to answer this time."

"Awww!" Pete said sadly. Rob snickered at him.

After a brief moment, Becky cautiously raised her hand.

"Becky!" Ben shouted enthusiastically. "Let's hear it!"

"Well," Becky started slowly, "I think it's from …Philippians?"

"Yeah, that's right," Ben said nodding his head in agreement. "Philippians two, verse thirteen."

"Oh, yeah! That's right!" Becky said with a smile. "So the verse goes something like…'For God is working in you, giving you the desire to obey him and the power to do what pleases him.' Am I close?"

"That was perfect!" Jill said with a smile. Jill held out her palm. "Gimme a high-five!" Becky laughed as she smacked her palm against Jill's in celebration.

"Awesome!" Ben said. "Can anyone tell me from what we talked about last week how God can be working in you like the verse says?"

Pete's hand shot up again.

"Alright, Pete," Ben nodded. "Go for it!"

"Well," Pete started, "last week we talked about who the Holy Spirit of God is and how he lives inside of us to help guide us in all truth. The Holy Spirit can help remind us of the things that Jesus told us about in the Bible, and he can help us to understand them better. That's one way God can work inside us."

"Great job, Pete!" Ben said approvingly. "Good memory as usual!"

"There's a person that lives inside you?" Rob blurted out as he turned to Pete. "I don't see nobody else sittin' in your chair except you!"

62

"That's because we can't directly see the Holy Spirit with our eyes, Rob," Ben pointed out. "But we can certainly feel his presence helping to guide us and comfort us when we spend time with God."

"So, who is this spirit then?" Rob asked. "Is he like some kind of ghost?"

Ben smiled.

"Well, Rob," Ben started, "some people call him the Holy Ghost. But the Holy Spirit is part of God, and he can be everywhere at once. He helps to give us understanding about God's plan and what God wants us to do, and the Holy Spirit also helps people to communicate with God when we pray, even when we have trouble praying clearly."

"This is what Jesus told his disciples about the Holy Spirit: he said 'If you love me, obey my commandments. And I will ask the Father, and he will give you another Advocate, who will never leave you. He is the Holy Spirit who leads into all truth' and Jesus says a little later 'when I am raised to life again, you will know that I am in my Father, and you are in me, and I am in you'. The Holy Spirit works and lives inside of people; he connects us to God and God to us."

Rob sunk back in his chair. "Sounds kinda creepy if you ask me," he mumbled.

"So, how else can God work in us to give us the desire to obey him and the power to do what pleases him? Emma? Do you know?"

"By giving us spiritual gifts?" Emma responded shyly from a chair near the back of the room.

"Good job, Emma!" Jill said with a smile.

"Yeah, that's great!" Ben agreed. "Last week we asked all of you to think about what kinds of gifts God may have given to you that would help you to serve him. So, do any of you think you might know what spiritual gifts you may have?" The room remained silent.

"Jill?" Ben asked. "Can you start us off? What's your gift?"

"Teaching is definitely my gift," Jill replied. "In fact, I'm planning on going to college next year to become a teacher."

"I knew it!" Rob whispered to Pete. "She acts like a teacher!"

"Shhh!" Pete said as he elbowed Rob in the side.

"Hey! I think my gift might be teaching too!" said James. "I like studying things and seeing how they work and then explaining it to people. I especially love to study science. Hey...maybe I'll be a scientist instead, and then maybe I could use my scientific discoveries to help get rid of hunger and diseases and stuff like that all over the world."

"Jesus certainly wants us to love others and take care of them," Jill said. "I think that would be a great way to serve him, James."

"I love arts and crafts," said Amelia. "I love building cool things out of ordinary stuff from around the house. I love to invent things too."

"That's great, Amelia," Ben said. "God needs people who are artistic and skilled in making all sorts of things. During the time of Moses, God chose many artists to make the first tabernacle and everything in it. It was a very important job. God gave those people the gifts to be able to engineer those items to be exactly what God needed them to be."

"Maybe you'll become an engineer, Amelia," Jill said with an encouraging nod. Amelia smiled wide in response.

"I think I've got a musical gift," said Becky. "I used it just a little while ago to serve God by helping to lead all of us in worship with the rest of the band…and with my dad too, of course!"

"I got a gift!" said Rob eagerly. "I don't know if it came from God or not, but I got one!"

"Okay," Ben said with a nod. "Tell us what it is."

"Well, it's actually easier to show you what it is," Rob said as he lifted the bottom of his shirt so that he could place his right-hand fist firmly under his left armpit. He then proceeded to quickly flap his left arm up and down as if he were a single winged chicken trying to fly. The sound that resulted was that of loud, repeated bursts of flatulence.

"Check it out! I can play the beginning of Jingle bells by doing this!" Rob said with delight.

Ryan seemed awestruck by Rob's performance. "Oh, cool! You can do an armpit fart!" he shouted as he also stuck his fist under his own armpit. "Let me see if I have that kind of a gift too!" The entire class started to laugh.

"All right! All right! Calm down everyone!" Ben said loudly as he waved both of his hands in the air to regain control of the students. "Come on! Stay focused here. And Ryan…please stop trying to get your armpit to make that noise, okay?" After a few more giggles, the class finally settled down.

"Now let's talk about something different," Ben said as he turned and walked over to the poster that he and Jill had stuck to the wall earlier. "Today we're going to learn about the fruits of the Holy Spirit which Jill and I have listed on this poster here."

Suddenly, a loud, long, low pitched sound of flatulence ripped through the room. Ben turned around to see that Ryan still had his fist shoved up under his shirt. Ryan, who seemed to be frozen in place, stared back at Ben with a frightened, wide-eyed expression.

"Ryan!" Ben said sternly, "Didn't I just tell you to stop trying to make that noise with your armpit?"

"Uh...actually...I didn't make it with my armpit," Ryan said bashfully.

"Ewww!" Pete and Rob said at the same time as they wrinkled up their noses and slid their chairs away from Ryan.

"My father has an old saying," Ryan stated. "He says 'better out than in'. And just hearing the noise of farts made me feel like I needed to do a real one, so...."

"Ryan, excuse yourself please," Jill interrupted gently.

"Excuse me everyone," Ryan replied shyly.

Many of the students began waving their hands in front of their noses. Sour looks of disgust appeared on their faces as a foul odor wafted slowly throughout the room. Ben asked James to open the classroom door a little ways to let some fresh air in.

Jill walked over to Ben. "I think this is a good time for me to get the snacks ready," she whispered.

"I wish I could go with you right now too," Ben whispered back as he wrinkled his nose.

Jill disappeared through the swinging doors that lead to the kitchen area which was located on the same side of the room as the poster.

"Hey! Where's she going?" Rob asked Ben.

"Jill is going to get your snacks," Ben replied.

"Snacks!" Rob shouted. "That's awesome! I heard that we get snacks at Sunday school! Are they free?"

Ben smiled slightly. "Yes," he said. "The snacks are free, but they are only for the people that can pay attention and focus!" The classroom instantly became silent. Ben turned back to the poster on the wall.

"So, getting back to the poster now. When we follow the Holy Spirit's guidance, we will develop these characteristics known as the fruits of the Holy Spirit. These fruits are to be enjoyed both by us personally as well as by those around us. The poster shows the nine fruits that are listed in the book of Galatians. So starting from the top of the list we have love, joy, peace, patience, kindness, goodness, gentleness, faithfulness, and self control. These are the traits that God will help to develop inside us as we follow him. With most people, it will take some time to develop all of these traits, but it's these traits that help to identify us as true Christians — people that are truly following Jesus Christ. Does anyone have any questions?"

"Why did you and Jill put a dot over the letter 'T'?" Rob blurted out.

Ben stared at the poster for a few seconds.

"Where do you see a dot over a 'T'?" Ben asked.

Rob jumped out of his chair and walked over to the poster and pointed to a small, black bump above the letter "T" in the word "control". As he pointed his finger, the little, black bump took flight and flew chaotically around the poster.

"It was a fly!" Ryan shouted excitedly.

"I'll get 'em!" Rob said as he began waving his hands through the air. With one wild swat, Rob knocked over a cup filled with markers and pens which sat on a small table near the poster. The objects rolled in various directions as they hit the floor.

At that same moment, Jill swung open the kitchen door and entered the room carrying a large tray of cookies, cups and a pitcher of water. Unable to see the floor directly beneath her, Jill stepped onto several markers, and her foot slipped out from under her. She quickly lost her balance. Instantly, Ben sprang into action.

"Move it, Rob!" Ben yelled as he raced to help Jill. Rob jumped out of the way just in time to allow Ben to catch Jill in his arms as she fell backward. Cookies, cups and water rained down onto the two youth leaders. They were both soaked. Jill peered up at Ben, who was holding her securely in his arms, and smiled. Ben looked down at Jill, shook his head, and began to laugh uncontrollably. Then Jill and the entire class also joined in the laughter.

"Wow!" Rob said as he grabbed a cookie off the floor and began to eat it. "Those two are really taking this well! Most of my teachers would have lost it by now, and I would have ended up in detention for sure!"

Pete shook his head with despair. "I just knew something like this would happen if I brought Rob to church!" he mumbled to himself. "He just doesn't fit in! He'll be kicked out for sure — just like I said he would!"

The church services ended, and Mrs. Johnson made her way downstairs to the Sunday school classroom to collect Pete and

Rob. As she entered the classroom, she saw Ben and Jill at the doorway. Pete and Rob were standing next to them. They were the last students in the room.

"Oops! Sorry I'm so late!"

"That's alright, Mrs. Johnson," Ben said with a weary smile.

"So, you two," Mrs. Johnson said as she looked at the boys, "how was class today?"

Ben, apparently unaware that Mrs. Johnson was asking the two boys this question, answered before Pete or Rob could say anything.

"Well, I learned a lot about patience," he said with a solemn tone.

"And I learned a lot about self-control," Jill added.

"Yeah," Ben agreed nodding to Jill sympathetically. "We definitely learned a lot about self-control today!"

Mrs. Johnson glanced up at Ben and Jill with an amused look. "Actually," she said, "I was asking the boys."

"Oh!" Ben said apologetically. "Sorry…I didn't mean to speak out of turn, Mrs. Johnson."

Rob looked up at Ben with surprise.

"What do ya mean that you guys learned about patience and self control today?" he asked. "Wasn't that what you two were just teachin' us about? Y'know…the fruit of the Spirit and all that other stuff that was on the poster? Love, joy, peace and stuff?"

"Hey!" Mrs. Johnson said with a pleased expression. "You *did* learn something today!" She patted Rob on the back and winked at Pete. Pete folded his arms across his chest indignantly and mumbled something under his breath.

"So, Robby," Mrs. Johnson started, "do you think you may want to come back to Sunday school next week?"

"Sure!" Rob answered. "It was awesome here today!"

"Really?" Ben asked in disbelief.

"Oh, sure!" Rob said with a cheerful expression. "You and Jill rock! You're both awesome teachers!" Ben and Jill looked at each other with a curious stare. "You two should really get married and have a lot of kids cause I think you're both really good with kids!" Rob added.

Ben blushed and laughed nervously. Jill, who also seemed embarrassed by Rob's suggestion, let out a short giggle and timidly pushed her hair neatly over her ears.

"Well listen, Rob," Ben started with an authoritative tone, "before anyone would get married and have kids or anything like that, you should really go on a date first, don't you think?"

Jill's expression suddenly lit up.

"Really?" she asked eagerly. "Did you say something about going on a date?"

Ben seemed taken by surprise. He turned to Jill.

"Uh...well...I was just trying to tell Rob that people in *general* should really go on a date first before they even consider marriage and kids. They should probably go on a whole bunch of dates actually. But...ah...I wasn't necessarily talking about...well, you know...*us* going on a date!" Ben laughed nervously again.

"Oh, no! Of course not!" Jill said quickly through a weak smile. Her cheeks flushed as she stared down at the floor.

Mrs. Johnson gently pulled Ben near her and whispered something quietly in his ear. Ben straightened his posture slightly and cleared his throat.

"But, uh…Jill. I mean if you, like, wanted to, y'know, go out on a date…" he stammered, "a date with me, that is…well, I think that would be, like, really cool…actually."

Jill hesitated thoughtfully.

"Well, where would we go if we were to, you know…go on a date?"

"We could go to the movies," Ben suggested. He glanced at Rob. "Well, we could go except I seem to be a little short on cash."

"I'm broke," Jill said quickly.

"Do you like to sail?" Ben asked.

Jill's face suddenly beamed with excitement.

"I would love to sail!"

"Great," Ben continued, "because the weather is still warm enough, and I've got a Sunfish sailboat at home we can use."

"Well, have a good time, you two!" Mrs. Johnson interrupted with a smile. "I've got to get these two boys home so that they can get ready for their own boating adventure."

"That's right!" Rob shouted. "Me and Pete get to go fishin' in a canoe today so we gotta go! See ya next week!"

"I look forward to it, Rob," Ben said with a hint of sincerity. "Have a good week guys!"

"Y'know, Rob" said Jill with a gentle smile. "I think you have a much greater, special gift inside you than doing an armpit fart. I can't wait to see what that gift is and how you might use it to serve God."

"Wow!" Rob said. "You think so?"

"You've got great potential," Jill replied.

"Oh, come on!" Pete said hastily as he shoved Rob out the classroom door. "Let's get him outa here before his head gets so big that we *can't* get him out!"

Questions:

1) Have you ever been to Sunday school at a church before? If so, what was *your* first time like? Were you nervous? Did you ever invite a friend to your Sunday school before? What did he or she think of it? If you have never been to a Sunday school before, do you think you might want to go sometime?

2) What does the Holy Spirit do in a Christian's life? Without looking, can you name all nine fruits of the Holy Spirit as listed in the book of Galatians (and also listed in the story)? Which fruits do you think you do a good job of showing to other people? Why?

3) If you are a Christian already, have you ever experienced the Holy Spirit working in your life? For example, do you think he has ever comforted you in times of trouble, helped you gain some important insight about Jesus, help remind you about a Bible verse when you really needed it, etc.?

4) What types of gifts or talents do you have that has, or could, help you to serve God? Do you think that any of these could be Spiritual Gifts given to you by God to help do his work on this earth?

Bible References Relating to this Story:

John 14:15-18   Galatians 5:16-26

John 14:26   Philippians 2:13

John 16:13-15   1 Corinthians 2:10-12

Chapter 5

The Fishing Trip

Rob, Pete and Mr. Johnson went fishing after church. The skies were slightly overcast, but the temperature was still relatively warm considering it was now the end of September.

Mr. Johnson untied the canoe from the car's roof racks and, with the help of both boys, slowly carried it to the water's edge. As they were getting the rest of the gear from the car, Pete's dad noticed that he had forgotten something important.

"Oops! It looks like I only brought two life jackets with us," said Mr. Johnson. "I forgot to grab the other one on the way out. That means that only two people can go fishing in the canoe at a time."

"Can me and Pete go first?" Rob asked.

"What do you think, Pete?" Mr. Johnson asked.

"Sure," Pete said. "I've done it plenty of times before. We'll be okay."

Mr. Johnson turned to Rob.

"Can you swim, Robby?"

"Sure. No problem."

"Good!" Mr. Johnson said with a smile. "Okay. So you two will go in the canoe first, and I'll fish from the shore. Here's the rules. Both of you need to wear your life jackets at all times. Neither of you are allowed to stand up in the boat once I push you out into the lake. Please be careful when you cast — try not to catch each other with your hooks. And don't go too far from shore, alright? You really shouldn't have to go too far out to catch some good-sized fish. Do you guys understand the rules?" Both boys nodded in agreement.

Next, they gathered their gear and climbed into the canoe — Rob in the front and Pete in the back. When they were settled securely on their seats with their paddles in hand, Mr. Johnson pushed the canoe out into the lake. Pete and Rob paddled about forty feet from shore before they cast their lines into the water.

As they fished, they talked about their Sunday school class which they had both attended earlier that morning.

"I thought for sure they were going to kick you out of class after you stole Ben's wallet and caused Jill to slip with the snack tray," Pete confessed.

"The snack tray thing was an accident," Rob said. "I didn't mean to do that."

"What about stealing the wallet? Was that an accident too?" Pete asked cynically.

"No way!" Rob replied with an offended tone. "I meant to do that!"

"But why?" Pete asked.

"It's just who I am," Rob said with a shrug. "I'm not proud of it. I know it's not right to steal from people, but what can I do? It's not like I'm perfect like you and your parents. It's not like I can change or anything, right?"

Pete started to say something out loud, but then stopped, and in a miserable, whispered grumble remarked, "Yeah, I remember, God. I made a promise." Pete had just been reminded about the promise he had made to his mother earlier that week which was to ask Rob if he had any questions about the Good News of Jesus Christ during their fishing trip. Apparently, Pete wasn't in any way thrilled about keeping this particular promise.

"What?" Rob asked loudly. "Did you say somethin'?"

"Uh...I was just going to say that the Sox are having a rough season," Pete said as he quickly changed the subject. "I don't even think they are going to get the wildcard spot this year."

"Yeah," Rob agreed. "The Sox stink worse than these socks I've been wearin' for the past two weeks. And that's pretty bad! I hope they win their next game. We could really use some good news right about now!"

"Yeah. Good news," Pete said nervously with a slight grimace. "So...speaking of good news and all that...what did you think about that talk you had with my dad last week? Y'know... the Good News about Jesus?"

"It's kinda weird, I guess. But I'm sort of interested in finding out more about all this Jesus stuff anyways."

"Whew! It's starting to get pretty hot out here!" Pete said nervously as he abruptly changed the subject once again.

"Hey!" Rob said with excitement. "I got a great way to cool you down!"

Rob carefully turned around in his seat to face Pete. Then he leaned over the side of the canoe slightly and smacked the top surface of the water with his hand in such a way as to direct a small sample of the cold water into Pete's lap. The canoe rocked back and forth slightly.

"Hey stop!" Pete yelled. "I don't want to get wet! Besides, you're scaring all the fish away!"

Rob laughed. "There's no fish in this spot! If there was, we would have caught 'em by now."

"We've only been fishing for a couple of minutes, Rob! You gotta be more patient if you want to catch a fish!"

"I'm bored," Rob declared. "So let's liven things up around here and have some fun instead! Like you just said, it's hot out here!"

Rob splashed more water at Pete. As Pete glared at him, he noticed that Rob's life jacket was no longer buckled.

"Hey! Your vest is unbuckled," Pete pointed out.

"I got hot in this thing, so I unbuckled it to let some air in. What's it to you?"

"You're supposed to have your vest buckled all the time when you're out on the lake in the canoe!" Pete shouted back. "Those are my dad's rules, remember?"

"Your dad didn't say that! He said we just have to wear them. He didn't say anything about buckling them! What's the matter, Pete? Do you think we're going to tip over and get wet?" Rob laughed mischievously and splashed more water at Pete.

Pete put down his pole and picked up his paddle.

"Well," he said angrily, "If you're hot too, I got a better way to cool you off faster! What do you think of this?" Pete swung his paddle and struck the surface of the water dousing most of Rob's body with a very large spray of cool water. Rob yelled out and raised both hands to cover his face. As he did this, his fishing pole dropped into the water.

"No!" Pete yelled out. "Grab it! That's one of my dad's poles!"

Rob quickly leaned over to grab the pole and the whole canoe rotated up onto its side.

"Don't!" Pete yelled out. "You're going to..."

It was too late. The canoe flipped upside down tossing both of the boys into the water. Pete surfaced and yelled out to his father who was fishing from shore. As Pete turned around to look for Rob, he felt something grab him around the waist and almost pull him under. It was Rob. Pete tried to keep his head above water as Rob tried to climb on top of him. Pete freed himself from him and swam a short distance away. He noticed that Rob was spending more time under water than above it. Rob surfaced long enough to yell for help. Pete then realized that Rob's life jacket was no longer on him. He also realized that Rob really didn't know how to swim. Pete swam back to Rob, took him by the arm and lifted him. Rob surfaced and gasped for air. He panicked and frantically tried to climb on top of Pete again.

"I can't swim! I can't swim!" he screamed.

"Calm down!" Pete shouted, "You're going to drown us both!"

Pete reached for the water filled Canoe which had righted itself, and he pulled it toward them. Once Rob realized that they weren't going to sink, he finally stopped thrashing about.

Pete's dad called out for the boys to hang on to the canoe.

"Just stay calm," he shouted. "Slide into the canoe. It will hold you both up even though it's filled with water. You two will be fine. I'm going to take the hook off the end of my line, and cast the line and sinker out to you. Pete, I need you to grab the line and knot it to the rope that's tied to the bow of the canoe. We have about twenty-five feet of slack to work with there. I'll reel the end of the canoe's rope into where I can reach it, and then I'll pull you two and the canoe into shore with the rope."

"He can't reach us!" Rob said. "He can't cast out this far!" He was very frightened.

"You don't know my father," Pete said. "Just trust him and try not to do anything else stupid!"

Pete's dad took the hook off the end of his line and then cast out to the boys. It was a perfect cast! The sinker bounced right off of the top of Rob's head.

"_Oww_!" he yelled.

"You deserved that," Pete said. "You didn't follow my dad's rules about your life vest, and you knew it. You also lied to us about being able to swim!"

Pete grabbed the bobber and found the end of the fishing line. Then he tied it to the end of the canoe's rope.

"Go ahead, dad!" Pete yelled out as he fed the rope out of the bow.

Pete's dad began reeling in the rope. The rope wasn't quite long enough to reach the shore, so his dad had to walk out into the water a short distance to grab it.

"Hold on you two!" he called out. He slowly began pulling the canoe and the boys to shore with the rope. Mr. Johnson chuckled.

"Y'know," he said loudly, "most of Jesus' first students were fishermen, and he told them that someday they would be the ones teaching other people about the Good News just as Jesus had done with them. So Jesus told these fishermen that he was going to make them the 'fishers *of* men'. He sent them out to get people '*hooked*' on the Good News of Jesus and '*reel*' them into the Kingdom of God. I wonder if that applies to boys too?" Mr. Johnson paused only to chuckle briefly before continuing. "Just wait until I tell the guys at work tomorrow that I went fishing this weekend and hauled in two eighty pounders! Normally, I throw back whatever I catch, but I guess you two are keepers, huh?" Both boys had somber expressions upon their faces and remained absolutely silent as Mr. Johnson laughed heartily at his own lackluster jokes.

Once on shore again, a soaked Pete and Rob shivered in the sun as they sat on a dock that jutted a short distance out from the lake's edge. The boys watched as Pete's dad emptied the water from the canoe. Once the canoe was empty, Mr. Johnson used a tree branch as a paddle and pushed off from shore in the boat to retrieve the two missing paddles and Rob's life vest.

Pete looked at Rob and shook his head in despair.

"What?" Rob asked defensively. "What are you looking at? It wasn't my fault! You're the one that swung the paddle!"

"You know," Pete began, "you're always going against everything you know is right, and you're always paying for it too! I don't know what my parents were thinking! You could never be a Christian! How could someone like you ever change?"

"Well, I don't think I want to be a Christian if I was gonna turn out to be like you!"

Pete looked startled.

"What?" he asked softly. "What did you say?"

"You heard me, Johnson! I don't wanna be no Christian if I'm gonna turn out acting like you! Are you even sure you *are* a real Christian? You sure don't seem like it to me! You're always on my case about how bad and rotten I am, and you're pretty crabby and impatient about it too! You know a lot about what the Bible says, and you've memorized a bunch of stuff out of it, but where's the fruit of the Spirit that you're supposed to have? Where's your love and joy and peace and patience that we talked about in Sunday school today? Didn't Ben tell us that it's those kinds of things that real Christians are supposed to have? I can see those kinds of things in your dad, but I don't see none of them in you!"

Pete stared blankly at Rob for a few seconds. His shoulders suddenly slumped, and his head drooped.

"You're right, Rob," he whispered. Rob looked surprised.

"I am?"

"Yeah," Pete replied glumly. "Lately I haven't been acting like a follower of Jesus. I go to church, read my Bible, say my

82

prayers, but I haven't been following or listening to his living Spirit. I've been following my own spirit instead." Pete bowed his head and tightly shut his eyes. "I'm sorry Lord. Once again, I'm *so* sorry!" Pete remained silent — head bent low.

Rob nervously inched away from Pete a short distance. "So…this is pretty weird," he said. "Should I, like, get inside the car just in case God's gonna wack you with a bolt of lightning or somethin'?"

"Something's been bugging me for months now," Pete responded, slowly lifting his head and opening his eyes. "It's like you said, Rob…I know a lot of stuff about what the Bible has to say about being a Christian, but lately I've been having trouble putting what I know into practice. It seems that I don't want to do what the Holy Spirit has been asking me to do. I could feel that he's wanted me to tell you about Jesus for a while now, but I haven't done it because I thought you were too much of a bad person to become a Christian. I didn't believe you could change your ways, but it seems that God thinks differently." Pete closed his eyes and bowed his head once more. "I guess I haven't been trusting you too much lately, huh God? I think I know better than you do, don't I? I've been feeling miserable lately, and now I know that, once again, it's because of my lack of faith in you. Thank you for helping me to see that, God."

"Hey, Pete?" Rob started cautiously. "I don't see nobody near this dock except you and me. What makes you think that God's around here listenin' to us?"

Pete opened his eyes and turned to Rob.

"When you told me you didn't see the fruit of the Spirit in me, the story of Jonah suddenly popped into my head. I believe the Holy Spirit reminded me of that story on purpose to show me who I've been acting like."

"Jonah?" Rob asked with a surprised expression. "You mean the story about the guy that gets swallowed by a whale? That Jonah?"

"Well, the Bible says he was swallowed by a big fish actually, not necessarily a whale," Pete replied with an authoritative air. Then he sighed wearily. "But yeah. That's the guy I'm talking about."

"Well, even I know that story!" Rob stated proudly. "I didn't know it came out of the Bible. I just thought it was from a little kid's book. So, what does this guy, Jonah, have to do with you? I thought that the whale…fish…or whatever it was swallows him whole and then pukes him out again on a beach somewhere. The end."

"There's more to the story than that," Pete began. "Jonah was a prophet of God."

"What's a Prophet?" Rob asked.

"Well, the prophets of the Bible were people who hear messages from God, and then they deliver the messages to whoever God wants them delivered to," Pete answered. "So, one day God asked this prophet named Jonah to go tell a message to the people who lived in this big city called Nineveh. These people were acting really bad according to God. So God told Jonah to tell them that God was angry with the way they were acting, and that God was planning on punishing them. But God also told Jonah to tell the people of Nineveh that if they were truly sorry about what they were doing, and turned to God and changed their ways, that they would be saved from God's punishment. But Jonah didn't want to follow God's plan because Jonah thought that these people were too bad to be saved. So Jonah ran away from God and Nineveh, but God reminded Jonah who was in charge. That's why he had a giant fish swallow Jonah — to keep him from running away. Jonah survived inside that fish for three days before it spit him out on land, so he had three days inside the fish to think about what he had done and to change his *own* ways and turn back to God."

"Whoa!" Rob exclaimed as he wrinkled his nose in disgust. "Three days inside of fish guts? That's, like, so gross! He must have smelled worse than my socks!"

"And I bet Jonah probably felt really uncomfortable being inside a fish too," Pete added. "He probably felt miserable. Kinda like the way I feel now."

"So, you don't think I'm good enough to be a Christian, huh?" Rob asked Pete sharply.

"I guess the point to the Jonah story is that it doesn't matter if *I* think you are good enough or not. I'm supposed to be doing what God wants me to do—not walking in the opposite direction from him. But now he's got my full attention." Pete looked directly at Rob. "So, Rob…it seems that God's pretty interested in you."

"God's interested in me?" Rob asked in disbelief. "Why?"

"I don't know," Pete shrugged. "He must have some good plans for you, but it's hard to say since neither of us can see into the future. Anyway, God wants you to get to know more about him. So…what do you think?"

"But don't I have to be perfect and all good and stuff if I decide to become a Christian?" Rob asked with sincere curiosity.

Pete smiled sheepishly.

"No. You don't have to be perfect. Nobody is. I'm a Christian, and I'm certainly not perfect."

"What?" Rob asked in disbelief. "But you're 'Pete the Perfect'! That's what a lot of kids at school call you, because you always follow the rules and never get in trouble!"

Pete rolled his eyes with embarrassment.

"Well, that's not exactly true, Rob. Like I said, lately I've been having a hard time doing what I know is right. You know that fifty dollar bill I showed you last month?"

"Yeah?" Rob replied with great interest.

"It wasn't really mine. I guess you could say I…I stole it from someone else."

"You?" Rob exclaimed in disbelief. "No way! That's somethin' I would do! No wonder you were acting so weird that day!"

"Yeah," Pete sighed. "I've got a problem with money. The Holy Spirit kept trying to remind me that day about what God says about stealing. I kept hearing over and over in my mind that day 'You must not steal! You must not steal!' So that's another case where I decided to ignore the Spirit and do things my own way instead. I'm a Christian, but lately I've been a pretty miserable Christian. So you see, I've got a lot of changing that I've gotta do myself." Pete looked directly into Rob's eyes. "So, Rob…you wanna join me? We can help each other to change…to be more like Jesus."

"I'm really confused about this Jesus guy," Rob said. "I mean, all this Christian stuff is …well…like really bizarre!"

"I'll help you understand," Pete said with an encouraging tone. "We can help each other. I can help teach you about Jesus and what the Bible says, and you can help me live up to the things that I teach you."

"You think that *I* can help *you* to follow God?" Rob asked with surprise. "Are you crazy or somthin'?"

"Not at all!" Pete responded. "You just gave me my first lesson for today. You taught me that we need true, honest friends who aren't afraid to tell the truth to help keep us on the right path. I think that if Jonah had a friend like that to help him, God wouldn't have needed to have him get swallowed by a fish in the first place! I'm glad I have a friend like that. Thanks for helping me today by pointing out that I wasn't acting like a true Christian."

Rob shrugged. "Okay," he said indifferently. Pete grinned at him.

"So you see, Rob, we all need to help each other so we can…keep our heads above water…if you know what I mean!" He nudged Rob gently several time in the ribs with his elbow. Rob snickered in response.

"Yeah, I know what you mean! You're a real funny guy, aren't you? Your sense of humor is about is good as your dad's," Rob said as he turned to the lake. "I suppose I should say 'thanks' for helpin' *me* today too — from drowning!"

As they stared out at the lake, the boys saw that Mr. Johnson had found the canoe paddles and was slowly making his way back to shore — with his fishing line trolling behind him in the water. "Looks like your dad finally got his chance to go fishin' in the canoe," Rob observed. Pete nodded in acknowledgment.

Rob looked down and silently watched the small, circular ripples grow and spread below him as he lightly dipped his toe in and out of the water. Then he firmly placed his hand on the back of Pete's shoulder.

"So, Johnson," Rob stated loudly, "you want to help teach me, huh?"

"Yeah, that's right," Pete answered.

"Well, besides teaching me about the Bible and Jesus and all that kind of stuff, maybe you can teach me about some of the other important things in life that I need help in."

"Like what?" Pete asked with a serious stare. "You mean like school stuff or something? You want me to help you with your homework?"

"Well, I was hoping you could teach me something about...learning how to swim!" Rob suddenly shoved Pete off the dock and into the knee-deep water. Rob laughed as Pete jumped up grabbed Rob's arm and pulled him into the water next to him.

"Actually," Pete giggled, "if you're really interested in learning about becoming a Christian, I think the first lesson that *I* should teach *you* today is about full body baptism! It involves dunking someone's head totally under the water. And I would be very happy to demonstrate that for you, but I need a volunteer, and you just happen to be the only one around!" The two boys laughed wildly as they splashed and chased each other through the shallow water.

Questions:

1) In the story, Pete thought that Rob was too much of a bad person to become a Christian. Have you ever judged someone else as being good or bad without getting to know what they're really like? Why?

2) Have any of your friends ever pointed out that you were showing bad behavior at any time? If so, how did you take it? Were you glad that they pointed it out, or did it make you upset? Likewise, have you ever told a friend that his or her behavior was poor? Was it hard for you to do? How did he or she take it?

3) In the story, Pete was told by two sources that he was not acting like a true follower of Christ. One source was Rob of course. Who was the other source?

4) If you are a Christian, who do you have (besides the Holy Spirit) to help you learn more about God's word, and to encourage you and keep you on the right track throughout your Christian life? Likewise, who are you helping?

Bible References Relating to this Story:

1 Thessalonians 5:19

Mark 16:15

Matthew 5:13-16

1 Peter 3:15

Romans 1:12

Jonah

Chapter 6

I Ain't Afraid of no Ghost!

"You wanna see a haunted house tomorrow night? Wanna see a ghost? I dare ya! I double dare ya!"

Pete and Rob were walking home from school as their classmate, Gordy Mayer, a thin kid with short, brown curly hair, dark brown eyes and a pale complexion, hovered wildly around them like an annoying fly.

"Gordy, you're so lame!" Pete said, shaking his head disparagingly. "You're always trying to dare someone to do something. Give us a break."

"Hey wait!" Rob yelled out. "Let him talk! I want to hear about this haunted house."

Gordy walked closer to Rob, waving his hands in the air with excitement.

"Listen up buddy! This is big-time scary stuff, and best of all...this is REAL!" he exclaimed wide-eyed. "The house I'm talking about is the old Jones house up on Crabapple Hill. The old lady, Mrs. Jones, died in that house five years ago and she's been haunting it ever since. Some people say that even during the day they can see her ghost standing at the attic window looking right down at them. And if you listen carefully enough, you can even hear her crying in the night for her dead husband. It's like really creepy and stuff! Since Mrs. Jones died, nobody's ever gone into that house and has come out alive! True story!"

"Wow!" Rob exclaimed. "Nobody?"

"Duh!" Pete said sarcastically. "Maybe that's because after Mrs. Jones died, they boarded up all the windows and doors so nobody *could* get in!"

"Well, yeah... but that's part of the challenge!" Gordy said undauntedly. "We need to find a way in so we can be the first ones to see what's inside there since they closed up the old place. I already talked to Ryan and Tony and they're gonna do it! We're all gonna meet up with each other at the Jones house just after midnight!" Gordy turned from Rob to Pete. "They're not afraid – not like *some* people I know!"

"Yeah, right!" Pete said defensively. "There are no such things as ghosts!"

"You believe what you want, Johnson, but I know the real truth about why you don't want to go...you're chicken!" Gordy yelled out. "Just admit it!"

"I am not chicken," Pete said calmly. "I'm just wiser than you!"

Gordy placed his fists under his armpits and began flapping his elbows up and down in unison while, at the same time, he started dancing bowlegged around Pete and Rob.

"Bawk, bawk, bawk! I'm Peter Johnson, and I'm a chicken!" Gordy chanted in a high, mocking voice.

Pete stopped in his tracks and laughed.

"Not only am I wiser than you, Gordy," Pete began, "but I also don't look as dumb as you do right now, either!"

Rob looked at Pete with an inquisitive stare.

"Well?" he asked. "What'd ya think?"

"Think about what?" Pete responded with annoyance. "Am I going to try to break into an old, abandoned house in the middle of the night to see something that isn't there? Do you think I want to be grounded by my parents forever or get thrown into jail? Forget about it!"

"Well, I think that Robby and I know who the *real* men are around here!" Gordy said smoothly. "So Robby, are you in? Or are you a chicken too?"

"I ain't no chicken!" Rob replied hotly.

"So, are you going to come with me, Tony and Ryan tonight or aren't you?"

Rob looked at Pete. Pete shook his head 'NO'. Rob looked at Gordy. Gordy's eyes grew almost as big as his wide smile as he frantically shook his head 'YES'.

"I don't know," Rob said with frustration. "Let me think about it."

"What's there to think about?" Gordy said. Gordy looked back and saw Meagan Pulaski and Becky Croteau walking a short distance behind them. "I bet if I asked one of those two girls right now, they'd say 'YES'. I bet they're not afraid of seeing a ghost like you are!"

"I ain't afraid of no ghost!" Rob yelled out defensively. "Okay, I'll go with you!"

"Good!" said Gordy cheerfully. "Meet us at the bottom of Crabapple Hill tonight at twelve thirty. Make sure your bike is in extra good shape in case we have to make a quick get-away!"

"Hey!" Pete yelled in protest. "What about your parents? They're not just gonna let you all just take off somewhere that late at night!"

"Not a problem!," Gordy said confidently. "We just got to sneak out, that's all. Our parents should all be asleep by then, right? You just have to stay awake that long and then sneak out quietly so they don't hear you. Ya see? Simple!"

Pete shook his head again.

"Oh boy! You guys are going to get into so much trouble! Do you really think you won't get caught?"

"Look," Gordy said seriously, "I always wanted to meet a real live ghost. Uh... what I meant to say was a real dead ghost! Er...well, whatever it is, I want to see it! Now I have the chance to make my dream come true! And tonight's a perfect night. It's a full moon and there won't be a cloud in the sky, so it will be easy to see. So, ya see? I thought this whole thing out," he said tapping his head with his index finger. "Robby, Tony, Ryan and I are all going in with or without you, Johnson!"

At 12:45 in the morning, four bicycles made their way slowly up Crabapple Hill. Affixed to each bike was a head-light which illuminated the road ahead. Gordy was in the lead. Next was a tall, slender boy with dark hair, dark skin and brown eyes, Antonio Sanchez (or Tony as his friends called him). Rob pedaled quickly after Tony and, a short distance behind Rob, a huffing and puffing Ryan McKenna struggled to keep up. At the top of the hill, the four boys parked their bikes under a giant sugar maple tree near the old house.

"Turn off your head-lights!" Gordy whispered loudly. "We don't want anybody to know we're up here!"

"But we won't be able to see!" Ryan whispered loudly.

"What are you afraid of, Ryan?" Gordy asked. "The moon's out. Once your eyes get used to the dark, you'll be able to see better."

Several seconds after each boy had turned off their head-lights, they saw the challenge that awaited them. Before them stood a tall, three story house covered in faded, cedar shingles. The paint on the trim-work around each window and door was chipped and worn. All of the doors and windows of the bottom story of the house had boards nailed across them, and there was a sign on the front porch that read "NO TRESSPASSING".

The wind started blowing, and the old tree next to them began to creak and groan loudly. The dead leaves that had fallen to the ground made a frantic clattering sound as they raced and swirled chaotically across the front lawn in little groups.

"Hmmm...Now how do we get in?" Gordy wondered as he scratched his head.

Rob quickly headed back to his bike.

"Okay, this was a blast! Now let's get out of here! You can call me chicken if you want, but I've had enough!"

"Wait!" Gordy whispered loudly. "Listen! I hear something! It sounds like it's coming toward us—from the road!" All the boys listened and sure enough, there was a strange noise approaching from the end of the dirt driveway – the noise was getting louder and louder. EEEK! EEEK! EEEK!

"What is that thing, Gordy?" Tony asked in a frightened voice.

An oddly shaped, dark object appeared in the distance, silhouetted by the moonlight. It became larger and louder as it drew closer to the boys. The boys, apparently very frightened by the approaching object, quickly scrambled for their bikes to make a quick exit.

"Hey, guys!" a voice called out. "Where are you going?"

Rob stopped in his tracks and spun around.

"Pete!" he cried out with relief. Pete rode to the boys on his squeaky bike with no head-light. "What are *you* doing here?" Rob asked. I thought you weren't going to come because you didn't believe in ghosts!"

"That's true," Pete said confidently. "But I figured that we should all stick together as a team and find out what the real truth is so we can stop the stupid rumors about this place. Like it says in Ecclesiastes four, verse nine, 'Two people are better than one, for they can help each other succeed. If one person falls, the other can reach out and help. But someone who falls alone is in real trouble'."

"Okay, that sounds good to me," Gordy said happily. "You're part of the team, Petey, ol' boy! But now we got the problem of trying to figure out a way to get inside. All the doors and windows are boarded up."

"You don't have a plan?" Pete asked in disbelief.

"Well, ah… no," Gordy said softly. "Look, I got us all here didn't I? Do I have to think of everything?"

"Okay," Pete said as he looked at the house. "Let's think about this. We got to be able to see what we're doing here. Even with the moon out, it's still way too dark to really see the house. Who's got the flashlight?" Rob, Ryan, and Tony all looked at Gordy.

"Oops," Gordy whispered apologetically.

"I got a flashlight at home," Ryan offered. "I can go back and get it! Would it be okay if I bring it back here in the morning after the sun comes up?"

Pete shook his head in despair. "Y'know, I didn't bring one either," he murmured. Pete looked over at the bikes next to the tree. "Hey!" he said as his eyes widened. "I've got an idea! Let's take off the bike lamps and use them like flashlights!"

"That's no good," said Gordy. "They're screwed on. We need a screwdriver or something to get them off."

"Let's see…," Pete said as he made his way over to the bikes. He knelt down next to one of the bikes and found one of the mounting screws on the lamp's handlebar clamp. Pete felt the screw head with his thumbnail. "I know!" He said as he reached his hand into his pocket and pulled out several coins. "We can use the edge of a coin like it's a screw driver tip!" He gave a coin to each of the boys and they tried to loosen the screws by sticking the edge of the coins into the screw heads and turning them. They could only loosen the one on Tony's bike.

97

"Well, one flashlight is better than none," Pete said.

They removed the headlamp from the bike and used it to look around the outside of the house. Behind the house, they quickly found the bulkhead doors that lead down into the basement. The boys noticed that the rusty old doors appeared to be latched shut with a padlock.

"This way is no good," Tony said. "It's padlocked shut, and we don't have a key."

"Oh, well, I guess we tried" Ryan said with a loud sigh, "Like my dad always says, 'nothing ventured, nothing gained'. Guess we'll have to try back another night! We should really be getting home now, isn't that right guys?"

"Wait a minute," Gordy said as he grabbed the lamp away from Pete. He kneeled down next to the padlock and inspected it closely. "Ha!" He cried out gleefully. "Look at this! It's not even locked shut! Somebody didn't even lock this thing!" Gordy removed the padlock from the latch. Next, he flipped the latch back on its hinge so that both doors of the bulkhead were free to open. "Tony, you're the biggest one here. Give me a hand opening these doors, will ya?" The bulkhead doors creaked slowly open as Gordy and Tony pulled up on each of them. The four boys now found themselves staring down into a dark pit leading into the basement.

"Wow!" Gordy said in disbelief. "That was easier than I thought it would be! We're in!"

"Who goes first?" asked Rob.

"I think Pete should go first," Gordy said, "He's like our leader now, you know."

"How did I become the leader?" Pete asked crossly. "I thought you were leading this whole crazy expedition from the beginning!"

"Well, I believe in sharing the leadership role. It's the polite and civilized thing to do in a team-like atmosphere, y'know. I'm sure a goodie-goodie like you would agree, right Johnson?"

"*You're* gonna be polite and civilized?" Tony asked with disbelief. "That's a first!"

"Thank you for sharing that fact with us, my good man!" Gordy said in a mocking voice as he took a graceful bow.

"Stop clowning around, you dork!" Tony replied angrily.

"It's okay, Tony," Pete said with a sigh. "Give me the light Gordy…I'll go first!"

One by one the boys descended cautiously into the basement. It smelled like mold and damp dirt. In the dim light they could see pipes, insulation and cobwebs hanging from the ceiling.

"Careful!" Pete called out. "It's a dirt floor with some rocks sticking up. Try not to trip on them."

"Ahhh!," Ryan screamed with a high pitched voice. The others jumped.

"What is it?" asked Gordy.

"I got cobwebs in my face!" Ryan complained.

"Oh brother!" Gordy said with dismay. "I thought you screamed about something important!"

"Look!" Pete said. He pointed the bike-lamp at the stairs that went up to the first floor of the house. Pete walked to the top of the stairs and opened the door. It led out into a dusty old kitchen. He turned around and held the light on the stairs so his friends could safely make their way up to the kitchen as well.

"Do you think the ghost of Mrs. Jones is watching us now somewhere in this house?" Tony whispered cautiously.

"Well, I know that God is watching over us now," said Pete confidently. "We should believe in God, who's real — don't believe in spooky ghosts that are fakes."

"Those are just words," Rob said with a trembling voice. "What's God going to do for us in this scary old place? You can't even see God! How do you know he's here?"

"God's everywhere," Pete replied confidently. "He knows we're in this house right now. And I trust him to help me and keep me safe. Like it says in the Bible in Psalm nine, verse two, 'This I declare about the Lord: He alone is my refuge, my place of safety; he is my God, and I trust him.' You guys call me your leader, but *my* leader is God who is real and with me right now."

"Wow!" Tony said with amazement. "Pete, you're like a walking Bible! When do you have time to memorize all that stuff?"

"That's what he's like in school too," Ryan noted. "He knows the answer to all the questions the teachers give him because he so good at memorizing stuff!"

"I think it's kind of annoying, if you ask me," Gordy said with an air of disdain.

"Nobody *did* ask you!" Tony responded hotly. "I like what Pete's got to say — especially in this creepy place!"

"Now what?" Rob asked. "Where do we go from here?"

"The attic of course," Gordy said in a low whisper. "That's where '*she*' is."

"Well, let's go," said Pete. "Let's get this over with. Just everyone be careful."

The five boys slowly made their way around the first floor of the house.

As the boys entered the living room, Ryan let out an ear piercing scream. The boys all jumped in terror.

"What is it now?" Gordy whispered loudly.

"Look!" Ryan yelled pointing into the darkness. "I see a ghost right over there in the corner!" The other boys could just make out a white, lumpy shape crouched down in a dark corner.

"Hold on!" Pete said has he aimed the lamp at the object. The light revealed a white sheet that was covering what appeared to be a sofa recliner. "It's just a piece of furniture covered by a sheet," Pete said.

"That's cruel!" Ryan yelled out. "Why would someone put a sheet over a chair? Is someone trying to scare us off?"

"Someone probably put a sheet over it to keep the dust off," Tony replied.

"Well," Gordy said rubbing both of his ears as if he were in pain, "if there *were* any real ghosts around here, they were probably scared off by Ryan's screaming!"

"I can't help it!" Ryan said. "I just got real scared — that's all!"

"Hey, look up there," Pete said as he pointed the beam of light on the wall across from them. There they saw one picture hanging on the wall. The picture showed a very young couple dressed in wedding clothes. "That must be Mrs. Jones and her husband on their wedding day," Pete said.

"They look like teenagers," Ryan said.

"Yeah, they do," Tony agreed. "They look like their real happy together, too."

"Blah, blah, blah!" Gordy said with annoyance. "If you guys are done strolling down memory lane, can we please try to find the stairs to…the *attic*!"

After a little more exploring, the boys found the stairs that led up to the second floor. They slowly climbed the stairs in single file. The stairs creaked loudly as they ascended. Immediately after reaching the second story landing, they found the door that lead up to the attic. Up they went, as quietly as they could despite the constant protest of the wooden stairs which creaked and groaned loudly under the weight of each footstep. Once they all made it into the attic, they swiveled the flashlight back and forth. Then, without warning, Gordy screamed out at the top of his lungs. Once again, all the boys jumped in terror.

"What is it, Gordy?" Rob yelled.

Gordy had seen the figure of someone standing in front of the attic window. Speechless and terrified, Gordy pointed at the figure and Pete aimed the lamp in the same direction. All the boys looked over to where Gordy was pointing. Then they saw it too. Everyone screamed. What they saw was not a mere piece of furniture simply covered with a bed sheet. Rather, it was the ghostly figure of a woman dressed in a flowing, white robe. She was looking directly at the boys. Her lifeless, glassy eyes seemed to have some type of hypnotic power that held the young adventurers captive in a petrified trance. Then suddenly, Gordy turned to Pete and yanked the bike lamp out of his hands.

"A ghost!" he cried out. "See? I told you so! I told you so! I'm out of here! You guys do whatever you want!" Gordy rushed down the stairs leaving the other four boys totally in the dark."

"Wait! We can't see!" Ryan cried out. "Don't leave us here, Gordy!"

"Come back, you loser!" Rob yelled out.

"Wait a minute guys!" Pete shouted. "Calm down!"

"But what about her?" Tony's voice cracked. "She's just standing there watching us!"

"Just let your eyes adjust to the dark," Pete said calmly. "Then we might be able to get to the bottom of this whole thing. Remember that God is here with us all right now! Psalm twenty-seven, verse fourteen says 'Wait patiently for the Lord. Be brave and courageous'. Everybody! Hold onto the person next to you." The boys listened to Pete, and they all held onto one another, squeezing each other's shoulder firmly. Pete shut his eyes and prayed as the other boys panted in terror: "Lord God almighty! Thanks for being here with us! Thank you for helping us and keeping us safe! I pray that we will all be brave and courageous like you ask us to be!"

After a couple of seconds the boys could just barely see around the room with the small amount of moonlight peeping through the attic window. As their eyes adjusted, they could just see the dark outline of the woman's head in front of them.

"There she is!" Tony whispered. "She's still there!"

Pete turned around to look at her. After a brief moment, he started to slowly walk toward the figure.

"Hey, what are you doin'?" Rob yelled out. "Pete, you could get hurt! She's right in front of you!"

Pete reached out his hand to the ghostly figure and touched it. It was cold and very hard. It was plastic!

"Hey guys!," Pete called out. "Come here! Look at this! It's only a mannequin in a wedding dress!"

"What's a mannequin?" Rob asked cautiously.

"It's a plastic dummy like you see in clothing stores," Tony replied.

The boys all gathered around the mannequin and touched it.

"Boy," Rob said, "*I* feel like a dummy now too! I was scared of *this*?"

"This looks like the same dress that was in the picture downstairs," Tony observed. "This must have been Mrs. Jones' old wedding dress. They never took it out of the house for some reason."

"This explains all those rumors about this being a haunted house," Pete said. "That would explain why some people thought they saw a ghost standing in the attic window. But now that we finally know the truth, let's get outta here!"

"But we don't have a flashlight," Ryan said.

Pete felt his way to the attic door.

"Remember, we're a team, so let's work together like a team! Everybody grab each others hand so you won't fall," he said. "I'll lead the way down."

The boys carefully retraced their steps and made it back down into the basement. They almost made it to the stairs that led outside when they heard a terrifying, whaling cry directly in front of them. The four boys screamed and grabbed onto each other.

"Don't leave me here!" a small voice pleaded. "Help me! Help me!"

"It sounds like a pitiful old woman's voice!" Ryan shouted. "It must be Mrs. Jones' ghost for real, this time!"

"No, you dork! It's me!" the mystery voice whimpered. "Help me! I'm hurt bad!"

"Gordy?" Pete called out. "Gordy, is that you? Where are you? Where's the flashlight?"

"It broke when I tripped over a rock," Gordy called out from the darkness. "I think I sprained my ankle! It hurts so bad — like you can't believe! I can't even stand up by myself!"

The four boys found him and carefully helped him up off the dirty ground.

"You should have stuck with the team," Rob said sternly. "If you were brave and courageous like the rest of us, this wouldn't have happened to you!"

Pete and Rob helped Gordy up the stairs and into the cool autumn air. On the way up, Pete explained to Gordy that the so-called ghost was only a plastic dummy wearing a wedding dress.

"What am I going to tell my parents when they see me like this?" Gordy asked as he rubbed his ankle. "I can't hide something like this! It's really starting to swell!"

"You're gonna tell them the truth," Pete said authoritatively.

"Yeah!" Rob, Tony and Ryan replied in firm agreement.

"In fact," Pete said, "we *all* need to tell our parents the truth about what we did tonight. It's the right thing to do."

"What?" Tony cried out in despair. "My dad will kill me!"

"I'm doomed!" Ryan cried cupping his face in his hands.

"You don't have to do it alone," Pete said with a big smile. "We're still a team, so we'll tell our parents as a team too! Remember, don't be afraid! God wants us to be brave and courageous! As long as we live in the truth, God is right there with us — even when we tell our parents."

"Well, that's not so bad then — if all of us are going to do it together," Tony mumbled.

"My dad always says that 'honesty is the best policy'," Ryan remarked.

"Do you think you'll be able to ride back, Gordy?" Pete asked.

"I think so," Gordy said with a slight grimace as he limped over to his bike. "It's almost all downhill to my house. I can coast most of the way."

"So long, Mrs. Jones!" Rob yelled up at the attic window. "Thanks for letting us visit, but there's not even a *ghost* of a chance that we'll ever come back here again!" The boys laughed and helped Gordy onto his bike. Then our heroes rode off together into the fading moonlight.

Questions:

1) What has been the most frightening thing that has ever happened to you? How did you handle it? Were you alone? Were you brave?

2) Who do you count on to help you when you get scared?

3) Have you ever prayed to God (silently or out-loud) when you have been in a scary situation to ask for help? What happened as a result of praying?

Bible References Mentioned in this Story:

Ecclesiastes 4:9

Psalm 91:2

Psalm 27:14

Chapter 7

The Fight

Pete waited patiently for Rob's release from school detention late Friday afternoon. Finally, at four O'clock, Pete saw his friend swing open the side door and walk slowly toward him. Rob's head drooped sadly. His face was downcast as it usually was after each detention. Rob slowly walked past Pete without saying a word. Pete gently patted his brooding friend's shoulder several times to encourage him.

"Hey, I know what we can do tomorrow," Pete said trying to cheer up his friend. "It will be a lot of fun, I promise."

"What?" Rob asked suspiciously.

"Well...," Pete began slowly, "the church is having a volunteer weekend to help the elderly people in town and..."

"Oh brother!" Rob interrupted shaking his head, "I thought you said that this thing was gonna be a lot of fun?"

"It will be!"

"Helpin' old people doesn't make me think of having fun. Havin' fun is doin' things like playin' video games, ridin' bikes and ..." Rob shoved Pete off the sidewalk and into a big puddle of water near a drain. "It's also pushin' your best friend into a mud puddle!"

Pete immediately jumped back onto the sidewalk next to Rob with a big grin on his face.

"Can't get rid of me that easy!" he said defiantly.

"Come on!" Rob protested. "Give me a break! I don't want to help no old people!"

"Just listen to the rest of it, Rob. You didn't even give me a chance to finish telling you everything!"

"Go ahead," Rob said, "but you ain't gonna change my mind."

"Well," Pete began. "We're going to rake leaves! You see, some of the older people in town can't even get outside anymore to do work around the house, so we have an opportunity to help them out."

"Whoopy-do!" Rob said sarcastically.

"Just think, Rob, of the fun we're going to have after we're done. We're all going back to the church for ice cream sundaes!"

"Uh huh," Rob said with a total lack of enthusiasm.

"There's five houses right in my own neighborhood that we can do together. My dad's going to be with us too."

"But besides ice cream sundaes, what's in it for me?" Rob asked. "Do I get money for doing this?"

"No," Pete replied. "We're all going to be volunteering, which means doing something helpful for others without expecting anything in return. It's a way for us to help out the community. Not only that, but God's word in the Bible asks us to help others and pray for them. Besides, I think it would be fun if we did it together."

Rob laughed. "I haven't even read the Bible yet, and I know that it don't say anywhere that Jesus commanded us to rake leaves for old people on Saturday — which just happens to be my day off from school!"

"Well...you're right. He didn't say anything in particular about raking leaves for anybody, but Jesus did command us to love each other," Pete countered.

"I don't even know any of these people," Rob protested.

"That's okay, Rob. You know me. And you know my dad." Rob remained silent. "I tell you what," Pete continued, "If you help us to rake leaves tomorrow, then after church on Sunday, we can play video games at my house the rest of the day, if it's all right with your mom."

"My mom don't care," Rob mumbled.

"What do you say then, Rob? Will you help out?"

"Yeah. okay. Whatever," Rob said halfheartedly.

"Sweet!" Pete shouted. "Meet me at my house tomorrow at seven O'clock in the morning. I'll get you a rake."

"Seven O'clock in the morning!" Rob cupped his face in his hands as if he were going to cry. "I must be a total idiot!" he cried out. "It's a Saturday mornin', and I got to get up just like we're goin' to school! I better be gettin' some pizza out of this deal too!"

"I'll see what I can do!" Pete said with a large smile.

Saturday morning came, and Rob arrived at Pete's house on his bike. After gathering the rakes, Mr. Johnson drove them all to the church. At the church, the volunteers prayed to God and asked God to help them to be a blessing to the people they were about to assist. Soon after, everyone left for their assigned houses to begin raking.

Later that afternoon, Pete and Rob decided to separate from each other and do a yard on their own. Both yards were next to each other, so they decided to have a race to see who could finish first. Rob won. He celebrated by running over to the pile of leaves that Pete was working on and jumped into them. Then he continued celebrating his victory by jumping up and down while throwing leaves above his head and chanting repeatedly "I won! I'm so awesome! I'm so great!" Leaves flew everywhere.

"Thanks a lot, buddy!" Pete laughed.

"I'm just getting you back for waking me up so early today!" Rob said cheerfully. Rob stopped his celebration and calmed himself. "Hey, I'll help you clean all this up in a second. I'm just gonna tell this lady that I'm done with her yard,"

Rob ran to the front door of Mrs. Stevens' house and knocked several times. After a short while, Mrs. Stevens answered the door.

"I'm done," Rob said.

"Oh, that's wonderful!" Mrs. Stevens said with a cheerful smile. "Wait right here. I won't be but a moment."

112

"Uh…well…okay," Rob said hesitantly.

Rob watched Mrs. Stevens through the screen door as she disappeared around the corner. A minute later, she reappeared holding a ten-dollar bill in her hand.

"What is your name, young man?" she asked.

"Uh… Rob," he said as he curiously eyed the money in her hand.

"Well, Rob. My lawn looks so wonderful! Thank you for doing such a good job and helping me."

Mrs. Stevens opened the door and handed Rob the ten-dollar bill. Rob's eyes shot open with surprise. "Oh, wait a minute!" he started. "I raked your yard for free. You see, I'm this thing called a volunteer … for the church. You don't have to give me no money."

"Please take it, Rob. It would make me feel very good to give it to such a hard worker!"

He gently took the ten-dollar bill from Mrs. Stevens and studied it closely as if to make certain it was real. "Well…okay," Rob said with a hint of uncertainty.

Rob started off the porch when Mrs. Stevens called to him.

"Rob? I have a question for you, dear."

"Yeah?" said Rob as he turned to face her.

"When Mr. Stevens was still alive, he used to do all of the outdoor work. I never had to worry about it. But he's gone now, and I'm getting on in years. I can't even get outside anymore. The windows need to be washed and the garage needs to be cleaned out. I would be willing to pay you to help me with those chores too."

113

Rob appeared to be very interested in this opportunity that was just offered.

"All I have to do is wash windows and clean out the garage?"

"That's right, Rob. Here…" Mrs. Stevens wrote her name and phone number on a piece of paper and handed the information to Rob. "Put that in your pocket. When you get home, give it to your parents and they can give me a call so we can work out all the details."

"My mom don't mind," Rob said. "She don't care where I go or what I do."

"Have her give me a call just the same," Mrs. Stevens said with a smile.

"Sure!" Rob said with excitement. "Bye!"

Rob ran across the lawn to Pete. He ran straight through the pile of leaves Pete had just raked together again.

"I thought you were going to *help* me with the leaves," Pete said with annoyance.

"Look what I got! Look what I got!" Rob yelled as he jumped up and down in the pile of leaves while holding the ten-dollar bill between his hands.

Pete frowned.

"Where did you get that?"

"Where do you think? The old lady that lives in that house just gave it to me!"

"But Rob, we're supposed to be doing this for free — as volunteers! You're not supposed to take money from these people!"

"I told her that, but she said it would make her happy if she gave it to me. And like you keep tellin' me all the time, 'treat

114

others the same way you would want to be treated yourself! I know that I always want to feel happy, so I took the money from her to make *her* feel happy too — just like she said. It was the Christian thing to do!"

Pete couldn't take his eyes off of the ten-dollar bill. He seemed to be in a trance and started to nervously bite his bottom lip as he focused on the money.

"Not only that," Rob continued, "but she said that *I* — Robert T. McGwyn — am a hard worker, so I really deserve it!" Pete snapped out of his trance, and faced Rob with an angry glare.

"We're all hard workers!" Pete shouted. He eyed the money again. "You should at least share it!"

"It's mine, and I don't have to! Besides, you and your family got tons of money already. You don't need any more!"

Pete became furious.

"Whose idea was it to ask you to come with us today, anyways?" Pete demanded. "It was mine, that's who! I deserve some of that money for just inviting you!"

"No way! She gave it to me! And not only that, but I'm coming back to do more stuff for her for more money cause she asked me to. After I'm done working for her, I'll have enough money to buy my own, brand new video game station. Then I won't have to keep coming over to your place to use yours!"

A painful and stunned expression swept over Pete's face.

"What kind of friend are you, anyways?"

"A rich one!" Rob said dramatically by raising his nose in the air and closing his eyes.

"You're a real jerk!" Pete said throwing down his rake.

"You want to make something out of it, Pete the Perfect?" Rob said with a threatening tone. "You have everything I could ever want. Two parents, a nice house, cool toys, lots of friends. I got nothin'! Now it's my turn to get something!"

"I'll give you something!"

In a fit of rage, Pete ran straight for Rob and tried to tackle him into the pile of leaves. Leaves went everywhere. The owner of the house came out and shouted at them to stop. Pete's dad, who was raking behind the house, heard the commotion and ran around the corner to find Pete and Rob rolling violently on top of each other through the leaves.

Mr. Johnson pulled the two boys apart. He demanded to know what had happened between the two of them. Both boys frantically began explaining their side of the story at the same time. Mr. Johnson stopped them both and had them speak calmly and one at a time. Then he told both boys that there would be no ice cream sundaes for either of them. He instructed them to rake up the leaves they had scattered around the yard during the fight. Both boys were angry and didn't talk to each other as they worked. When Mr. Johnson left to apologize to the owner of the house, Pete whispered over to Rob, "Don't bother coming over tomorrow!"

"Don't worry!" Rob whispered hotly through his clenched teeth. "I don't need you *or* your video games anymore! I'm rich now—and I'm just gonna get richer! Come to think of it, I don't need your dumb ol' church either! I ain't comin' tomorrow!"

Mr. Johnson and Pete returned home that afternoon after they dropped Rob off at his home. Mr. Johnson had Pete sit down next to him.

"Okay, we need to talk about what happened today. Just you and me."

"What did *I* do wrong, dad?" Pete blurted out.

"Now that's a good question. Maybe you can answer that yourself. After all, you call yourself a Christian. You claim that you are a follower of Jesus Christ. Is this something that Jesus would have done?"

"But Rob…"

"Don't worry about Rob and his problems right now," Mr. Johnson said. "Just focus on yourself. Why did *you* do what you did?"

"I did what I did because I got mad that he got money for working and wouldn't share it with me. It was my idea that he came with us in the first place! I should have got some money too! If Rob was a Christian, he would have shared with me!"

"How long has Rob been a Christian?" Mr. Johnson asked.

Pete was silent for a moment. "Well…," he began thoughtfully, "I don't actually even think he really is a Christian yet. He's only gone to church for two months, and he still asks me a ton of questions. He hasn't really even read the Bible yet. I guess he's still learning."

"That's right," said Mr. Johnson. "And so are you. You're growing up in a Christian home, Pete, so you already know about who Jesus is and how he wants us to behave, but you still have a lot to learn about putting what Jesus asks you to do into practice, don't you?"

"Yeah, I guess I do," Pete whispered softly as he looked down at the floor.

"And as a Christian, you have a huge responsibility to Rob. You're Rob's closest friend. You also happen to be his closest example of what a Christian is."

Pete eyes shot open wide as if he had just woken from a bad dream. Then he looked down at the floor again in despair.

"Oh great!" he said sadly. "I messed up again! And I did it over money!" He shook his head sadly. "Because of me, Rob probably thinks that all Christians are greedy and love money more than they love other people. I even tried to keep the fifty dollars I found in the baseball cards I bought at the yard sale last summer when I knew it wasn't mine. What is it with me and money? Dad, you said you would help me with this problem!"

Mr. Johnson paused for a moment with a thoughtful expression on his face before he leaned back in his chair and nodded in agreement.

"Yep. You're absolutely right. I did say that. I guess I didn't realize how hard this money problem is for you — until now. This was the first real fist fight you've been in. This money issue must be pretty serious."

"Yeah," Pete said glumly. "I'm the one who started the fight. And I just happened to get into it with a friend that I said I'd help bring closer to Jesus and teach him about his ways. Now I'm actually pushing him farther away from God. He told me he doesn't even want to go to our church anymore. I'm acting like a real hypocrite! Man, how many times do I have to mess up before I get it right?"

"Well," Mr. Johnson began, "fights and other conflicts happen sometimes between even the best of friends, and sometimes even between Christians. Doing the things that Jesus

118

commands us to do and being good at it takes a lot of practice, doesn't it?" Pete nodded. "We all mess up from time to time, Pete, and that certainly includes adults like me. Sometimes I wish I could just go back in time and keep myself from making huge blunders that I got myself into, or keeping the promises that I made to people, but God doesn't allow us to do that. We just have to accept what we've already done and try our best to do the right thing to handle the damage we created." Mr. Johnson paused briefly. "So, having said all that, I have a question to ask you Pete. Will you forgive me?"

"Huh?" Pete looked at his dad with a confused expression. "You're asking *me* to forgive *you*?"

"Well, I told you that I would help you with you're problem, and I really didn't, did I? I got too busy and neglected it. I should have kept my word to you, son, like I promised. I think mom and I are probably the closest example of what a Christian is to you, and I feel terrible for letting you down. So I need to ask you if you'll forgive me."

"Uh…well, of course I will, dad."

Mr. Johnson nodded his head. "Y'know Pete," he said, "I think that when people ask others for forgiveness, it must make Jesus very happy simply because it's the best way to begin fixing the damaged relationships that sometimes happen between people. Asking for forgiveness and forgiving others is truly a great demonstration of people loving each other in the way God wants us to. Keep that in mind the next time you see Rob, okay?" Pete nodded in thoughtfully agreement.

"So, let's start addressing this problem you're having with money right now. Here's what I'm going to do. I'm going to pray each day that God will strengthen you so you will become better at resisting the hold that money has on you. I'm also going to make it a point to ask you how you're doing with this problem each week, and, afterward, we can both pray about it together. And whenever you feel like the temptation of money is becoming a problem for you, please promise me that you'll talk to me about it right away, alright? There's no need to be embarrassed about any of this with me. Remember, I'm not perfect either." Pete smiled.

"Let's not leave your mom out on this," Mr. Johnson continued. "She really needs to know about this situation too. She can help keep both of us on track and pray with us as well. It's always nice to have people that really care about you to help keep you accountable to the promises you've made. I find it's a huge help to me personally. Are you okay with all of this?"

"Yeah," Pete responded soberly. "I'll take all the help I can get."

"Oh, and I have another idea!" Mr. Johnson continued. "How would you like to draw a poster together that we can hang on your wall that will show Luke, chapter sixteen, verse thirteen?"

"I haven't memorized that verse yet," Pete said. "What's it say?"

"It says, 'No one can serve two masters. For you will hate one and love the other; you will be devoted to one and despise the other. You cannot serve both God and money.' "

"Alright," Pete said with a smile. "I like that idea! That will help me memorize that verse since I'll see it every day when I wake up and just before I go to bed."

"Alright, then!" Mr. Johnson said with a smile. "I'll get the markers and some construction paper. I'll bring mom back with me also, and then we can all pray about it together."

"Dad?" Pete said. "What about me and Rob? Do you really think he'll ever forgive me for what I did and said to him today? I don't want to lose him as a friend."

"Well, there's only one way to find out, right?"

"Yeah," Pete replied thoughtfully.

As Mr. Johnson left to gather the art supplies, Pete, closed his eyes and prayed privately.

"I'm sorry Lord, for acting the way I did today. I didn't do a very good job representing you. I really messed up. Please forgive me. And please don't let me lose Rob as my friend. Even though we had a big fight today, I pray that Rob and I will become closer friends than ever before."

"And thank you for helping me with my problem. Now I see how bad it really is, and now I have someone that I can count on to help me to really deal with it. I guess that's one good thing to come out of all of this. Thanks for listening to me. Amen."

The next Monday, an hour after classes had finished at school, Rob left detention and made his way to the side door exit. He appeared surprised to see Pete waiting for him just outside the doors.

"Hi, Rob!" Pete said cheerfully.

"What do you want?" Rob asked coldly.

"I want to walk home with you like I always do," Pete said.

"Why? Are you gonna try to pick my pocket on the way, Mister Moneybags?"

Pete laughed softly. "Yeah," he said. "Guess I deserve that after the way I acted towards you the other day."

"When we went on our little fishin' trip together, you said you wanted me to help you live up to what you're supposed to do as a Christian."

"Yeah," Pete nodded. "I asked you to hold me accountable in case I started ignoring God again."

"Well," Rob said coolly, "I'm very happy to help you out once again. On Saturday, you acted like a big, dumb jerk! Somethin' tells me you ain't gonna win the Christian of the year award anytime soon!"

Pete swallowed hard and lowered his head.

"Look," he said, "I'm sorry about the fight we had on Saturday. I want your friendship more than I want your money. And I'm happy you got a job where you can earn some more. That's a great blessing for you. Anyways, I was hoping that you could forgive *me* — I did act like a big jerk to you. I don't want to lose you as a friend, Rob. I'm sorry. Really! I'm sorry. Will you forgive me?"

Rob stared at Pete silently for several seconds before he spoke: "Johnson, you are *so* weird! I've never met *any*one like you before! What is it with you anyways?"

Rob stared silently at Pete for several seconds more. Then he spun around quickly and continued walking down the sidewalk away from Pete. "Come on!" he called out. "We can't stand here all day! We got to get down to the Dairy Bar on the corner before it gets too crowded."

"Why?" Pete asked.

"Special treat today!" Rob called out. "We're both havin' ice cream sundaes before supper!" Rob stopped and turned back to face his friend with a large grin. "And *I'm* buyin'!"

Questions:

1) Have you ever been in a fight with a close friend? After the fight was over, how did you feel? Did your friend ask you for forgiveness? Did you ask your friend to forgive you? Why is it important that we forgive each other?

2) Have you ever wanted something (money, a toy, food, etc.) so badly, that you just couldn't keep your mind from thinking about it most of the time? How do you feel when this happens? Does it affect your relationship in any way with friends, family, or God? If thinking about something all the time bothers or frustrates you, what do you do about it to keep it from bugging you?

3) Name three things from the story that Rob's dad did to help him with his problem? Who do you have to help you with your problems when they come up? Who is someone that you could help if they were to have a problem?

4) Name some ways that you serve God and others.

5) At the end of the story, why did Rob think that Pete was so weird?

<u>Bible References Mentioned in this Story:</u>

Deuteronomy 13:4

Matthew 6:9-15

Luke 16:13

1 Timothy 6:6

2 Timothy 3:16-17

Colossians 3:13

Chapter 8

I Want a New Family!

Near the end of November, Pete signed up to participate in his church's Christmas concert as part of the choir. Pete, who had invited Rob over to his house for the afternoon, decided to asked Rob if he would be interested in singing in the concert as well. Rob looked at Pete with surprise.

"What? Are you crazy? I hate singin'! I don't even sing on Sundays at church, so what makes you think I wanna sing in front of a bunch of people at Christmas?"

"Well," Pete started, "like my mom says, 'you'll never know if you're going to like it unless you try'."

"Uh-uh! No way!" Rob said violently shaking his head.

"Fine. Have it your way. Just thought I'd ask."

"Is it okay if I just watch you guys practice, even though I'm not gonna sing?" Rob asked.

"It's fine with me," Pete said. "We'll be practicing at the church Saturday nights at seven O'clock."

"What time are you done?"

"I don't know," Pete said shrugging his shoulders. "Depends on how much actual practicing we get in and how much fooling around we do. It could be eight-thirty or nine."

Rob sighed out loud. "Too bad my mom don't have a car," he began. "You guys are just gonna have to drop me off at my house late that night and then pick me up again first thing in the mornin' to bring me back to church. Too bad I just can't stay overnight with you guys. Then you wouldn't have to run all over town."

Pete's eyes lit up and a huge smile crossed his face.

"That's a great idea!" he said with excitement.

Rob's eyes suddenly lit up as well.

"Really?"

"Yeah!"

"Oh, man!" Rob shouted as he raised his arms above his head and jumped up and down. "This is going to be so totally cool! We can have a pizza party! We can stay up all night and eat pizza and watch movies!"

"Yeah!" Pete shouted back eagerly. "Let's go ask my mom right now!"

The two boys ran into the kitchen where Pete's mom was sitting at the table working on a crossword puzzle.

"Mom!" Pete yelled.

"Pete," Mrs. Johnson said with a gentle sigh, "please don't yell. I'm trying to concentrate."

"Mom, can Rob stay overnight at our house next Saturday? Please?"

Pete was practically jumping up and down as he asked the question. His mom thought for a second, and then looked up at the two enthusiastic boys in front of her.

"Well, *I* don't have a problem with that. Make sure it's okay with your father."

Pete and Rob smacked each other's hands together in the air in a 'high-five' fashion, and then they both danced around the kitchen in a celebratory manner. Pete's mom rolled her eyes and shook her head.

"Pete, I told you that you would still have to make sure it's okay with your dad. You heard me say that, right?"

"Sure I did, mom. But we all know that dad is just going to tell us to ask you to see if it's all right. And you already said 'yes'! So it's in the bag! Rob, you're staying over!"

"Wait one minute!" Pete's mom said brusquely. "Even if your father and I do say it's okay for Robby to stay over, isn't there one more person that we need to ask?" Both boys thought long and hard. Finally they both shrugged with blank expressions on their faces.

"What about your mother, Robby?" Pete's mom asked. "Don't you think that we should ask for her permission too?"

Rob stared at Mrs. Johnson with a look of annoyance.

"But Mrs. Johnson...we've been through that before! My mom don't care where I go or what I do. She don't care about

127

me at all. She don't even want me! If I was never born, she'd be real happy. And that's okay cause I don't want her neither!"

Pete's mother had a concerned look on her face.

"Listen to me Robby," she began, "I don't really know your mother that well, but I do know there are always two sides to every story, and the truth is usually found somewhere in-between. But so far I have only heard your side."

"But it's true!" Rob protested. "She hates me and I hate her right back! She must have been the reason my dad left! Anyone that acts like she does would make anybody go away! She just doesn't care about nothin'— especially ME!"

Pete's mom put her pencil down and straightened up a little. Rob was becoming very agitated.

"Well," Mrs. Johnson said calmly, "your mother feeds you and takes care of you, doesn't she Robby? It doesn't look to me like you're wasting away. I wonder if she is truly as terrible as you make her out to be."

"She is!" Rob retorted defensively. "She gives me food and clothes because it's the law, but she don't work for it or nothin'! We have Section Eight housing assistance! We get most of our food from food stamps! Most of our clothes come from the Salvation Army! She don't do a thing! I have to wash my own clothes if I want clean clothes, and I have to make my own dinner most of the time too. You know what I eat for dinner almost every night? Boxed macaroni and cheese that I have to make myself! That's all we can afford cause she won't even try to get a job! Her life would probably be easier for her without me, but she'll never get rid of me because that would mean she would get less welfare money to live on! And that's the truth! If

128

I was ever given a choice, I would never have picked her as my mother!"

"Whoa!" Pete exclaimed under his breath with a look of shock upon his face.

Mrs. Johnson actually appeared to be a little shaken for a moment as well, but she regained her composure quickly. "We can't pick our parents, Robby," she said calmly. "But I do know this… the Bible tells us that we should honor our parents, whoever they are. Ephesians six, verse one through three says 'Children, obey your parents because you belong to the Lord, for this is the right thing to do'."

"I shouldn't have to obey someone that's as bad as my mom is!" Rob snapped back. "She doesn't even love me, so why should I bother obeying her? She's too lazy to love anything! You just don't understand, Mrs. Johnson! You don't even know her!"

"You know, Robby…you're absolutely right," Mrs. Johnson continued after a thoughtful pause.

"I am?" Rob asked in disbelief.

"Yes, you are. I really don't know your mom very well. I only know her through the short phone calls we have when I ask if it's all right to have you over or to get permission to take you to church. She seems a little shy on the phone. And I've only seen her when she waves from the window when I pick you up. She's probably not much of a social butterfly, is she?" Rob shrugged but remained silent. "Anyway, you just made me think…I really should get to know your mom a little bit better. I'll call her. In fact, I would like to invite her over here sometime."

"How's that gonna work? She don't even have a car. She don't drive!"

"I do," Mrs. Johnson stated flatly.

Rob looked incredulous. "Are you really serious?" he asked. "I can't believe that someone as perfect as *you* would want to have anything at all to do with someone as awful as *her*!"

"Oh, I don't know…," Mrs. Johnson said as she stood up and walked over to Rob and lightly swatted his shoulder with her crossword book. "After all," she said with mock arrogance, "don't you think it's pretty amazing that someone as perfect and wonderful as me would allow a scrappy, troublesome young man like *you* into my perfect home?" Rob, who looked bewildered by the question, turned to Pete for help. Pete glanced at him and shrugged helplessly.

"Why are you so quiet all of a sudden, Mr. McGwyn?" Mrs. Johnson asked, suspiciously eyeing Rob. "Is it that you really don't think I *am* wonderful and perfect? Is that it? Come on! Speak up! It's true, isn't it?"

"Well…I…uh…," Rob stammered nervously. Mrs. Johnson laughed and playfully mussed-up Rob's hair with her hand.

"I'm just having fun with you, Robby!" Mrs. Johnson said with a grin. "Seriously though, I think it's pretty amazing that Jesus, who actually *is* perfect, would want to have anything to do with *any* of us considering the way we all disobey God from time to time! From God's point of view, none of us are perfect." She smiled slyly at both boys and then left the kitchen.

Pete seemed amused. He giggled and grinned at Rob.

"What?" Rob asked with an irritated tone.

"I just think it's pretty funny," Pete replied. "You just got fooled by the mom-ster! I'm so glad it was someone else this time instead of me!"

"D'ya know what I think is pretty funny?" Rob asked calmly in response.

"What?" Pete asked naively.

"Seein' the look on someone's face when I give them a wedgie!"

With that, Pete quickly spun around and ran down the hall laughing hysterically as Rob chased after him.

Saturday afternoon arrived. Mrs. Johnson and Pete drove to Rob's house, which was almost two miles away, to collect Rob. Rob and his mother lived in one-half of a slightly disheveled, two story duplex located by a busy intersection near Kingston's city center.

After their arrival, Pete waited next to the car as Mrs. Johnson and Rob's mother, Mrs. McGwyn talked on the small porch by the front door. Mrs. McGwyn was a short, heavyset lady with slightly tousled, strawberry-blonde hair streaked with grey. Her eyes were the exact same color of blue as Rob's. Wrinkles revealed themselves easily at the corners of her eyes when she smiled, and she appeared to limp somewhat when she walked. Rob's mother appeared much older than Pete's mom.

Rob suddenly burst through the front door carrying a ragged duffle bag and impatiently pushed his way past the two moms.

"Take it easy there, Robby!" Mrs. Johnson called after him sternly. "I have the keys to the car, so you're not going anywhere until I'm finished talking with your mother, young man!"

"Well, at least I'm outta that house!" Rob mumbled without turning around. "The sooner we get outta here the better!"

"You be nice now, Robby," Mrs. McGwyn said meekly, almost inaudibly. "Remember your manners today."

Rob grunted in acknowledgment. He greeted Pete with a 'high-five'. Both boys jumped into the car and started making plans of their own.

Soon afterward, the boys arrived at Pete's house where, in the midst of light snow flurries, they played basketball in the driveway until suppertime.

Later that night, Pete's dad drove Mrs. Johnson and the boys to the church for choir practice. Rob sat near the front of the church as the choir assembled on the stage. There were three musicians present that accompanied the choir. Mr. Croteau, one of the school's music teachers, played the guitar, his ten year old daughter, Becky, played the electric bass. A young man named Glenn played an electronic keyboard.

As the choir began, Rob found himself tapping his feet to the beat. As he looked at the chair in front of him, he saw several pencils on top of a notebook. Rob picked up two pencils and started tapping them loudly upon the plastic chair in front of him.

After practice ended, Mr. Croteau approached Rob.

"Hi. You're Rob, right?" he asked.

"Yeah," Rob responded suspiciously. "What's up?"

"I heard you tapping to the songs we played tonight. Do you play the drums by any chance?"

"Uh, no. I don't know how to play anything musical," Rob mumbled shyly.

"Well," said Mr. Croteau, "would you like to learn? We could use a drummer for the Christmas concert."

"Well, I don't even own any drums."

"Not a problem," Mr. Croteau responded. "You can use the school's drum set. I can teach you how to play."

"But the concert is only a couple of weeks away!" Rob grimaced. "I can't learn to play the drums that fast!"

"Well, you won't know if you don't try."

"Yeah...someone else just told me somethin' like that last week," Rob said as he eyed Pete who was talking with a couple of boys from the choir.

"You don't have to be a professional drummer, Rob. I can teach you two easy rhythms that will work for all the songs we just practiced. From what I heard you do tonight, it seems to me that you might have a natural musical talent. You may have real drummer's blood in you!"

"Really?" Rob's face brightened. "I always wanted to try playing real drums!"

"Good! Plan on practicing in the auditorium on Tuesday's and Thursday's right after school."

"Yeah, that sounds good!" Rob said excitedly. "I'm used to stayin' after school anyways cause I'm always...uh...well I used to always have to stay for detention."

"Well, no more detention then," Mr. Croteau smiled. "I need you to practice. Having a drummer would really help the out the Christmas concert. Tomorrow, I'll get you a permission sheet to

133

take home and get signed. Once you get it back to me, we'll start the lessons. Sound good?"

"It sounds awesome!"

On the way back to Pete's house, Rob told the Johnson family what had happened after practice. Mr. And Mrs. Johnson congratulated Rob. Pete shook his head skeptically. *"You ... play the drums?"* he said. "This I gotta see!"

"Mr. Croteau said I have drummer's blood in me," Rob said proudly. "Who would have thought that me, Robert T. McGwyn, would be a famous drummer?"

Pete rolled his eyes. "Oh brother!" he said. "Success has gone right to his head!"

"By the way, Robby," Mrs. Johnson began, "I've been talking to your mother this past week. We had some great conversations. She really likes talking about you, by the way."

Rob's dreamy smile quickly faded into a frown. "What did she tell you?" he asked. "Did she tell you how I'm always gettin' into trouble? Did she tell you how I'm always causin' her grief, and how I'm such a big pain in her..."

"Actually," Mrs. Johnson interrupted abruptly, "your mother is quite proud of you, young man. She thinks the world of you."

"Yeah, right," Rob mumbled unconvinced.

"Robby, would it be alright with you if I invited her to the Christmas Concert since you're going to be in it now? I think she would really love to see you up on stage."

"I don't care," Rob responded blandly. "You can ask her, but if anything is good on TV that night, she ain't gonna come."

"Well then, Robby, since you say you don't care, I'll be asking her."

That night, after eating pizza and playing video games for an hour, Mr. and Mrs. Johnson put the boys to bed. All four of them prayed together. The Johnson's even prayed for Rob and his mom. Rob watched both parents kiss Pete goodnight and tell him that they loved him. Then both parents hugged Rob and wished him a 'good night'. They switched off the lights and left the bedroom. Rob sat up on his cot and whispered loudly across the room to Pete.

"Hey! What happened to the part where we get to stay up *all* night and watch movies and stuff? We're gettin' a raw deal here!"

"My parents said it was time to go to bed," Pete replied.

"And you listen to them?" Rob said with surprise. "At my house, I go to bed whenever I want. My mom don't care how late I stay up. Even if she tells me to go to bed, I don't listen to her. It's not like she's gonna do anything to me if I don't do what she says."

"But I love my parents," Pete said. "Remember that Bible verse my mom talked about last week? To honor your mother and father? Well, that's what I try to do because that's what God wants us to do."

"But you have a good mom. She really *is* perfect. And you have an awesome dad. I don't have either! You're way lucky, Pete. You guys are the perfect family, and you have the perfect life!"

"Well, I wouldn't say that we're…"

"You know what I should pray for?" Rob interrupted abruptly.

"What?" Pete asked.

"Well," Rob started cautiously, "I want a new family, so maybe I should pray that I could belong to a new family! Y'know...a real family. Kinda like...well...like yours! Y'know, a family where there's nothin' wrong, or weird, or screwed-up with it. So...do you think that your mom and dad could maybe adopt me or something? I mean, the other day you told me that sometimes you wished you had a brother or sister. How about me? I'd be a perfect brother for you cause we already like each other. Don't you think I would make a good brother?"

Pete bolted straight up in bed and stared over at Rob's figure in the darkness.

"Rob, listen to me for a second. If you truly trust Jesus and do what he asks, then you already are part of my family. The family of Jesus Christ."

Rob thought for a moment.

"What the heck are you talking about, Pete? I wanna be part of *your* family! Y'know, the Johnson family? I want to be Robert T. Johnson. I want it to be for real – like it's all legal and stuff."

"But this is real, Rob!" Pete pointed out. "Don't you believe that Jesus is real or do you still think that all this stuff about Jesus is too weird to believe?"

"Man, I don't know!" Rob said with sad frustration. "I'm still thinkin' about it." He cupped the sides of his head with his hands and stared down at his legs.

"Hey," Pete whispered softly. "You want to hear a bedtime story?"

"Get out! I'm not a baby!" Rob mumbled under his breath.

136

"No, I'm serious," Pete said. "Throw me the flashlight that's on my desk." Rob threw the flashlight over to Pete, and Pete grabbed his Bible from the bed stand. "This story is from Luke, chapter eight, and it's about who Jesus considers his family to be." Pete illuminated his Bible, flipped quickly through the pages and then began to read.

"Then Jesus' mother and brothers came to see him, but they couldn't get to him because of the crowd. Someone told Jesus, 'Your mother and your brothers are outside, and they want to see you.' Jesus replied, 'My mother and my brothers are those who hear God's word and obey it.'," Pete closed the book and switched off the flashlight.

"That's it?" Rob asked loudly. "Not only do we have to go to bed early, but my bedtime story is only three sentences long!" he said sarcastically.

"Shhh!" Pete held his index finger to his lips. "What the story says is that if you follow God's commands, then you are part of the family of Jesus. And if you're part of the family of Jesus, then you're part of my family too. My brother in Christ — for real!"

"So what's these commands that I'm supposed to follow again?"

"Well, you know...you've got to love God with all your heart, and you've got to love others around you too."

"I'm tryin' to do that," Rob responded.

"What about your mom?" Pete asked.

"Hey!" Rob snapped back. "That's not fair! She don't even love me, so why in the world should I love her?"

"Because God asks us to," Pete replied calmly.

"You know," Rob said with annoyance, "the more I think about it, the more I think I'm not cut out for this Christian thing at all!"

"Listen Rob, please give God a chance and see what he can do in your life. In just a couple of months I've already seen some changes in you, and there's more that's gonna happen if you stick with it. You've just got to work on this 'mom' thing. I mean, if you can't even love and honor your own mom who you *can* see, then how are you going to ever love and honor God who you can't see?"

"It's easy for you to say all that stuff cause you *have* awesome parents. You don't understand what my mom's like at all," Rob said. "It's too hard for me to try to love someone who's supposed to love me like a real parent – but doesn't! I feel like I'm all alone in this whole thing."

"No you're not," said Pete confidentially. "Remember what we talked about before, on the fishing trip? We said we were going to help each other, and I'm helping you to understand what Jesus wants us to do. And I'm not giving up on you because I want you to be my brother."

"What was that?" Rob asked. "What did you just say?"

"Look, Rob. I'm asking you if you'll be *my* brother. I'm praying that you'll be my brother in the family of Christ."

Rob sighed.

"You're confusin' me, and I'm startin' to get tired," Rob responded in an exhausted voice. "Let's just stop talkin' about it for now, okay? We might as well just go to sleep since nothin' else exciting is goin' on here." Rob rested his head on his pillow and thought for a long time about what Pete had just said to him.

The Christmas concert finally came and Rob had learned four rhythms on the drums in four weeks. Mr. Croteau said that Rob did indeed have drummer's blood since he learned drumming so quickly. The stage in the front of the church was decorated with garlands and colorful lights. People were starting to arrive for the concert. Rob sat at his drum set and kept an eye on the front door. Finally, he saw Mrs. Johnson and his mother enter the building. They sat near the back.

Pete and Becky Croteau made their way over to Rob.

"So, how do you feel?" Pete asked Rob.

"I don't know. Kinda nervous, I guess."

"Yeah, me too," Pete admitted.

"Add me to the list!" Becky said with a nervous smile.

Rob looked around at the large crowd before him.

"I've never done anything like this before in my whole life, you guys. I never thought I'd be sittin' in front of a whole crowd of people who came to see me play in a concert. And I never thought I'd ever wear a tie neither!"

"It looks really good on you, Robby!" Becky said with a reassuring smile.

"Thanks," Rob replied shyly.

"I always knew there was a musician deep, down inside of you somewhere!" Becky said brightly. Rob smiled with an air of pride. "I hear you get to have another sleep-over at Pete's tonight," she continued. "That's got to be a pretty exciting thing to look forward to."

"Yeah!" Rob agreed. "I love it over at his house!"

"Hey, look in the back!" Pete said suddenly. "I see your mom's sitting back there, Rob!" Rob shrugged as if he didn't care.

"It was really nice of your mom to drive her to the concert, Pete," Becky commented.

"How much you wanna bet she ain't gonna stay for the whole thing?" Rob asked darkly.

"Just give her a chance, you dork!" Pete said as he playfully shoved Rob's shoulder. "Come on Becky! Your dad just showed up at the front of the stage. We gotta get into our places. It's show time!"

At seven minutes past seven O'clock, the concert began. Rob was very nervous and sweaty, but his beat was solid and true. Halfway through the second song, he saw his mother make some sort of commotion at the back of the church. Then he saw his mother and Mrs. Johnson rise and quickly leave the building. Rob's face contorted into an angry scowl. At that moment, he banged the drum so hard that everyone in the church looked over at him with a curious glance. He took a deep breath, settled down and played normally again.

After the concert, Mr. Johnson took the boys home. Rob was noticeably quiet.

"What's wrong, Rob?" Pete asked, "Something's bothering you. What is it?"

"My so-called mother!" Rob said angrily through clenched teeth. "I know her so well! I knew she was gonna leave! I told you, didn't I? Do you see now what I have to put up with?"

"Maybe there was a good reason why they left early," Pete said.

"I doubt it. She didn't even make it through the second song! I hate her!"

"Hey, hey! Hold on there!" Mr. Johnson interjected loudly from the driver's seat. "Why don't you two find something else to talk about for a little bit, okay? We'll ask why they left early when we all get home."

When they arrived at Pete's house, Mrs. Johnson met Rob at the door.

"I dropped your mom off early, Robby. She had to leave."

"What's new," Rob muttered.

"Well, there's something you should know. Come on, step over here for a second," Mrs. Johnson pulled Rob aside so she could have a private word with him.

"Robby, your mom had to leave because she couldn't keep herself from crying at the concert. In fact, she cried all the way home."

"What are you talkin' about?" Rob asked with a concerned look on his face. "What's wrong with her?"

"Well," Mrs. Johnson replied, "When the crowd clapped after the first song, she just couldn't help herself. She was so overcome with all kinds of emotions at that moment, she simply broke down. I was the one who suggested taking her outside the building so she could have some privacy and settle down. At first, she kept going on and on about how badly she feels that she isn't the kind of mother that she would like to be for you. She told me that she doesn't know why she is the way she is. She has felt so ashamed about herself for such a long time now, that it's very hard for her to even leave your house to go out and do even the most simple tasks. It's a terrifying experience for her just to do a little shopping. All these things just came pouring out of her while she was watching you play the drums in front of all those people."

"Great!" Rob said with annoyance, "Why did it all have to come out right then during the concert?"

"Because Robby," she was so proud of you. Just seeing her talented son up there in front of all those clapping people was enough to finally let her release all those hard emotions that she has been holding back for such a long time. Actually, I'm glad we missed most of the concert, because it gave us time to talk about all sorts of things that are important to her. We talked mostly about you."

"Me?" Rob asked suspiciously. "What about me?"

"Well," Mrs. Johnson continued, "for one thing, she told me that the only thing that she ever did right in her whole life was to have you, Robby." Rob stared blankly at the floor. "Robby, your mom loves you. She may not say that to you very often, but I can tell you that after listening to her, you're the most important thing in her life."

"Your mother told me tonight that she wants to change her life around. It's probably going to take a lot of time, but she's determined to make a change for the better. She's going to make an appointment with a counselor that may help her address some of her problems." Mrs. Johnson placed her hand gently on Rob's shoulder. "And I'll be there to help support her as well. I like your mom, and I'm glad that the Holy Spirit encouraged me to meet her. I want to encourage her to change her life for the better. I think you do too, don't you?"

After a brief pause, Rob softly whispered a simple "Yeah".

"I think that you, Mr. Robert T. McGwyn, will be the biggest help of all to her," Mrs. Johnson said as she gently squeezed Rob's shoulder. "Don't give up. Remember, God's love is very powerful, and it can do amazing things if we allow it to work freely through us. His love flows extremely well through people with humble spirits and forgiving hearts, people who allow it to flow freely inside of them without letting anger, fear or pride dry it up. This means, Robby, that if you really want your relationship with your mother to improve, then you are going to have to do a lot of changing yourself. Maybe to start with, try looking at your mother in the same way that Jesus sees her: as a potential child in the family of Christ."

After the Johnson's dropped him off at his house the next day after church, Rob walked slowly to the front door and placed his hand on the doorknob. He heard the sound of the television set blaring from the living room. He knew that when he stepped inside the house, he would see his mother sitting on the couch, her back to him and her eyes glued to the television screen. He softly opened the door and quietly entered the house.

Usually, when Rob arrived home, he would run up the stairs directly to his bedroom without saying a word to his mother. On this day, however, he stood silently at the foot of the stairs for a moment. He paused to study his mother from behind as she sat on the couch watching her television show. He sighed slightly, closed the door behind him and turned to climb the stairs.

"Robby?" came his mother's small voice.

"What?" Rob answered indifferently.

His mother turned her head toward him and stared at him out of the corner of her eye. Rob saw the light from the television screen twinkle brightly through several teardrops that clung to her face.

"You did real good last night at the concert. Real good. I was real proud of my boy up there on the stage. Real proud."

She sniffed, wiped the tears from her eyes, and turned slowly back to the television.

Rob paused silently for a moment as if he were considering the words his mother had just said to him. Perhaps Mrs. Johnson was right about his mother after all? Rob slowly started up the stairs. He stopped halfway up and held onto the railing tightly.

"Thanks…mom," he said softly.

Rob continued up the stairs and entered his bedroom. He reached under his bed and removed a torn and crumpled picture of himself and his mother that had been taken when he was just two years old. In the picture, his mother was holding him on her lap. Though she was smiling, Rob's mother wasn't looking at the camera at all. Instead, she was affectionately gazing down with loving eyes at her little son.

Rob placed the old, beaten photograph next to a new picture of the Johnson family he had propped up on his desk several weeks ago. Then, he found his kids' study Bible that Mr. and Mrs. Johnson had recently bought for him, and he cut out a cartoon drawing of Jesus from one of the pages with a pair of scissors. Rob placed the picture of Jesus on the desk between the two photographs. Rob looked at all three pictures and smiled.

"Robert Thomas McGwyn," he announced to himself softly, "I'd like to proudly introduce you to my new family!"

Questions:

1) Do you sometimes get frustrated with members of your own family? Do you think that your family members sometimes get frustrated with you, too? Does this mean that you don't love your family members, or that they don't love you? Do you think that you frustrate God sometimes? If so, do you think that God still loves you anyway?

2) Did you realize that if you love Jesus and practice following his commands each day, that you have become an adopted member of the family of God, our Father in Heaven? How does that make you feel?

Bible References Relating to this Story:

Ephesians 6:1
Luke 8:19-21
Romans 8:15-17
Matthew 7:1-5

Chapter 9

It wasn't me!

Yellow Snow

Pete zipped up his winter coat and put on his gloves. He grabbed his backpack and ran out the front door of the school. There was only a half-day of school today due to the teacher workshop classes scheduled for the afternoon. Pete ran as fast as he could through the crowd of kids making their way down the sidewalk. Most of them would have to take the bus home, but Pete lived close enough to walk – or in this case, run!

Pete caught up with his friend, Rob, who had snuck out a back door of the school a few seconds before everyone else was allowed to leave.

"Hey!" Pete yelled, "Wait up!"

"I can't wait today, Pete!" Rob called back as he sprinted down the sidewalk. "I'm in a hurry!" Pete caught up to him.

"Hey, Rob! Just listen for a second! Me, Gordy and Ryan are going to build a snow fort after lunch at Haley's Field. We're going to make at least one hundred snowballs and have the biggest snowball fight in recorded history. You wanna be part of it?"

"No thanks," Rob said. "I got to get to the music store downtown. I'm not even gonna eat lunch today."

147

"But if you help us," Pete began, "then we can have two even teams when we do the snowball fight. And we need help making all those snowballs too."

Rob turned and grabbed Pete by his arms. Pete stopped abruptly.

"Dude," Rob said calmly as he stared directly into Pete's eyes. "I said I gotta go. Doesn't it say somewhere in Proverbs that 'When you gotta go, you gotta go'?"

"Uh...no," Pete answered hesitantly. "I'm pretty sure that saying isn't in the book of Proverbs."

"Well, it's probably in the Bible someplace. With a book that big, it's gotta be in there somewhere. Anyways, I said 'no'."

"Well, can you at least tell me why you're in such a big hurry to get to the music store?"

"I'm gonna get me some brand new drumsticks to practice with so I don't have to keep using those beat-up, old sticks from the church!" Rob declared proudly.

"Oh! So *that's* what you're gonna do with the money you made from working for Mrs. Stevens last month, huh? Good idea!" Pete said with a smile.

"No," Rob replied. "I spent most of that money on junk food. I spent the rest of the money on a tie and a shirt for the Christmas concert, remember?"

"So...," Pete started slowly, "how are you going to pay for the new drumsticks then?"

"I'm just gonna to walk down to the music store and take 'em. I ain't gonna pay anyone for nothin'."

"You're going to steal them?" Pete asked with a shocked expression on his face.

148

"Yeah. It's not like I haven't stole stuff before. Here's my plan: If I get to the music store during lunch, there's usually only one guy at the counter, and if it's the guy that's usually there, he'll be practicing his guitar with headphones on. When this guy practices, he usually has his eyes closed while he nods his head up and down mumblin' to himself. Pretty weird, huh? Anyways, that's when I can grab the sticks and slip 'em into my coat and get out of there without gettin' caught. That's why I got to get down there right now. I've got to grab 'em while it's still lunch time and there's only that one clerk in the store."

"But Rob!" Pete protested earnestly. "That's stealing! You know that stealing is a sin! What are you thinking? What happened to trying to change your life to live the way God wants us to?"

"Hey, that's no problem," Rob said with an air of authority. "Accordin' to your dad, if I steal somethin', which I know is wrong, but I repent and ask God to forgive me, then he will forgive me. So I don't have anything to worry about, right?"

"The Bible says that those who have become part of God's family don't make a practice of sinning!" Pete exclaimed. "And when you repent, you have to mean it; you have to be sorry for real! You just didn't understand what my dad meant!"

"Yeah, well I guess I don't understand anything in the Bible then," Rob said with a hint of annoyance. "Y'see, I memorized a verse too — a simple verse from First John, five fifteen," Rob said proudly. "It says somethin' like this: 'since we know Jesus hears us when we make our requests, we also know that he will give us what we ask for'. That's from the Bible, so it must be true, right?"

149

"Yeah," Pete replied cautiously. "But..."

"Well," Rob interrupted, "I've prayed for a bunch of things, and I didn't get any of them! Not one! I prayed that I would be rich and famous and pass all my tests in school! I prayed that I would get more muscles so I could be the strongest kid in town. And I prayed that I would be invited to one of Meagan Pulaski's parties, and that I would get my own, real drum set to practice on at home so I don't have to keep practicin' on plastic buckets. I would have been happy if I could just be rich like I prayed for! If I was rich, then I could just buy the sticks. But it doesn't look like that's gonna happen any time soon. Y'know, I'm still not convinced that this whole God-Jesus thing is for me because it sure doesn't seem like anyone is listening to any of *my* prayers."

"But, Rob, listen...," Pete said as he tried to reason with his friend.

"You listen, Bible boy! Maybe you're in with Jesus like the best of friends, but he don't seem to be doin' much with me and *my* prayer requests! And since none of my prayers are coming true, I decided that I'm gonna make them come true all by myself — with or without Jesus' help!" Rob turned and started down the sidewalk again.

"Wait!" Pete shouted. "Just listen to me for a minute! I want to help you to understand what that Bible verse really means!"

"And I want to become a famous drummer in a famous band," Rob replied confidently. "I'm gonna get those sticks, and nothing's gonna stop me!"

Pete watched his friend walk further away from him. "I've got to do something fast!" he said to himself. "God?" Pete whispered. "Please don't let Rob steal those sticks! He doesn't understand you yet, but he's trying. You know he's trying! He's still new at all this stuff. Please give me the right words to say to him right now that will bring him back to you. Thank you for listening to me and helping me, Lord Jesus!"

Rob was getting farther away every second. Pete started to run after him but then he stopped after a short distance. He cupped his gloved hands around his mouth and called out to Rob.

"Hey Rob!"

Rob ignored him and continued walking away.

"Yoe! Robby!"

No change.

"Robert T. McGwyn! Stop for a minute!"

Rob shook his head and kept moving on. Pete was desperate, but he was suddenly inspired by an idea that popped into his head. He dropped his backpack at the edge of the sidewalk and scooped up a large handful of snow. He shaped it into a snowball and packed it hard. Then he yelled at Rob with all his might.

"Robert T. McGwyn! You are the biggest loser that ever walked the face of the earth! And that's loser with a capital 'L'! You're nothing but a sissy and big cry baby! A loser like you could *never* be famous!"

Rob immediately stopped in his tracks.

"Turn around and face me, *loser* — if you dare!" Pete shouted. Pete went into his pitching stance and waited. Rob slowly turned around. As Rob was turning, Pete aimed and fired his snowball with all his strength. The frozen missile raced silently toward Rob and slammed him squarely in his face. Rob staggered backward. Pete looked surprised. He had never

151

before thrown a snowball that well aimed, with that much speed and distance in his entire life. For a brief moment, Pete was very pleased with the results!

"Wow!" he said to himself. "That was awesome! Thanks God! I think that got Rob's mind off of stealing for now!"

Pete watched Rob blow a big chunk of packed snow out of his mouth and scrape splattered snow away from his eyes. Then Pete could clearly see the look upon Rob's face. It appeared to be an unfriendly look. Oh, yes. It was indeed a very unfriendly look. Rob coughed and spat on the ground. He stuck a finger up each nostril of his nose to dig out the rest of the splattered snowball. Then Rob's angry voice filled the air.

"Oh, you're dead now, buddy boy!" Rob yelled out. "I'm going to kill you, Johnson!"

"Oh boy! This could be a problem!" a worried Pete mumbled to himself. Then he prayed again anxiously: "Father God, what have I just done? It looks like he really *is* gonna kill me! What do I do now?"

Rob hollered something that sounded like a battle cry and then ran at Pete with great speed and ferocity. Pete sprinted off the sidewalk and tried to escape by running down the snow covered hill onto the school's sports field below.

"You can run, Johnson, but I'm gonna catch you. And when I do, you're in for it big time!"

Rob caught up with Pete near the bottom of the hill and tackled him face first into the snow.

"You can forget your lunch, Petey-boy, cause I'm going to force feed you a homemade snow cone!"

Pete squirmed around frantically as Rob sat on Pete's back. Rob grabbed the back of Pete's collar and lifted Pete's face out of the snow for a second, and then he forced it back into the snow again. He did this over and over.

"Stop!" Pete yelled as Rob pulled his face out of the snow.

"Why should I, you freak?" Rob said angrily as he shoved Pete's face back into the snow.

When Rob raised Pete's face out of the snow again, Pete yelled out hysterically, "This isn't really something that Jesus would do!"

Rob paused for a moment to catch his breath.

"So, Pete the perfect," Rob began thoughtfully, "are you sayin' that what you just did to *me* is somethin' that Jesus would do? I don't think so! I don't understand the Bible as good as you, but I do know *two* things that Jesus would *never* do," Rob leaned over close to Pete's ear. "Number one: Jesus wouldn't have called me nasty names like 'loser' or a 'sissy' like you just did, you dumb jerk! Number two: Jesus wouldn't have plastered my face with a snowball! And don't try to tell me that's because he lived in a desert where they ain't got no snow!"

"I didn't mean it!" Pete cried out desperately. "I was just trying to stop you from making a big mistake! I didn't want you to go back to stealing things again!"

"You know, Bible-boy, none of this had to happen. I wouldn't have to steal nothin' if only Jesus had answered my prayers in the first place and gave me everything I asked for! I know this might seem hard for you to believe, but I really *don't* want to be poor or a loser my whole life! You hear that God?"

Rob yelled fiercely as he looked up to the sky. "I don't want to be poor or a loser no more!"

As Rob took a deep breath in an attempt to calm down, his gaze fell back to earth. Something brilliant and glistening in the snow next to his leg suddenly caught his eye. As he focused on it, his angry scowl slowly changed into a placid smile. His eyes widened in astonishment. It seemed as though a wave of peacefulness eased his tense body.

"Wow!" Rob said joyfully. "There *is* a God after all!" Eagerly, he reached out and scooped the precious discovery into his gloved hand. He examined it closely. It was a truly valuable find! It had all of the precious attributes of which he was seeking at the time. It was cold. It was snowy. It was bright yellow!

"Hey!" Pete cried out. "Can you get off of me now? Please?"

"Just one more thing," Rob said wryly. "I can see that you have been havin' a real bad day so far. So I want to give you somethin' that will help make it all better, okay pal? It's somethin' very refreshing that will help cool you off."

Pete shivered and his voice cracked.

"Oh, I think I'm cooled down enough right now — especially my face!"

"Sure you are," said Rob with mock sympathy. "But I insist. I just know you're gonna get *real* excited about what I just found for you."

"What is it?" Pete asked warily.

"Oh, nothing much. Just some ... *yellow snow*!"

"**NOOOO!**"

Rob was correct. Pete did get very excited. Pete's legs and arms swung back and forth wildly, but Rob wouldn't let him

154

move. He forced Pete's arms to his side and then held them securely with his knees.

"Open up!" Rob commanded. "Yellow snow is best served cold!"

"Help me! Someone help me!" Pete screamed. "He's gonna force feed me frozen DOG PEE!"

Rob leaned forward and put the handful of yellow snow right in front of Pete's face so that he could see it clearly.

"Just try to think of it as a lemon snow-cone, buddy, and it won't be so bad goin' down," he said with a villainous laugh. "So, let's get this over with and we can both go home. Open up...LOSER!"

"Lord, help us!" Pete yelled out before tightly closing both his eyes and his lips as the yellow snowball slowly made its way toward his mouth.

At just that moment, Rob heard several girls giggling from the sidewalk at the top of the hill.

"Look at those two idiots! Boys are *so* immature!"

Rob turned around and saw Meagan Pulaski, Sarah Mills and Amanda Grant standing on the sidewalk above him. Rob didn't know what to say, so he simply stuck out his tongue at them.

"Oh, like that's *so* mature!" said Sarah. "I'm *so* impressed with your command of the English language," she said sarcastically.

"Obviously there's no sign of intelligent life here," said Amanda with a laugh.

"Aw, just go away!" Rob yelled back.

"Did you hear that?" Megan asked as she pretended to be surprised. "The big one on top can talk! Maybe they're not as primitive as we thought they were!"

"Well the smaller one on the bottom can't be that smart," said Sarah. "He doesn't look too bright with his head stuck in the snow like that."

"It's definitely brain freeze," said Megan nodding her head thoughtfully. "That would explain a lot. His brain must have frozen up like an ice cube."

"And it's probably the same size as an ice cube too!" Amanda blurted out. The group of girls began giggling uncontrollably.

Pete opened his eyes and lifted his head so he could get a better view of the group of young female hecklers on the sidewalk above them.

"Hey! We don't need to listen to your dumb comments!" he shouted.

"Yeah!" Rob agreed. "Get lost! This doesn't have anything to do with you!"

"We're not going anywhere," Megan replied defiantly. "This is way too entertaining to miss. I mean, this is just like watching the monkeys play at the zoo!"

"I'm warning you!" Rob replied angrily. "Get lost!"

"Make us! We'd like to see you try!" Megan challenged them.

Rob rolled off of Pete. The two boys looked at each other and smiled.

"Pete, grab some more of that YELLOW SNOW!" Rob yelled so that the group of girls would easily hear his remark. "Let's go show the girls what we found!"

"Oh, you two are *so* disgusting!" Meagan said slowly backing away.

"Get 'em!" Rob yelled out. "Charge!"

Both Rob and Pete rushed up the hill toward the girls while carrying handfuls of yellow snow. The girls screamed and ran down the sidewalk as fast as they could. Rob and Pete looked at each other and laughed.

"Well," Rob began as he brushed the snow from his hands, "after this, I don't think Megan will *ever* invite me to one of her parties. There's another prayer that's never gonna come true."

Pete smiled at Rob and shook his head.

"Rob, what I was trying to tell you earlier is that praying and asking for things in Jesus' name isn't like magic. Jesus isn't like a genie in the lamp. You don't control him, and you don't get three wishes to ask for anything you want."

"Then how come the Bible says you'll get whatever you ask for? I was really starting to get into in all this Jesus stuff, too."

"Well," Pete began, "You have to read the *whole* Bible passage and understand everything it says, not just one little piece of it." Pete walked over to his backpack, removed his gloves, and pulled out a small Bible. "You said that First John five fifteen tells us that if Jesus is listening when we make our requests, we can be sure that he will give us what we ask for."

"Look for yourself," Rob stated confidently. "It's right in there!" he said tapping the top cover of the Bible.

157

"I believe you," Pete said as he opened the book and flipped through the pages near the end of the book. "But let me read the verse just before that — verse fourteen which is part of the same passage. It says 'And we are confident that he hears us whenever we ask him for anything that pleases him."

"Okay," Rob said skeptically. "If that's true, where's all the stuff I asked for?"

"Don't you see?" Pete asked. "Were you asking for those things to please Jesus? No! You were asking for those things to please yourself! Jesus knew that you were asking for those things for selfish reasons and not because you love God or because you're trying to help other people. It's supposed to be all about God, not all about Rob! God gives freely to us when we ask for things that please him! You have to look at the whole passage to really understand what God wants us to do, not just a small part of it."

"But you and your parents told me that you are praying for me so that I would understand God better, and be more like Jesus," Rob argued. "You weren't being selfish when you prayed for that, and it still hasn't come true! I was gonna steal something today! I haven't changed at all!"

"Wow!" Pete said as he smacked his hand against his forehead in disbelief. "Can't you see it? Of course you've changed!"

"I have?" Rob asked in disbelief.

"Rob, have you taken a good look at yourself lately?" Pete asked. "These days, you're not in detention anymore. Instead, you're helping the church choir. You've learned to play the drums, you've made new friends, you're doing better with your

158

mom, you've earned your own money from having a job, and you've been having more fun than you ever had in your whole life. You said so yourself just the other day. That's a lot of change for you in only four months!"

"But, I'm not acting like Jesus," Rob said with a hint of disappointment.

"To be changed into the kind of person that Jesus wants you to be can take a real long time. Sometimes it happens over a person's entire life," Pete replied. "As long as you're always trying to improve each day, you're doing fine. Don't be so quick to give up on yourself or on Jesus when things don't seem to be going the way you want them to."

Rob though for a moment.

"Okay, Pete. If I was praying the wrong way all this time, then how am I supposed to pray?"

"Well, when I'm not trying to rescue a friend from doing something crazy," Pete started as he subtly nodded toward Rob, "I usually start my morning prayer by praising God and giving thanks to him. Then I ask 'God, what would you like me to do for *you* today?', and I quietly listen for him to respond; usually he puts something in my mind that he want me to do. Then I pray for people I know: my family, friends, and my church family and myself. And then I give thanks again in Jesus' name. I usually pray a couple times a day. And most of my prayers during the day aren't long — probably less than a minute or so. A lot of times I pray when I'm just walking down the street. I know I can talk to God anytime and anywhere. And I know that if I'm doing what pleases him, God will hear me."

Pete was quiet for a second, as if he were considering something to do or say. Then he looked at Rob boldly.

"So, Rob. Would you like to pray with me – I mean, right now? Then you can see what I'm talking about."

Rob's eyes shifted nervously from left to right.

"What are you talkin' about? Don't you know there's people around? They'll think we're a couple of yahoos!"

"That's okay. I'll pray for both of us," Pete responded. "I don't care if people hear me talk to God."

"Well, do it then," Rob whispered loudly as he walked a short distance away. "I'll just...stand over here." Rob appeared a little embarrassed.

Pete gave thanks to God and took some time to pray for Rob. He prayed especially that Rob wouldn't give up on the opportunity to learn more about Jesus as well as the opportunity to become a Christian. When he opened his eyes, Rob had disappeared. Suddenly, someone yanked his coat collar from behind and dropped a snowball down his bare back. It was Rob. Pete yelped and Rob laughed.

"At least it wasn't yellow snow!" Rob chuckled. "And by the way, I wasn't really gonna make you eat dog pee. I just wanted to torture you a little bit for calling me a loser."

"You really had me fooled!" Pete exclaimed. "And I'm sorry about all those things I called you. I was just trying to get your attention, that's all."

"Actually, I think it was God trying to get my attention," Rob said thoughtfully. "Anyways, who cares now? We got a snow fort to build. Come on! Let's get some lunch and then meet the guys."

Pete smiled.

"Sweet!" he said. "Let me get my backpack, and we'll take off."

"Hey, by the way...thanks for praying for me," Rob said softly with a smile. "Y'know, I'm still not sure about this whole Christian thing, but, just like you prayed, I'm not giving up. So at least that's one prayer that's gonna come true today! No one's gonna steal away my chance to get to know Jesus better — not even me!"

Questions:

1) Do you pray to God everyday on your own? What are your prayers like — what do you say? How do your prayers differ from Pete's? Do you listen to hear what God might have to say to you?

2) Is it all right to ask God for things for yourself? What kinds of thing do you think are all right to ask God for? Have you prayed for anything simply for selfish reasons? How do you think God feels when we pray to him with selfish reasons?

3) That same night that Jesus was arrested, he had prayed to God to ask if he wouldn't have to suffer what was to come shortly after (being whipped, made fun of, and nailed to a cross to die, for example). Do you think that this was selfish of Jesus to ask this? Read all of Luke 22:41-42 and then decide.

4) Do you find it hard sometimes to understand the meaning of certain verses in the Bible? Would reading the entire chapter that the verse is in help you better

understand its meaning? Would knowing who the verses were written by, to whom they were written, and what time period they were written also help? Who can you ask that may help you understand Bible verses better? Is it good to ask a couple of different people about the verses you are trying to understand? Why?

5) Did you know that on the night before Jesus died and sacrificed himself for us (at the Last Supper) that he prayed for you? You can read this in John 17:20-21.

Bible References Relating to this Story:

1 John 5:14-15

James 4:1-3

Philippians 2:3-5

1 John 2:3-6

Chapter 10

The Altar Call

"A newspaper man is gonna be there? Finally! I'm gonna be famous!" Rob yelled with excitement. "If our church band is gonna be in the newspapers, then everybody is gonna know me! People won't think I'm a loser anymore!"

"I never thought that you ever *were* a loser, Robby," Becky replied calmly.

"Plus," Pete cautioned, "even if you *do* get an interview with the reporter, it doesn't mean you're going to make it into the paper for sure."

Becky and Pete stood on the front porch of Rob's house while Mr. Croteau waited for the kids in his van parked by the curb. They had stopped to pick up Rob on the way to the Kingston Church Valentine's party which was taking place at the church that afternoon. The church band, of which all three kids were members, was scheduled to play the music for the event.

"Well, after he hears how I play the drums, the newspaper man won't be able to help himself; he will *have* to interview me!" Rob stated confidently. "He might even want to get my autograph or somethin'!" Pete and Becky looked at each other and burst out laughing. "What?" Rob asked indignantly. "You two don't think I'm good enough to get into the paper?"

"It's not that, Robby," Becky said with a gentle smile. "But I think you need to practice working on your humility a little bit more."

"Humility?" Rob said with a puzzled look. "What's humility? I don't know the meaning of that word!"

"Exactly!" Pete said loudly in agreement.

Becky giggled and patted Rob lightly on the shoulder. "Don't worry about it now," she said. "My dad's waiting for us. Grab your sticks and let's go. We have to get to the church early so we have time to set everything up."

"I already got my sticks in my back pocket, so let's get outta here!"

Becky noticed that Rob's upper body was only covered by a loose-fitting, thin tee shirt. "What about your coat?" she asked him. "It's the middle of winter. You really should wear a coat or something."

"What are you? My mother?" Rob replied, mildly irritated.

"Oh! That reminds me about something else you should do," Pete chimed in. "You should also make sure you tell your mom that you're leaving now, and tell her when you'll be back."

Rob rolled his eyes. "Gimme a break!" he said with exasperation. "My mom don't…"

"Stop!" Pete said as he held the palm of his hand in front of Rob's face. "Please, please, *please* don't tell me that 'my mom don't care where I go' or that 'my mom don't care what I do'! You say that every time we do something like this! You're supposed to be working on getting along better with your mom…remember?"

Rob looked down for a moment as if he were trying to think of a rebuttal. "Okay," he relented stubbornly after a brief pause. "You wanna come in for a second while I do all these *chores* you guys just gave me?"

"Okay," Pete said quickly. "This will be the first time that I've ever been inside your house!"

Becky signaled to her father that they were going into the house. Her father nodded in approval, and then Pete and Becky followed Rob inside to the kitchen.

"It's kind of messy in here," Rob said. "We just haven't had time to clean in a while. I'll be back in a second. I'm hoping I can actually find a coat in all this mess."

Rob ran up the stairs as Pete and Becky stood still —very still — as if they were almost too frightened to move. Only their heads slowly swiveled to the left and right as they peered nervously around the kitchen. What they witnessed must have seemed to them to be wildly chaotic — well beyond anything they would be used to seeing in their own homes. There were dirty dishes piled high in the sink. The floor was gritty and generously littered with dirt and crumbs. A large area of the stovetop was covered with multiple layers of spaghetti and cheese sauces with an occasional old, hard noodle stuck on here or there. There were several areas on the floor where tiles were missing. The garbage can overflowed with milk cartons and empty boxes of macaroni and cheese dinners. In the corners of the ceiling hung dusty cobwebs, and several of the walls had a few small holes in them. Becky quickly grabbed Pete's arm with alarm after she spotted two cockroaches exit the sink and scurry across the countertop.

"Wow!" Pete whispered. "I didn't realize that he…well…that this is what his house was like. I mean, my mom's been over here before, but she never told me that…it was like *this*!" Becky nodded soberly and remained silent. The house was very quiet. Pete turned toward the living room and noticed a large television set on the floor nestled amongst several pizza boxes and soda cans. "The TV's not on. Maybe his mom isn't here."

Rob rumbled quickly down the stairs. He was now wearing a light jacket. "Well, it's not very thick, but it's better than nothin'," he said.

"Is your mom home?" Pete asked.

"Yep. She's nappin' upstairs in her bed." Rob chuckled. "She fell asleep with that Bible your mom and dad gave her. It's opened up and lying right across her face! She looks hilarious!"

"Did you take it off her face?" Pete asked.

"No. I didn't want to wake her up."

"Well, if you don't want to wake her up, why don't you leave her a note then to tell her where you are," Pete suggested.

Rob sighed heavily.

"Ya mean now I gotta to try to find a pen and some paper to write on? Look at this place! I don't even know where to begin!"

166

Pete reached into his pants pocket and pulled out a pen which he handed to Rob.

"Here," Becky said as she removed a folded paper from her pocket. "You can use this to write on. It's blank on the back."

Rob unfolded the paper and saw that it was a flyer for the Kingston Church Valentine's party. "Oh, cool! I didn't know someone made advertisements for this thing! Let me read it." Rob read aloud from the top of the flyer which were several verses from Matthew eleven: "Then Jesus said, 'Come to me, all of you who are weary and carry heavy burdens, and I will give you rest. Take my yoke upon you. Let me teach you, because I am humble and gentle, and you will find rest for your souls. For my yoke fits perfectly, and the burden I give you is light'." Rob paused for a moment as if he were considering the verse, and then continued reading the bright pink, bold words that followed immediately after: "Do you need some time to kick back, relax and have some fun? Could you use some Good News right about now? Join us at the Kingston Community Church on Saturday, February 15th from one O'clock to three thirty and find out who truly loves you during this Valentine's season — and for an eternity beyond! Come and relax for a casual gathering and enjoy yummy refreshments and fun, toe-tapping music. Best of all, discover who Jesus Christ is and how he can change your life forever!" Rob smiled as he glanced down to the bottom of the page. "Hey! They printed the verse from John three sixteen!" he said. "Even *I* memorized that verse!" he stated proudly as he closed his eyes tightly and thrust the flyer behind his back so that it would be impossible for him to cheat as he recited the verse. "'For God so loved the world that he gave his one and only Son so that whoever believes in him will not perish but have everlasting life'. How did I do?"

"Impressive!" Pete said with a big smile.

"Excellent!" Becky agreed.

"Well, what can I say? I'm awesome!" Rob said boldly.

Pete and Becky looked at each other. "Humility!" they said at the same time with a nod and a smile.

Rob looked at both of his friends suspiciously for a moment, and then shrugged indifferently. "Whatever," he said coolly.

Rob glanced down at the flyer again and smirked at the picture of a pink, candy heart at the bottom of the page. Inside the heart, the words read 'BE MINE! LOVE, JESUS'.

Rob brushed aside some plates and cups on the kitchen table. He set the flyer down on the tabletop, and then he drew an arrow pointing to the time and date of the party which was printed on the front of the flyer.

"Purple ink?" Rob asked as he looked at the arrow he just drew.

Pete shrugged. "What's wrong with purple ink? My mom got a bunch of purple pens for a big discount at the office supply store. That's all we have in the house right now."

Rob raised his eyebrows with surprise.

"Wow. Purple ink. That's weird. Anyways, here's your purple pen back. We're all set!" Rob handed the pen back to Pete and headed toward the front door.

"That's it?" Pete asked in disbelief. "How's she even going to see the flyer when it's being surrounded by so much...stuff?"

Rob sighed loudly and spun around. "Alright already!" he said as he hastily swept the flyer off the Kitchen table. I'll put it

168

on top of her Bible, all right? She won't miss it then considerin' her Bible's lyin' right on top of her face! Don't worry…I'll take care of it," he said as he eyed Pete crossly, "…for *Pete's* sake!"

As Rob ran upstairs to deliver the note, Pete glanced at Becky who was studying his face closely. Her arms were folded over her chest and she had one eyebrow raised in an inquisitive manner. Pete did a double take.

"What?" he asked nervously. "Why are you looking at me like that?"

"Purple? Really?" Becky teased him with a playful grin.

"Gimme a break!" Pete said defensively. "It's just a pen that happens to write in purple! It's just a color! Why is everyone making such a big deal about it?"

*   *   *

After setting up the stage in the large Fellowship Hall at the church, Pete, Rob, Becky and the other band members practiced several of the songs they were going to play at the party. As they finished their last practice song, Becky noticed a young woman making her way around the room with a camera hanging from her neck and a notebook and pencil in her hand. Becky tapped Rob's shoulder lightly.

"Look, Robby! The newspaper reporter is here!"

Rob anxiously looked around the room. "Where? I don't see him!"

Becky laughed. "It's not a him…It's a *her*!"

"A *girl* newspaper man?" Rob seemed doubtful.

169

"Why not?" Becky asked indignantly as she placed her hands on her hips and narrowed her eyes at Rob.

Rob looked at Becky's eyes and then shrunk back. "Well, I'm not sayin' that girls can't be newspaper men…"

"I think what you meant to say was newspaper *reporters*, right?" Becky said correcting him.

"Oh! Yeah! That's what I meant! It's just that I was expectin' a guy, that's all."

Pete walked up behind Rob.

"Hey, Rob. We have some free time now, so why don't you go over and introduce yourself to the reporter? You said you wanted to be famous and get into the paper. So here's your big chance!"

"Naw. Not now," Rob said with a hint of embarrassment.

"Why not?" Pete asked. "This is a perfect opportunity. Look. She's all alone and she's not talking to anyone right now. Go introduce yourself to her while you have the chance!"

Rob slipped quietly behind Pete and Becky and stooped over slightly as if to hide himself from the reporter. "I said 'no'! I'm not ready to do somethin' like that right now!"

Pete turned around and smiled impishly at Rob. "You're chicken, aren't you?"

"Gimme a break, Johnson!" Rob retorted as his face grew ruddy with humiliation.

"Bawk, Bawk!" Pete said softly with a bold smile.

"I ain't got nothin' to say to her right now, that's all!" Rob whispered hotly. "Now stop askin' me! What are ya tryin' to do? It sounds like you want me to ask the reporter to go on a date or somethin'! Why don't *you* go talk to her, big man?"

"It's because she's a pretty woman, isn't it?" Pete blurted out with a laugh. "You're embarrassed to go over there and meet her because you're too shy to talk to a pretty woman!"

"Why don't you go soak your head in the punch bowl, Johnson!" Rob retorted.

"This is what you should do, Rob," Pete giggled as he continued to tease Rob. He reached his hand into a nearby dish of small candy hearts and removed a pink one. "You don't even have to talk to her! Just hand her this piece of Valentine's candy and it will explain everything! It's got 'TRUE LOVE' written on it! See if she'll put *that* in the newspaper for you!" Pete continued to giggle almost uncontrollably as Rob struggled to cover Pete's mouth with his hand.

"Shut it, Johnson!" Rob whispered loudly, his face turning bright red with embarrassment. "She's gonna look over here if you don't shut it!"

"Speaking of valentines," Becky interrupted with an impish grin of her own, "Meagan Pulaski received a very, *very* nice valentine's card from a secret admirer yesterday. It simply gushed with romance and praises. She let me read it, you see." Becky tilted her head slightly upward and batted her eyelids dramatically in a flirtatious manner. She let out a long, exaggerated sigh of satisfaction. "Whoever wrote it," she continued, "is definitely a true romantic! He certainly has a very artistic and colorful flare for expressing both his passion and individualism! You see, the handwriting on this particular valentine's card was written in…*purple* ink. So, I keep asking myself 'now *who* do you suppose might have sent her that card'?"

"HA!" Rob shouted as he pointed at Pete. "It's you, Pete, and your pathetic, purple pen! Hey! I gotta a great song for you and Megan for this valen-times! It goes like this…" Rob cleared his voice and sang out joyfully, "Peter an' Meagan sittin' in a tree! K-I-S-S-I-N-G! That spells kissin' if you haven't figured it out yet, buddy-boy!"

Now it was Pete's turn to turn bright red with emotion.

"Look at his ears!" Rob laughed. "He fits right in for valen-times with those big, pink ears of his!"

"Alright, alright already!" Pete said with irritation as he covered his ears with his hands. "Let's just all forget that any of this conversation ever happened, all right?" Pete glared at Becky.

"Sorry!" Becky squeaked brightly. She pretended to zip her lips shut with her fingers and thumb.

Mr. Croteau approached the kids. "Okay, you three. It's show time! Take your places on the stage."

Pete, Rob, and Becky took to the stage with the other musicians and began to play. The crowd grew larger as people continued to stream into the church's Fellowship Hall.

Part way through the band's second song, Rob's eyebrows shot up in surprise and his jaw went slack. He almost missed a beat as he stared in awe as he witnessed his very own mother enter the church building. Mrs. McGwyn limped slowly into the entrance of the Fellowship Hall, relying heavily on her cane for support. She seemed to have arrived by herself. Rob watched as Pastor Moore, who was greeting people at the entrance, rushed to help her. The pastor led Mrs. McGywn to a seat near the back of the room and sat down with her. They talked together for a while, and then the pastor stood and introduced Rob's mom to several other people near the doorway.

The church band took a break after playing for an hour. Rob rushed off the stage and ran over to his mother who was still sitting in the same seat at the back of the Fellowship Hall. She was talking to an older woman that Rob had never seen before.

"Well, here's your son!" the woman declared with a large smile. "What a talented drummer you are!" Rob simply stood motionless and stared at the woman and then at his mother.

"Go on now, Robby," Mrs. McGwyn said as she lightly tapped Rob's sneaker with the tip of her cane. "What do you say, son?"

"Thanks," Rob mumbled.

"I've seen you here on Sundays with the Johnson family, but we've never officially met," the woman continued. "My name is Jenny Lister."

"Hi," Rob mumbled quickly.

"His name's Robby," his mother said turning to Jenny.

"It's nice to meet you, Robby," Jenny said with a nod. "You truly did a wonderful job up there." There was an awkward, silent pause as Rob stared at the floor in an attempt to avoid eye contact with Jenny.

"Well, you probably want to talk to your mother now that you're on break. I'll let you two alone for now," Jenny said as she smiled again and left to mingle with the other guests.

"Mom!" Rob whispered loudly as he sat down next to his mother. "How did you get here?" Rob looked around the church as if he were frantically searching for someone. "Who brought you? Mrs. Johnson? Is she here somewhere?"

"No one brought me," Mrs. McGwyn replied. "I actually walked all the way here by myself."

"But that's almost two miles!" Rob exclaimed with amazement. "What about your bum knee?"

Mrs. McGwyn raised her cane in front of him. "This comes in handy," she said. "I haven't used it in a real long time. But I had two good reasons to get out of the house today. One reason is that I wasn't gonna miss another one of your concerts. I'm sorry I missed so much of your first one back at Christmas. I really enjoy listenin' to your band. You're all doin' real good up there today, Robby. Real good!"

"So...what's the other reason you came?" Rob asked curiously.

Mrs. McGwyn reached into her pocketbook and withdrew the flyer for the party that Rob had left with her earlier that day.

"This invitation you got me."

"That was just somethin' to tell you where I was gonna be today. It wasn't really to invite you or nothin'."

Mrs. McGwyn read the top of the flyer aloud: "'Come to me, all of you who are weary and carry heavy burdens, and I will give you rest. Take my yoke upon you. Let me teach you, because I am humble and gentle, and you will find rest for your souls.'" She put the flyer back into her pocketbook. "Sounds like an invitation to me. Maybe not from you, but from him." Mrs. McGwyn pointed at a large wooden cross which was standing nearby. "I think I'm ready, Robby, to change my life around. I want to give myself over to Jesus. Mrs. Johnson has

174

been good about helpin' me understand about what it means to follow Jesus and how followin' him can change you around. And the pastor here, he told me that today he's doin' an altar call for anybody that wants to make a public confession about their faith in Jesus."

"Altar call?" Rob asked. "What's that?"

"It's just like your mom said."

Rob spun around to see Pete and Becky standing behind him. Pete and Becky both said hello to Mrs. McGwyn, and then Pete continued with his explanation: "In our church, an altar call is when new Christians are invited to say publicly that they want to follow Jesus. Usually the pastor gives a short sermon about what it means to be saved by Jesus. Then he invites people who want to give their lives to Jesus to come up to the front of the church to publicly tell everyone that they believe in the power of Jesus to take away their sins and save them from God's punishment."

"Our altar calls are supposed to be like a celebration," Becky added, "which is why we have a party. And our church does it around Valentine's day because Valentine's day reminds us about love—like the love that Jesus has for us. "

"Can't you just believe in Jesus without standing up in front of a bunch of people and tellin' them that?" Rob asked.

"Sure," Pete shrugged.

"So what's the point of this whole altar call thing then?"

"Well," Pete began, "the reason our church does altar calls has to do with several passages in the Bible which mention that anyone who publicly acknowledges Jesus and confesses that Jesus is their Lord will be saved."

"Wait a minute!" Rob interrupted. "Can't a person just ask Jesus to let them be part of his family while they're praying in the privacy of their own bedroom when nobody else is around? Wouldn't they still be saved then?" he asked sharply.

"Sure," Pete responded cautiously, "but Jesus also says in Matthew ten, verse thirty-two 'If anyone acknowledges me publicly here on earth, I will openly acknowledge that person before my Father in heaven.' That quote comes from Jesus himself. So my question is why *wouldn't* a person want to take Jesus up on that kind of promise?" Rob remained silent as if he were pondering the question. "Well," Pete continued, "I guess one reason might be that a person may feel too shy and afraid to stand in front of a group of people."

"Would you be too afraid to go up in front of all these people, Robby?" Mrs. McGwyn blurted out suddenly.

Rob glared at his mother and then at Pete. "I ain't afaid of nothin'!" he snapped back hotly.

"Well, that's good cause if you wanna go up with me, Robby, you can," Rob's mother offered. "We can go up together so it won't be that scary for either of us havin' to get up in front of everybody."

"I said I ain't scared of nothin', and I ain't gonna go anywhere today except back to play some more music on the stage!" Rob said in a loud voice. "Look," he said with a calmer tone, "I'm only here to play music for the party. That's why I came here today. That's it!" He spied the refreshment table across the room. "And I also came to eat cookies. That's it...music and cookies! So if you will all excuse me..."

Rob turned his back on his mother and his two friends and strode off to get some snacks.

His mother shook her head sadly. "Yep," she said glumly, "He's such a big chicken sometimes." Becky opened her mouth as if she were about to say something to defend Rob, and then quickly closed it again. She sat down silently next to Rob's mother and smiled weakly. "You seem like a real nice girl," Mrs. McGwyn observed. "Are you in Robby's class at school?"

Pete tapped his chin thoughtfully as he watched Rob travel across the crowded room. Suddenly, his eyes sparkled with an insightful glimmer.

"You two stay and chat," Pete said as he abruptly interrupted Becky and Mrs. McGwyn's conversation. "I'm kinda hungry too. Do either of you two want anything?" Both Mrs. McGwyn and Becky said 'no thanks', and Pete turned and hurried after Rob.

Pete approached the snack table just as Rob stuffed four cookies into his mouth at once.

"Wanna coof-hee?" Rob blurted out with a muffled voice, showering Pete with a spray of cookie crumbs that freshly jettisoned from his mouth.

"Maybe later," Pete said with a look of disgust as he flicked away crumbs from his shirt with the back of his hand. "Thanks for sharing, though," he said sarcastically.

"Sure!" Rob said as he reached for a cup of pink lemonade.

"So, Rob," Pete said in a low, serious tone, "something just occurred to me. Y'know, I haven't asked you this question for awhile, but I suppose this is as good a time as any."

"What question?"

"Well…do you…I mean, have you actually, uh…I thought that maybe — from the way you were talking over there — that maybe you have, y'know…"

"Come on, Johnson!" Rob said impatiently. "Spit it out!" He took a sip of his lemonade and immediately spat it back into his cup. "Yuck! That's way sour!"

"Look…what I'm trying to ask you, Rob, is…have you accepted Jesus Christ as your Lord and Savior? I know you haven't been too sure about the Christian thing up to this point."

Rob seemed taken aback by the question and stood still for a moment before replying. "Yeah," he shrugged indifferently. "I did."

"Have you prayed about it at all?"

Rob seemed slightly embarrassed and he lowered his voice to almost a whisper.

"Well…yeah! I guess I've been prayin' about it ever since you showed me how to pray a few weeks ago."

"What did you say in your prayer?" Pete asked with deep interest.

"Well, I told Jesus that I couldn't believe that he would want to have someone like me in his family, but that I would love to be part of it if he would have me. And I've been tellin' him that I'm real sorry that I can't live up to all of his commands perfectly, but that each day I would try to practice following the commands he gave us because that's what he wants us to try to do even though it can be real hard sometimes. So, yeah. Basically I told him that I want to be saved, and that I want to be part of his family, and I want him to be my Father and Lord."

Pete smiled broadly from ear to ear and slapped Rob so hard across the back that Rob spilled a little of his drink on the rug. "I've never been as happy and proud of anybody in the world as I am with you right now, Robert T. McGwyn!"

"Alright already!" Rob said as his face flushed with embarrassment. "Just calm down ! And please don't tell me that I got to go up in front of a bunch of strangers and spill my guts for them about this whole thing! It's something that I did that's just between Jesus and me. And, well...you too now. I don't want to tell any of this personal stuff in front of no strangers!"

"Your mom's not a stranger, and Becky and Mr. Croteau aren't strangers. In fact, you could consider that everyone that goes up to the front of the church today are all members of your new family that you were just talking about! You'll be in good company! We'll all be cheering you on, including your new Father in heaven, Jesus! It would make him very happy to celebrate this awesome news with the rest of us today!"

Rob looked around at all of the people in the church and shook his head with despair. "Naw. Not gonna do it!" he said firmly.

"But why?" Pete asked with a desperate tone.

"Because," Rob responded.

"Because why?"

"Because...maybe I *am* just a little bit...afraid of doing something like that right now."

Pete looked slightly disappointed. "Well, okay," he shrugged. "At least you're honest about it. I'm still way happy for you, though. It would be great to share this good news with all these people. I mean, this *is* a party after all, and I would love all of us to celebrate this big change in your life together. This would just be a great time to do it. But it does take a lot of courage to tell people that you love Jesus. So, if you're…uncomfortable with doing that sort of thing…"

Rob nodded in agreement.

"Well," Pete continued, "I'm still glad that your mom's going to make her confession. To tell you the truth, I'm a little surprised that she's the one that is going to publicly confess her love for Jesus rather than you. I thought for sure she was way more shy than you are."

"I think she actually is way more shy than me," Rob said thoughtfully.

"Well, not anymore," Pete said with a grin. "She's brave enough to go outside the house — alone — and walk two miles on a bad knee in the middle of winter to get here. She must really love Jesus! And she's the one that's going to get up in front of her new family and…"

"Guilt trip!" Rob said pointing an accusing finger at Pete. "Now you're trying to 'guilt' me into getting up there, aren't you? Admit it!"

Pete shrugged. "It's just an observation. That's all. I just thought that this would be a good time and a good place for you to practice some courage and bravery for Jesus, y'know, in the company of your family — especially considering the sacrifice Jesus has made for you. But it's your decision. Whatever you decide to do, I just want you to know that I'm still way happy and proud of you…brother." Pete smiled at Rob and gave him an encouraging slap on the back. He glanced at the clock on the wall and then headed toward the stage. "Come on! Stop filling your face with sugar. It's time for us to get back up on stage."

The band played again for half an hour before Pastor Moore took to the stage and gave a short sermon about the gospel of Jesus and briefly explained what it means to become a follower of Christ. After the sermon, he asked the band to softly play the old hymn *Great is thy Faithfulness*, which, as practiced by the band beforehand, did not require the use of drums throughout the song's performance. This freed Rob to simply sit and focus on the proceedings of the altar call uninhibited.

Pastor Moore invited any new Christians who wanted to publicly acknowledge Jesus as their Savior and Lord, to come to the front of the Fellowship Hall where he would pray with them individually.

At this point, Mrs. McGwyn, who was still seated at the back of the Hall, grabbed her cane and struggled to stand. Rob watched as Jenny Lister hurried over to his mother to help her up. Pete, who was softly singing at the time also witnessed this and glanced over at Rob. Rob quickly glanced back at Pete as his cheeks flushed with color.

"Oh brother! I guess I gotta go help her," Rob murmured to himself with a sigh. "I guess that would be the right thing to do. This is so embarrassing!"

Rob slowly lifted himself from his stool and staggered slightly as he took several steps away from the drum kit. He saw Becky turn to him with an encouraging smile and a friendly wink. Rob then looked to Mr. Croteau, who was directing the band. Mr. Croteau smiled warmly and nodded to Rob as if he knew Rob's intentions and was cheering him onward.

Rob quickly jumped off the stage and zigzagged through the stream of people making their way up the center aisle. He met his mother at the half-way point and relieved Mrs. Lister as he took his mother by the arm. Mrs. Lister smiled and whispered in Rob's ear "good man!" She gently patted Rob on the back several times as Rob started walking his mother slowly toward the front of the Fellowship Hall. When they reached the front of the hall, they noticed that someone had placed a chair near the stage for Mrs. McGwyn to sit in.

After sitting, Rob's mother looked up at Rob with hopeful eyes and asked with an almost inaudible voice "staying?" Rob hesitated for a moment as he looked out over the crowd of faces smiling with encouragement and joy. He turned back to his mother and hesitated briefly before nodding 'yes'. Mrs. McGwyn smiled and gently gave her son's hand a reassuring squeeze.

Suddenly, a brilliant flash of light exploded next to Rob from his right-hand side. He quickly turned to see the newspaper reporter kneeling on the floor only a few feet away, her camera aimed directly at him and his mother. Rob quickly turned back as Pastor Moore approached. The pastor handed the McGwyns a copy of the confessional prayer (as he had done with the others standing at the front of the hall), and then invited anyone else in the room who wished to confess that Jesus is their savior to join in as well. This is how the prayer read:

Dear Father in heaven, thank you for leading me in this celebration of my new life today. Thank you for accepting me into this family of believers and as a part of your Holy body of which you are the head.

Your promise, written in Romans ten, verse nine, tells us that if we confess with our mouth that you are Lord, and if we believe in our heart that God raised you from the dead, then we would be saved. Jesus Christ, I do confess that you are the Messiah whose coming the prophets foretold. I do confess that you are the Son of God. I do believe that you suffered for me and died to save me from my sins. I do believe that God raised you to life, and that by God's good plan, gave you all power and authority as Lord and King over heaven and earth. Father Jesus, I confess before this crowd of witnesses today that you are my Lord and Savior.

Even though I am a sinner, you love me. I am grateful and humbled that you have saved me from the terrible punishment I deserve. Though I sincerely regret the sins I have committed against you, I am filled with joy that, through your infinite loving grace, you have given me the eternal salvation of my soul.

Please help transform me into your likeness. May my greatest desire be to faithfully follow and serve you so I may bring honor, glory and praise to your matchless name.
Amen.

*   *   *

Near the end of the party, the reporter approached Rob, Pete, Becky and Mrs. McGwyn.

"Hi, folks!" she said in a cheerful voice. "My name is Melanie. I'm a field reporter for the Kingston Times. I was hoping I could talk a little bit with you and your mom," she said looking directly at Rob.

Rob's eyes grew big. "You...you wanna talk to me?" he asked in disbelief.

"Well, yes," said the reporter. "I'd like to talk to both you *and* your mother if you have some time."

"Okay!" Rob said with excitement.

Melanie smiled.

"You probably noticed that I took a picture of you two just before you prayed with the pastor." Both Rob and Mrs. McGwyn nodded. "Would either of you mind if I were to use that picture in our newspaper?"

Rob and his mother looked at each other and shook their heads 'no'.

"I guess it's fine with us," said Mrs. McGwyn said with a shy giggle.

"Great!" said Melanie. "It was a really awesome picture of both of you." She opened her small notebook and withdrew a pencil from her pocket. She looked at Rob's mother. "May I have your name please?"

Mrs. McGwyn's face flushed with color, and she laughed nervously. "Good gravy!" she exclaimed. "Nobody's ever wanted to interview me before!" Becky gently placed her hand on Mrs. McGwyn's shoulder to help strengthen her. Mrs. McGwyn smiled up at Becky and then turned back to the reporter. "Well, my name is Anne McGwyn, but most people who know me real good just call me Annie."

"Do you spell McGwyn M-C-G-W-I-N?" asked the reporter.

"Nope," Mrs. McGwyn answered quickly. "Everybody makes that mistake. Just change out the 'I' for a 'Y', and you'll have it right."

"Great!" said Melanie with a smile. "Thanks, Annie. Now how about your name?" she said looking at Rob.

"It's 'Robert T. McGwyn'," Rob stated proudly. "And McGwyn is spelled the same way as my mom's last name," he added thoughtfully.

"Well, I'm glad to hear that," Melanie said with a chuckle as she wrote the information in her notebook. "Thank you, Mr. Robert T. McGwyn. May I ask you why you and your mom came here today?" Rob turned toward his drum set on the stage and stared at it for a moment. He then turned to his mother.

"Me and my mom went up in front of all the people here today to tell them that we love Jesus, and that we want to be part of his family," he stated confidently.

"Great," said the reporter. "May I quote you in the paper with that statement, Robert?"

"Sure!" Rob said happily. Pete and Becky both raised their eyebrows with great surprise.

"Can I ask *you* a question, Melanie?" Rob asked. Melanie stopped writing and looked at Rob.

"Sure."

"Well, I was wondering…are you a Christian too?"

Melanie smiled politely and shook her head.

"No. But I have to say that this party was a great way to celebrate the folks that have just become new Christians. I met a lot of really nice people here. I personally had a lot of fun covering this story. I wish more of my fieldwork was as pleasant as this event was. I interviewed a lot of folks here and they all seemed genuinely upbeat and happy. You guys are all truly like one big, happy family. Y'know, sometimes it seems like there's so much bad news out there, that it's very refreshing to get a good news story every once and a while like this one to report on."

"Did you see me play the drums up on the stage there?" Rob asked eagerly.

"Yes, I did," Melanie responded.

"I was pretty good, wasn't I?"

Pete and Becky looked at each other with a slight smile. "Humility!" they said in unison. "That's the Robby that we all know and love!" Becky added with a twinkle in her eye.

Melanie laughed. "*All* the musicians up there were just fantastic!" she said.

"Want my autograph?" Rob asked boldly.

"And to think we couldn't get him to talk to her two hours ago!" Pete whispered to Becky.

"Yeah! And now we can't get him to shut up!" Becky giggled.

Melanie laughed again and nodded.

"Okay. Sure, Robert. I'd love to get your autograph. Do you want to use one of the pages out of my notebook to write on?"

"Nope!" Rob grabbed a flyer that was left on top a nearby table. Then he walked over to Pete and extended his open hand. "Pen, please!"

"But it's purple," Pete reminded him.

"I don't care. Just hand it over, lover boy."

Pete glared over at Becky as he fished the pen out of his pocket.

"What?" Becky said shrugging defensively. "I didn't say anything this time! I promised, remember? My lips are sealed!"

"I wish his were!" Pete mumbled as he thrust the pen firmly into Rob's hand.

"Thank you, my good man!" Rob said with an air of elevated dignity as if he were an important celebrity.

Rob wrote quickly on the front of the flyer and then handed it to Melanie. Melanie read the remark with great interest.

"Thanks, Robert," she said nodding. "Y'know, you peaked my curiosity. I may just take you up on this suggestion. I've never actually tried this before. Maybe I should. Thank you."

"Sure!" Rob said enthusiastically.

Mr. Croteau approached the group. "Sorry," he said with a grin, "but I have to recruit these young folks to help pick up this place."

Becky, Pete and Rob said their goodbye's to Melanie before they returned to the stage to pack their instruments and load the van with all of the musical equipment.

Ten minutes later, the van was packed, and it was almost time to leave the church. Pete and Rob had a brief moment alone in the Fellowship Hall before turning off the lights and locking the door behind them. Unable to contain his personal curiosity any longer, Pete asked Rob what he had written on Melanie's flyer.

"I wrote 'if you really want a Good News story, read the Gospel of Jesus! Signed Robert T. McGwyn. And I circled the verse from John three, sixteen."

Amazing!" Pete exclaimed. "You've just became an evangelist! And to think...just a little while ago you were too afraid to let *anyone* else know you were a Christian...and now, everyone in the city who reads the paper will know by the end of next week!"

Rob gulped nervously. "Yeah!" he said. "When I came here today, I wanted to be famous for being a great drummer, not for being a Christian. I guess some of the people I know might look at me differently now, huh? I guess things are gonna change for me...and my mom."

"They already have," Pete said. "And there's more changes to come...for *all* of us. But don't look so worried! You have a lot of people around you who are cheering you on! You met a whole bunch of them today."

"I have another question for you," Pete continued. "Why did you participate in the altar call when you were so definitely against it just moments before?"

"Well," Rob began, "when I stood up to help my mom, I felt real scared — like I was gonna pass out or somethin'. Then I saw Becky and Mr. Croteau smile at me like they were cheering me on — just like you just said. Then I started praying to myself. I said 'God? If I'm brave and courageous, and I do this thing, then I gotta ask that you help me. Give me the peace you promise to give to us — like you say you will in the Bible.' And when I was standin' up in front of everybody with my mom, I actually picked my head up and looked at all the people in front of me. Normally that kind of thing would freak me out! But everyone was all smilin' and happy to see us up there. And that's when I got the peace that I asked for. I could really feel it!

And then I told my mom that I'd stay with her and do the altar call. After I read the prayer out loud with everybody else, I didn't feel embarrassed anymore about lettin' people know that I love Jesus. It was like somethin' that happened all of a sudden."

Pete smiled and nodded his head silently.

"Come on you two!" Becky shouted from the exit door. "Rob, your Mom's in the van and we're all ready to go. Don't forget to turn off the lights and shut the door!"

Just before they exited the building, Rob quickly turned around and stared into the large Fellowship Hall. "I almost forgot something!" he said. He cleared his voice and shouted, "Happy valen-times Jesus! I'm yours!"

Questions:

1) If you are a Christian, have you ever made a confession that you are a follower of Jesus in front of a person or group before? Was the person or group Christian as well? Were you nervous or scared before you made your confession? How did you feel after you made your confession? How did the person (or people) react to it?

2) If you're not a Christian, do you think that it would be hard or embarrassing to publicly confess that you are a follower of Jesus if you became a Christian, or do you think that it wouldn't be hard to do at all? Do you think you would you be concerned with what people would think or say about you after your confession, or wouldn't it bother you?

3) Why would it be important that other people —
especially in the family of Christ — were to know that
you are a follower of Jesus?

4) How did Rob's Prayer to God in this story (which was
to give Rob peace as he helped his mother make her way
to the front of the fellowship hall) differ from his prayers
from the previous chapter? Was his request granted this
time around?

<u>Bible References Relating to this Story:</u>

Matthew 10:32

Luke 12:8

Romans 10:9

Ephesians 1:5

Romans 15:5

Chapter 11

Jesus Freak

God smiled. His enormous hand reached down and touched Rob's face. The whole world was filled with the light emanating from the Lord, and Rob squinted as he looked up to witness God's brilliant, radiant face directly. Everyone on earth looked on in total amazement as God gently caressed Rob's face with his gigantic, mighty finger which protruded from an enormous, heavenly, white cloud above. Then God withdrew his finger into the cloud, and, in a booming voice louder and deeper than thunder, God spoke: "This is my son. And with him I am very pleased!"

Everyone on earth knelt down in front of Rob in reverence.

"Whoa!" Rob said with a dreamy smile. "This is so intense!"

Rob turned around to see all of the people of the earth bowing down to him. There were billions and billions of people! Out of this multitude, Rob saw his friend Pete, who was kneeling near him. Pete's head was bowed toward the ground.

"Hey, Pete!" Rob yelled out excitedly. "Check this out! I'm awesome! I told you I'd make it really big someday! I'm, like, the most famous person here on earth! Come on up here! You're my best friend, and I want everybody to see you too!"

Pete kept his head bowed down.

"I'm not worthy! I'm not worthy!" Pete declared in a low, monotone voice.

"Sure you are!" Rob argued. "Isn't that right God? Can't Pete come up here with me?"

God's mighty voice suddenly thundered throughout all the earth: "Get up!"

"Y'see, Pete!" Rob called out joyfully to his friend. "God wants you to get up here with me just like I asked! So...get on up here, and make it snappy! You don't want to make God wait!"

Suddenly the whole earth shook violently. The masses of people before Rob cried out in terror.
Once again, God's voice filled the air: "GET UP! GET UP NOW!"

"Uh oh, Pete!" Rob said with worry in his voice. "Get a move on! I think you better get up here right now!"

"NO!" God said loudly as peals of thunder shook the ground. "Robert T. McGwyn...I want *YOU* to get up! Stop foolin' around and GET UP!"

Rob looked confused.

"Uhh...what's that God?" he asked. "What do you mean when you say you want *me* to get up? Get up where?"

"If you don't get up now, you'll be late for school," the voice thundered. "Hurry up, or you won't have time to eat your Toasty Pops!"

Rob's eyes shifted back and forth suspiciously.

"God?" Rob asked softly as he stared into the brilliant light from above, "do you know that you sound just like my mother?"

"I *AM* YOUR MOTHER!" the voice boomed.

Rob cried out in terror and his eyes shot open. His heart pounded hard as a dose of adrenaline coursed through his body. He was in bed. His mother had turned on his overhead light and was frantically shaking him awake.

"Now stop foolin' around and get your butt outa' bed!" she said sternly. "As it is, you're gonna to miss your breakfast!"

"Stop it, mom! Come on! Leave me alone!" Rob covered his eyes with one hand and swatted at his mother with the other until she stopped shaking him.

"Are you really awake?" she asked. "You're not gonna fall asleep as soon as I leave are you?"

"No, I'm definitely awake! You almost scared me to death!" Rob said angrily. His mother nodded and left his room. Rob squinted at his overhead light and sighed. "How could I ever think that God's glory was just a cheap ol' light bulb?" he muttered with disappointment as he turned over on his pillow. A few seconds later, he was sound asleep again.

Rob was late for school, so he decided to take a short cut that morning by crossing through Haley's Field. Now that it was covered with several layers of winter's snow, the field rather looked like an enormous, white, arid desert.

193

Since Rob was late, he walked briskly. His stomach growled loudly in the crisp air. Since his mother had forgotten to buy more Toasty Pops, and since he decided there wasn't anything else worth eating in the house, Rob skipped breakfast completely and left his house extremely hungry. Despite the constant complaining of his nagging stomach, Rob found that he was fully willing and able to focus on praying.

He had been reading the Gospels in the Bible —Matthew, Mark, Luke and John — which tell about the life and times of Jesus Christ. He had mentioned to his Sunday school teachers over the past week that the Gospel verse he liked the best was from the book of Matthew, chapter seventeen, verse five when God speaks to Peter, James and John about Jesus. In that verse, God declares "This is my dearly loved Son, who brings me great joy. Listen to him." This sentiment was reflected in both his dream and his prayer that morning:

"Dear God, Thanks for the great dream I had this mornin'! I think that Jesus is like the biggest hero ever! I do want to be just like your Son and do the same things that he did in the exact, same way that he did them in the Gospel books! Then I know you'll be pleased with me in the same way too! Please make me perfect just like your Son, Jesus so that I'll be able to serve you real good today. Amen!"

As Rob reached the middle of the field, he heard someone huffing and puffing behind him. He turned around to see the large, hulking shape of Eric Beauclair sprinting through the snow waving his hand.

"Wait up, dude!" Eric called out.

Rob rolled his eyes with an air of annoyance. Eric was nothing but big trouble.

"What do *you* want?" Rob asked suspiciously.

"You can help me."

"How?"

"You know that test we got today in Mrs. Hudson's class?"

"Yeah."

"Well, I want you to get a copy of the test this morning so I can study it before I take the test this afternoon. My parents told me that if I fail another one of Hudson's tests, they'll ground me until I'm old enough to start collecting Medicare!"

"What are you crazy or something?" Rob cried out in disbelief. "What makes you think I can get you a copy of the history test from Mrs. Hudson?"

"You have her for homeroom in the mornings. Everybody knows that on the day of her tests she leaves copies of the test in the black notebook at the corner of her desk. You sit right next to her desk. When she's not looking, steal a copy of the test. It'll be easy! I even have an apple that you can put on her desk — kinda like a gift to her — if she happens to catch you near the folder. You can always tell her you were just giving her an apple because she's such an awesome teacher. That way, you won't get in trouble."

"What makes you think that *I* would steal a test?" Rob asked indignantly.

"Oh, come on!" Eric laughed. "You're Robert T. McGwyn! King of detention! It's not like you haven't done things like that before! Everyone knows you're a thief. Stealing stuff is just part of who you are."

"Oh yeah?" Rob shouted out defiantly. ""Well, I've changed! I don't do that kind of stuff no more! I haven't been in detention for two whole months now!"

"Yeah, right!" Eric said sarcastically. "I don't think you *can* change. I'll believe it when I see it!"

"Well, you better believe it cause it's true!" Rob stated confidently.

"Playin' hard ball with me, huh?" Eric said as he unzipped his backpack. "Fine McGwyn. Just hold on a second. I'll change your mind for you! If you steal a copy of the test, I'll make it worth your while, okay?"

"What are you talkin' about?" Rob asked.

Eric pulled a full package of chocolate, frosted Toasty Pops from his backpack and waved it in front of Rob's eyes.

"Yum! Just for you, McGwyn! I bet you didn't even eat this morning like you usually don't when you're late. You're starved, aren't you?"

"Yeah," Rob admitted. He fixed his eyes on the box and he felt his stomach rumble. He imagined himself tearing the top off of that box and wolfing down the entire contents of chocolaty, yummy goodness. He could almost taste the sweet, creamy frosting swirling around his tongue.

"These Toasty Pops are yours if you get the test for me. What do you say... buddy?"

Rob remembered in the book of Matthew how Jesus was tempted by Satan (also known as the devil). In the book, Jesus wandered in the desert for forty days and forty nights without a bite to eat. Satan challenged Jesus to use his Godly power to turn the desert stones into bread so he could eat and satisfy his hunger. But Jesus rejected Satan's suggestion right away. Jesus told Satan that people needed more than just food to strengthen their lives; they must also feed on every word of God as well. Rob took a stand and decided to do likewise despite the protest of his whining stomach.

"No," Rob said. "I won't do it."

"You're a tough customer," Eric said slyly as he slowly pulled another object out of his backpack. "But the Toasty Pops was just the beginning. Do you know what this is?" he asked as he waved the item in front of Rob's nose. Rob saw that it was one of the newest videogames just released to the stores. He wanted to buy one, but all the stores had sold out of them. Besides, he didn't have enough money to purchase it anyway.

"This is called 'Master World'," Eric said with an air of authority similar to a professional salesman. "I'm sure you recognize it. All the kids are just begging their parents to get this game. As you may have heard, this is the game where you can take control of all the countries of earth one-by-one and make them do as you command. Today, you, Robert T. McGwyn, can be the ultimate ruler of the world! Everything and everyone on earth will be under *your* control! It's really an awesome game! So here's the deal…this video game and the Toasty Pops for a copy of the test. Nobody can say 'no' to that!"

Rob sighed sadly. He squeezed his eyes shut and turned away from Eric.

"I can say 'no' to that, and I will! No deal!" Rob jumped back a bit as if he had actually startled himself. "Wow, I can't believe I just said that, but, man, does it feel good! I actually feel like I *am* Jesus!"

197

Eric looked confused.

"*You're* Jesus? What are you talking about, weirdo? Are you trying to make me think that you've gone insane or something? I don't buy it!"

Rob turned around to face Eric again.

"Don't bother trying to tempt me, Eric," Rob replied confidently. "You see, I'm working for God today, and I'm going to do everything like his Son, Jesus, did. So just walk away!"

Eric's loud laughter echoed across the field.

"You're working for God today?" he chuckled. "That's a good one! Do you really think that if there was a God that he would want to hang out with a loser like you?"

Eric's devious grin was suddenly replaced by an expression of deep thought as if he were trying to remember something.

"Wait a minute!" he said. "Come to think of it, someone told me the other day that they saw you in the paper. Yeah, that's right! You *are* famous — or maybe *infamous* is more like it! They said you were joining up with one of those weird, creepy Jesus fantasy cults!"

"It's no fantasy!" Rob earnestly protested. "Jesus is real, and he loves me. He loves you too, and you would know that, Eric, if you just would give him a chance like I have." Rob's eyes grew large and a wide smile exploded across his face. "Hey! Yeah! That's a great idea, God! Hey, Eric! I can tell you more about Jesus if you're…"

"Give me a break!" Eric interrupted angrily. "Why don't you go and throw yourself off a cliff, McGwyn! Let's see if God and all his angels will save you then, you crazy zealot! All I wanted was a copy of the test, not a sermon about your weird, hocus-pocus religion!"

Eric hastily stuffed the Toasty Pops and the video game into his backpack and zipped it closed. "You know, you're right," he said with contempt. "You really have changed — into a real wacko, that is!"

"But…"

"But nothing! Why don't *you* get away from *me*, you crazy Jesus freak! I'm taking my Toasty Pops and Video game and giving them to someone else!"

Eric stormed off in a huff. Rob smiled with satisfaction as he watched Eric hurry to the school building quickly leaving him behind.

"Well, Jesus," Rob said to himself, "I did exactly what you did when you met the devil in the desert. It was like…I'm you! We're like exactly the same, and it was pretty cool! I'm gonna try being you for the rest of the day! I can't wait to see what other cool things will happen!"

Rob finally made it to his classroom. Upon entering, he noticed that Mrs. Hudson was helping a student near the back of the room. As he approached his desk, he observed a very suspicious looking character slowly making his way toward the front of the classroom. It was Kyle Cassidy, and Rob could tell, he was up to no good. Kyle carried a bright red apple in his right hand, and his eyes darted back and forth suspiciously, watching everyone around him. He made sure that Mrs. Hudson had her back to him as he took one little step at a time closer and closer to her desk. Kyle eventually made it to the corner of Mrs. Hudson's desk – the corner of the desk where she kept the copies of the history exam! Rob watched as Kyle nervously fumbled for the black folder on top of the desk that held the history test for that day. He quietly slipped a paper out of the folder and quickly hid it behind his back while at the same time placing the apple on top of the desk. He noticed Rob watching him, and so he raised his index finger to his lips as if to signal Rob to keep quiet. As Kyle did this, Rob noticed that there were very visible traces of dark crumbs around his mouth. Then Kyle slowly crumpled up the paper in his hand into a tight ball, shoved it into his pocket, and slunk off silently back to his desk.

Rob shook his head with disgust as he sat down next to Pete. "I just can't believe it!" he said.

"What's that?" Pete asked.

"I just saw a crime happen right in front of my own eyes!"

"A crime? What kind of crime?"

"Kyle just stole a copy of the history test."

"What?" Pete cried in disbelief.

"Yeah, I'm serious!" Rob whispered loudly. "I saw him do it! Kyle was pretendin' to give Mrs. Hudson an apple, but when he was dropping the apple off on her desk, he grabbed a test sheet and put it in his pocket!"

"Why would he need a copy of the test?" Pete asked. "Kyle's not failing history."

"I think I know why he's doing it," Rob said. "I think Eric Beauclair put him up to it. Look at the brown stuff around Kyle's mouth."

Pete squinted slightly and focused on Kyle's lips.

"It looks like he's been eating dirt," Pete observed.

"I wouldn't put it past him," Rob replied. "But I know what that crummy stuff actually is from my own experience — he's been eatin' chocolate Toasty Pops! That's what Eric tried to bribe me with on the way to school. Eric said I could have them if I would steal the history test for him."

"So, what are you going to do?" Pete asked. "Are you going to tell Mrs. Hudson? That's what I would do."

"Yeah, but what would Jesus do?" Rob asked thoughtfully tapping his chin.

"Uh…I think that Jesus would tell the teacher," Pete replied. "It's kind of a no-brainer."

"I think I'll wait for now," Rob decided, nodding his head confidently. "I'm comin' up with a plan as we speak, and it's the kinda plan that I think Jesus would approve of."

Pete looked at Rob curiously. "What plan?" he asked. "Are you gonna pray about it or something? Y'know, it's always a good idea to pray when you have hard choices to make, but in this case, I don't really think that you have to…"

"Just trust me on this one, Pete," Rob interrupted with a reassuring tone.

"Uh…alright," Pete said hesitantly. "Well, let me know what you come up with anyway. I'm really interested."

During Lunch, Pete and Rob watched Kyle's every move. Kyle sat with Eric Beauclair, just as Rob had expected. They witnessed Kyle pull the crumpled piece of paper out of his pocket and hand it to Eric.

"I knew it! Eric's cheating!" Rob said as he pounded the table top with his fist.

"So, what are you going to do about it, Rob?" Pete demanded. "You can't wait forever! What about that plan you had? You gotta do something!"

"I know exactly what I'm gonna do about it," Rob said. "In the Bible, Jesus gets mad at the guys sellin' stuff at the temple in Jerusalem because they were tryin' to make a quick buck off of people who were goin' there to worship. Those guys were only interested in getting rich, and they really didn't care about God or his house of worship at all. Jesus said that they were turnin' his house of prayer into a den of robbers! So he flipped over their tables and all the stuff they were sellin' and chased them out of the temple area." Rob stood up. "I see some robbers right over there! I caught them right in the act, and I'm going to do something about it!"

"Hey, Rob?" Pete said with a worried expression as he tugged gently on Rob's shirt. "I think I know what you're thinking about doing right now, and I think we should think about it a little more ... don't you think?"

Rob vigorously rubbed his hands together.

"You know what I think? I think it's time for Jesus to show up and deliver some truth and justice! My plan is to do exactly what Jesus did at the temple right here and now! If Jesus could flip over tables, so can I!"

Pete noticed the determined look on Rob's face.

"But, Rob, I think…" Pete began.

"There's no time for thinkin', Pete! There's just time for doin'! And you better not try to get in my way, or I'll start flippin' out with this table that we're sitting at right here! You get me?"

"Okay..." Pete said softly as he slowly stood up, attempting not to irritate his friend further. "Well," he said, "if you'll excuse me for just a second, I...uh...well I'm gonna go see someone about something."

Rob noticed Pete's eyes casually glance over to the lunchroom monitor who was making his way through the crowd of children on the other side of the cafeteria. Pete's stare quickly turned back to Rob. Both boys locked eyes with each other for a brief moment, pausing as if each one were daring the other to make the first move. Then, like a flash of lightening, they bolted in opposite directions at the same time. Rob ran for Eric and Kyle's table, and Pete desperately weaved through the crowd toward the lunchroom monitor.

Rob reached Eric's table within seconds and pointed at them.

"Eric and Kyle!" he yelled out in an accusatory tone. "I've got somethin' to say to you!"

Startled, Eric and Kyle jumped slightly.

"Hey! Look who it is!" Eric said in a loud, mocking voice when he saw it was only Rob. "If it isn't the world famous Jesus Freak of Kingston Middle School!"

"You're both robbers and cheaters!" Rob stated authoritatively. "You stole a copy of Mrs. Hudson's history test so you could find out the answers before you take the test. This lunchroom is a place meant for *eating*! But you turned it into a place for *cheating*! You're both gonna pay! Everybody, get away from the table! Now!"

Everyone but Eric and Kyle quickly moved away and formed a circle around the table.

"Fight! Fight! Fight!" the crowd of children chanted gleefully.

Eric shot up out of his seat.

"Whad'ya gonna do, ya wimp? I don't have a test paper!"

Rob grabbed onto the long table-top and tried to flip the whole thing over in front of Eric and Kyle. Apparently, it was heavier than he thought it would be. Everyone around him, including Eric and Kyle, began to laugh as Rob struggled to lift the table even an inch off the ground. Rob prayed out loud for God's help: "God! Please help me with your strong and powerful hand!" The voices of the laughing children suddenly ceased, and Rob felt a large, powerful hand rest firmly on his shoulder. "Is that you God?" Rob grunted while still struggling with the table. "Wow! You answered that prayer real fast!"

The powerful hand on Rob's shoulder was attached to a powerful arm, which effortlessly spun Rob around. Rob peered up to see the Lunchroom monitor, Mr. McIntosh, glaring down at him. All of the kids in school called him Big Mack. Rob always said that Big Mack could be a great pro-wrestler if he ever were to change his career. Rob seemed to forget all about Eric and Kyle, as he stared in fearful awe at Big Mack's huge, tank-like, muscular form immediately before him.

"You got a problem, kid?" Mr. McIntosh growled in a low voice.

"No sir," Rob whispered weakly, "I ain't got no problem."

Pete poked his head out from behind Big Mack's big back.

"Come on Rob! Tell him about the test!"

Rob blinked a couple of times to rouse himself from his stupor. Then he remembered his mission. "Oh!" He reached over and pulled the crumpled piece of paper away from Eric.

"Hey!" Eric protested.

Rob presented the paper to Mr. McIntosh.

"Eric and Kyle stole this from Mrs. Hudson."

Mr. McIntosh looked at the paper closely. Then he looked squarely at Eric and Kyle.

"Did you two steal this?" he asked. Kyle and Eric looked at each other but remained silent. "All right," Mr. McIntosh said in a low, loud voice. "All three of you come with me. Ms. Hornsby, would you please watch the lunchroom while I take these three 'scholars' to the Principal's office."

Rob was dismissed from the school late that day having spent most of the afternoon in the principal's office. Although all the other children had already left for home, Rob saw that his friend Pete was faithfully waiting for him near the side door exit.

"Wow!" Pete said. "That took a long time! What happened in the principal's office, anyways?"

"I got in trouble for creatin' a disturbance in the lunch room. They called my mom, and all that stuff."

"But what about the stolen test? What happened to Eric and Kyle? Did they get into trouble too?"

"No."

"What!" Pete exclaimed in disbelief. "How come?"

"Because Kyle's not too bright," Rob began. "He accidentally stole a stupid ol'lunch menu that was on top of the tests. Kyle didn't even look at what he was stealin'. The principal didn't believe me when I told them that he was trying to steal the history test. Eric and Kyle both said that that's not what they were trying to do. They said I was crazy. They said it was me who was trying to steal from them! So I'm gonna get detention for something I didn't even do. It's only detention for one day, but still…I'm so mad right now! I was doin' so good by not gettin' into trouble! Kyle is a worm and Eric is a major mega-dork! I was only trying to do the right thing, like Jesus would have done. So how come I'm the one that's getting punished?"

"Well," Pete began, "in the book of First Peter, the Bible says, 'God called you to do good, even if it means suffering, just as Christ suffered for you. He is your example, and you must follow in his steps'. You were trying to do a good thing today. God knows that. But, the way you went about doing it was probably not the best way…in my opinion, anyway."

"What do you mean?" Rob asked. "I was trying to do exactly what Jesus did in the Gospels. Didn't you just say we're supposed to follow his example?"

"Yeah, but following someone's example doesn't mean you have to try to become exactly that same person. And that's impossible to do with Jesus anyway because he's perfect and we're not. Face it Rob…you're not Jesus Christ!"

"I had a dream that I was Jesus just this morning," Rob said with a wistful grin. "I thought it was great being the Son of God!"

"But then you woke up, right? And you were still Robert T. McGwyn, a human being and a *follower* of Christ. Not Jesus himself, right?"

Rob grunted glumly in agreement.

"Hey, I'm not Jesus either," Pete continued. "No Christian is! Sure, Jesus is part of each of us through the Holy Spirit that lives within us, but none of us are *fully* Jesus Christ! We were all created to be different from one another. So when we follow his example, we have to do it as the individual and unique people that God created us to be. In your case, Rob, you have to follow Jesus' example as Robert T. McGwyn, using your own personality, gifts and talents to live for Christ in your own unique way. So even though you and I follow the same example that Jesus shows us, we might act it out in different ways. "

"Follow Jesus' example in our own individual and unique way, huh?" Rob mumbled to himself as he considered what that meant.

"Hey!" Pete continued thoughtfully, "Speaking of following Jesus Christ's example, I know a really awesome way for you to end the day in a way that I know Jesus would really love!"

"How's that?" Rob asked with a suspicious look.

"By praying for Eric and Kyle."

"Aw, man!" Rob interrupted shaking his head in despair, "Somehow I just knew you were gonna say somethin' like that! Why should I pray for someone that just got me in trouble? I don't even like them, and I know for sure that Eric definitely don't like me!"

"Well," Pete said, "remember Jesus's example when he was suffering on the cross? He prayed for the people who were crucifying him! He actually asked God to forgive them! Jesus said 'You have heard that the law of Moses says, 'Love your neighbor' and hate your enemy. But I say, love your enemies!

Pray for those who persecute you! In that way, you will be acting as true children of your Father in heaven'."

"Alright, alright!" Rob interrupted hastily. "You don't have to keep preachin' at me and quotin' Bible verses! I already know all about that stuff! I know that's what I should do, but it doesn't mean it's gonna be easy! I'll try to pray for them...maybe later tonight... in my own 'Individual and unique' way as you put it."

"Hmmm. I think I'd love to hear *that* prayer!" Pete grinned.

"Well, prayin' for Eric ain't gonna be easy. Not after today!"

"Remember *my* run-in with Eric Beauclair a couple of years ago?"

"Sure I remember!" Rob said as a smile spread across his face. "That was the day when we first met! Eric was pickin' on you at lunch that day to impress his friends. Remember? It was the first day of school, and the lunch room monitor was absent. The cafeteria was like a zoo — every man for himself! I was sittin' all by myself at the table right behind you. And then Eric comes up and pushes your head down into your cup of vanilla puddin'! It looked like you had gross snot runnin' all down your face and shirt!"

Pete sighed solemnly. "Yep," he said. "Everyone was laughing at me. I was so humiliated; I thought I was going to cry right in front of everyone in the lunch room."

"But remember what I did then?" Rob grinned. "When Eric was bendin' over holdin' you down, I poured a whole carton of apple juice down the back of his pants. I called him 'sticky buns', remember?"

Pete laughed and shook his head. "Yeah, I remember," he said.

"Everyone in the lunch room started laughin' at him instead of you," Rob continued.

"Well," Pete began, "it took me weeks to get over that whole thing! I really wanted to hurt Eric back somehow and come up with a plan to humiliate *him* instead so he could see what if felt like to be humiliated in front of his friends. I wanted revenge! But that would have actually been the coward's way out. I would have been just as wrong as he was and no better than him. If I had done something like that, you wouldn't have even believed that I actually *was* a Christian. I would have been no different than Eric."

"Anyway, I asked my dad for help, and he and I started praying about it, and finally I could pray for Eric, but it took some time. One thing that I'm discovering about being a Christian is that following Christ's example isn't for weaklings! Being able to love, forgive and pray for all the different kinds of people in the world — even people that have hurt you — takes a lot of courage. It takes a strong person to be a Christian!"

"Yeah!" Rob responded quickly. "After today, I really feel more like punching Eric's lights out than praying for him!"

"I know," Pete chuckled. "But that's your human nature talking, not the Holy Spirit. The Holy Spirit wants to develop the fruit of the Spirit in you. Remember? Love, joy, peace, patience, kindness, goodness, gentleness, faithfulness, and self control."

"Like I said before," Rob began, "I'm ain't givin' up on Jesus. But, man! It's gonna take me a whole lot of time and a whole lot of practicing to get good at this stuff. This thing about trying to love everyone all the time and forgive people is really tough for me!"

"Y'know what, Rob? Tomorrow's another day and we'll both get another chance to practice again. Like my mom's saying goes, 'Practice makes improvement'!"

"Yeah," Rob said slowly. "I guess tomorrow I can practice being patient while I'm in detention. Speakin' of that, do you wanna hang around and wait for me tomorrow when I finally get out?"

"Sure! Of course I will," Pete said with a mischievous grin. "That should be easy! After all the practice I've had doing that over the past year, it should be a piece of cake!"

"Hey! You're makin' fun of me, aren't you?" Rob said as he punched Pete in the arm.

"Ow!" Pete said with a grimace as he rubbed his arm. "Yeah, I suppose I was."

"Oh, by the way," Rob said jokingly, "I just want you to know that I punched you with love! Just some extra practice on the side, y'know. That was my own '*unique*' way of showin' it!"

"Yeah, right!" Pete laughed sarcastically. "I think that's enough practice for today. Let's go home! I think I've had all the loving I can handle from you for one day!"

Questions:

1) What person do you look up to in a way that you would want to be more like him or her? Why? What things did you admire about that other person? Do you try to change the way you act to become more like that person?

2) What types of easy things could you do to practice acting more like Jesus? What type of things would you find difficult for you to practice to be more like Jesus? (For example, in the story, Rob suggested it would be very difficult to love Eric enough to pray for him after Eric helped get him into detention again).

3) How would you handle the bad actions of a bully while still following Christ's example?

4) What type of unique personality do you have? Are you outgoing, shy, funny, loud, quiet, get mad easily, laugh easily, make friends easily, etc? How can you use your unique personality to faithfully serve God?

Bible References Relating to this Story:

1 Peter 2:21-25
Matthew 4:1-11
Matthew 21:12-13
Matthew 17:1-9

Chapter 12

What happened to Peter Johnson?

Rob waited impatiently in front of the Johnson family's door.

"Wow!" said to himself shaking his head. "I know they're home. What's takin' them so long to answer the door? Maybe the doorbell ain't working." He pounded on the door with his fist several times. No answer. He rounded the corner of the house and peeked through a window. He rapped gently on the window pane several times and called out for Pete.

Rob finally saw Mr. and Mrs. Johnson run down the stairs together. He watched as Pete's parents hugged each other tightly. Mr. Johnson whispered something in Mrs. Johnson's ear, and Mrs. Johnson silently nodded her head. Then the two parents kissed each other and turned to answer the door.

"Whoa! Gross!" Rob blurted out as he scrambled back to the front steps. "That's, like, way embarrassing! I hope they didn't see me peekin' in the window while they were kissin'!"

The door slowly opened.

"Oh!" Mr. Johnson said with surprised look on his face. "Sweetie, uh... Rob's here."

Mrs. Johnson appeared next to Mr. Johnson.

"Hi, Robby. I'll bet you're looking for Pete, huh?"

"Yeah," Rob replied. "I haven't seen him for almost a week now. Is he sick or something?"

Mr. and Mrs. Johnson looked at each other for a moment.

"Well, uh, I...," Mr. Johnson stammered as he looked to his wife.

"Come on in, Robby," Mrs. Johnson said calmly as she ushered Rob inside and shut the door.

"Are you two alright?" Rob asked.

"What do you mean?" Mrs. Johnson asked in a casual manner as she straightened her posture slightly and forced a weak smile.

"Well, you're eyes look kind of puffy and your nose is kind of red. Do you have a cold? My mom does. She feels terrible."

"Well...It's something like that," Mrs. Johnson gently replied.

"So where's Pete?"

"Upstairs. In his room," Mr. Johnson said.

"Is he feelin' bad too?"

"Listen Robby," Mrs. Johnson began. "Pete's going through a little bit of a hard time right now, so he may act a little different from what you're used to. He may not be as playful as he usually is."

214

"Why? What's wrong with him?" Rob appeared very concerned.

"He received some news the other day that was a pretty big shock to him," Mr. Johnson said. "It's just going to take some time for him to adjust to it."

"What news?"

Pete's father was about to answer, but Mrs. Johnson quickly interrupted.

"We'll let Pete tell you about that, Robby. When he's ready, he will tell you himself. Right now, he could really use a good friend like you to be with him. So why don't you go on up."

"Okay," Rob said with a puzzled expression.

He turned to the stairs and made his way up to the second floor. At the top of the stairs, Rob stopped and turned back to Mr. and Mrs. Johnson. Mr. Johnson had his hand around Mrs. Johnson's shoulder in a sympathetic manner as if he were trying to give her moral support. Mrs. Johnson nodded toward Rob to continue. Rob turned and walked down the hall to Pete's room.

"This is, like, so weird!" Rob mumbled to himself. He knocked on Pete's door. There was no answer. "Not again!" Rob said. "Doesn't anyone around here answer the door? Look Pete! I know you're in there, and I'm coming in whether you're ready or not!" Rob called through the shut door.

Rob slowly opened the door and saw Pete sitting on his bed with his back to him. Pete was looking at his baseball card collection, and gently scratching his sleeping cat, Charley, on the head. Toys and books covered his bed. Rob closed the door and walked over to his friend.

"Hey, you're looking at your cards," Rob said in an effort to start a conversation. Pete nodded silently. Rob made some space on the bed and sat down next to him. He looked at the card that Pete was presently holding.

"Hey! That's Jackie Robinson!" Rob said with excitement. "That's the most valuable card in your whole collection. Your grandpa gave you that card, right?"

Pete nodded. "Yep," Pete replied softly. "My grandfather. You met him once, remember?"

"Sure I do," Rob said with a concerned look on his face. "Is he...uh...okay?"

"Yeah," Pete answered. "He's fine."

There was a short moment of uncomfortable silence before Pete spoke.

"I look a little bit like my grandfather, don't you think?"

"Well...sure you do." Rob said with a puzzled expression on his face. "Well, I guess you do. Well, to tell you the truth, Pete...I didn't really look at him all that hard, so I don't really know."

Pete smiled slightly and offered the baseball card he was holding to Rob. "Go ahead. Have a look at it if you want," he said.

"But you never let me hold Jackie before!" Rob exclaimed.

Pete slowly moved the card closer to Rob. "It's okay. Go ahead."

"Wait a minute!" Rob exclaimed. "This is too messed up! That's not like you to just let me hold Jackie! What's going on around here!" Pete was silent. "Why doesn't someone just tell me why you guys are all acting so weird? First it's your mom

216

and dad actin' strange. Now it's you. What happened to the people that used to be so much fun to be with? Or are you all really space aliens that took over the Johnson's bodies or something? Just tell me what's going on around here, Pete!"

Pete looked at Rob for the first time since Rob entered his room.

"I'm not really Peter Johnson."

"So…," Rob began playfully, "what you're telling me is that you really are a space alien in Pete's body?"

"No! Of course not!" Pete laughed lightly for a brief moment.

"Got you to laugh!" Rob shouted exuberantly.

Pete smirked. "Yeah! Guess you did. I haven't really laughed that much in days."

"Why?" Rob asked. "What's botherin' you?"

"I found out last Sunday that I was adopted."

Rob stared intently at Pete for a moment with a blank expression. Then he shook his head and started to laugh. "Okay," he chuckled, "You got me back! I have to admit you had me fooled — but just for a tiny second!"

Pete smiled at Rob. "It's true," he said softly. "I'm adopted."

Rob's smile transformed into an expression of bewilderment. "But you're…you're Peter Johnson!"

"Well...," Pete thought for a moment, "Yeah. Legally my name is Peter Johnson. I don't know the last name of my birth father. But my birth mother's name is Kelly. Kelly Spae."

"Wait a minute," Rob said hesitantly. "You mean, like, this is for real?"

"Yeah. It's for real."

Both boys remained silent for a moment.

217

"Of all the people in the world," Rob blurted out suddenly, "I never would have guessed that you...well, you know. The Johnson Family is like the most perfect family I've ever met!"

"Well, I guess the world's not always a perfect place," Pete shrugged.

"So, how do you feel about this whole ... thing?"

"Kinda strange," Pete said. "I'm getting used to it, though. I'll probably be back in school tomorrow."

"So...do you still call Mr. and Mrs. Johnson 'mom' and 'dad'?"

"Of course!" Pete laughed. "Nothing's changed between us. I just feel really kinda goofy about the whole thing right now. That's all. I'm sure it won't be long before I'm back to my old self."

"So...how did you find out that you're adopted?" Rob asked

"Rob, didn't you ever wonder why I never had a brother or sister like a lot of families do?"

"No!" Rob said defensively. "I don't have no brothers or sisters neither! None that I know about anyways."

"Well *I* always wondered why I didn't have any," Pete continued. "I asked my mom once why I didn't have any brothers or sisters, and she said that she couldn't have children. So I asked her how she had me, and she would say the same thing every time. She would say that I was special — like the brightest star in the heavens. A true gift from God."

"But how did you find out you were adopted?" Rob asked again impatiently.

"My dad has a safe that he keeps important stuff in. He keeps it in his bedroom closet. Two days ago I was looking for a box to hold some of my new baseball cards, and I looked in his closet for a spare box. Well, the safe was open, and so I decided to see what kind of stuff he kept in there. I saw a file named 'Peter' so I took a peek at what was inside it. That's when I found the adoption papers. And that's when my mom walked in and found me reading them."

"Whoa!" Rob said. "Was she mad at you for looking in the safe?"

"No," Pete responded. "She looked really scared, actually. I asked her what the papers meant. Then her and my dad and I all sat down for a talk. That's when they told me that I was adopted. They said that they planned on telling me when I was a little older, but ... I guess I beat them to it."

"How come you don't remember your first mom? Y'know...Kelly."

"Because I was a newborn baby when I was given to my mom and dad. Kelly didn't even hold me."

"But why?" Rob asked with great concern. "Why would Kelly just, y'know...give you away to someone else? My mom and me don't get along a lot of the time, but she never tried to give me away!"

"Well," Pete began slowly, "My parents said that they would tell me the whole story some day when I'm older. But, what they did tell me the other day was that Kelly wasn't looking to have any kids at that time. She was still in college. She was scared and felt pretty hurt and confused. She actually didn't want to have me at all. She was going to ... well ... she was going to see a doctor to have an operation to make it so that I wouldn't be born."

"What?" Rob cried out in disbelief.

"Yeah, I know," Pete said. "Pretty scary stuff, huh?"

"So what happened?" Rob asked, staring intensely at Pete.

"Well," Pete continued, "Kelly's college roommate worked part time at a place that helped pregnant women that weren't sure if they wanted to keep their babies to understand what kind of choices they have. So she talked to Kelly about her different choices."

"Like what choices?" Rob asked.

"Well, like adoption! That's why I'm here now. Kelly changed her mind and decided to have me. My parents had been on a list to adopt a baby for just over a year. Then I came along. My mom couldn't have babies, and her and my dad had been praying about adopting a baby, a boy or a girl, that really needed a good home. And so, with God's help, we got matched up! That's why mom always says 'I'm a true gift from God'."

"I'm sure glad God gave your parents a boy!" Rob said with relief. "A girl just wouldn't be as much fun to play with. I would never get used to all those tea parties and all those boring dolls!"

"Yeah," Pete chuckled. "We turned out to be kinda like brothers, didn't we? I wonder if God planned that too?"

"Of course he did!" Rob stated confidently.

"I guess we have one more thing in common now, Rob."

"What's that?"

"Neither one of us really knows our true birth-father."

"Yeah," Rob sighed softly. He stared blankly at the floor. Both boys remained silent for a moment before Rob spoke again: "So, whatever happened to Kelly?"

220

"My mom and dad keep in touch with her. I didn't even know it, but mom and dad send her a Christmas card every year. They always write 'We thank you and God for the special gift you gave us', and then they put a school picture of me in the card and send it to her."

"So," Rob began, "are you ever going to meet Kelly in person?"

"Yep," Pete replied. "Tonight, actually. For dinner. She should be here any time now. Yesterday, I asked my parents if I could meet her."

"Whoa!" Rob exclaimed. "Are you nervous or anything?"

"Way!" Pete replied as he looked over to his friend. "I'm scared to death."

"Then why did you ask to meet her?" Rob asked. "I don't get it!"

"Because I …I just need to. I don't know. I just feel like I need to meet her, cause otherwise, I'll always be wondering about who she is, what's her story, what's she look like, and am I like her at all. I just need to meet her and then maybe I can stop thinking about this whole thing so much."

Pete glanced over at the bedroom door.

"My parents almost said 'no', but we prayed about it and they changed their minds," he whispered. "We've been really relying on God to help us through all of this stuff. It's been real hard this past week. We've been doing a lot of praying. I think this whole thing is really stressing out my parents, especially my mom."

"Why?" Rob asked.

"Because," Pete said loudly as he pointed at the bedroom door, "*she's* my mom. Kelly may have had me, but that's my *real* mom. And that's how I really feel about the whole thing. My mom just has to really believe that somehow. Do you know what I mean?" Rob nodded. "But this whole thing has been tearing me up inside too," Pete said as he looked somberly at the bedroom floor. "But I just need to know who Kelly is...I just need to know. I've spent half the day praying that this whole thing will turn out okay somehow; that me, my mom and my dad will be able to deal with this whole thing alright and then be able to get on with the fun part of life again."

"Hey," Rob said. "You've been helpin' me a lot the last few months. Is there something I can do to help *you* now?"

Pete thought for a moment.

"Do you like spaghetti and meatballs?"

"Yeah," Rob replied. "But what's that got to do with helpin' you?"

"I want to invite you to dinner tonight. Is that all right?"

"Well, I'll have to call my mom to ask her, but I'm sure she'll say 'yes'. But, I don't get it. How's that gonna help you, Pete?"

"Just trust me," Pete said as he smiled at his friend. "It will help me more than you know. I suppose I should ask my mom if it's okay to invite you, too."

"You're mom's awesome, Pete. Of course she'll say 'yes'!"

"I know that," Pete agreed, projecting his voice loudly. "I'm the luckiest kid in the world! I guess the best thing to come out of this whole situation is that I know more than ever how lucky I am to have her as my mom!"

Rob raised both eyebrows inquisitively.

222

"Well, why don't you just tell her that?"

Pete grinned and winked slyly at Rob. "I just did!" he whispered back.

Pete turned toward the bedroom door. "Hey, mom?" he called out in the same loud voice. "Can I invite Rob to stay for supper... please?" Pete paused for a moment. There was no response.

"Uh...Pete? I don't think she's there," Rob said doubtfully.

"Of course she is," Pete responded. "I know my mom better than anyone! She's been there all along, isn't that right Mom?"

The door slowly opened and Mrs. Johnson poked her head inside the room.

"Yes," she replied softly. "Ever since you were my baby boy."

"You see?" Pete said to Rob with a confident smile.

Mrs. Johnson smiled and nodded her head gently. A very small tear delicately hugged her cheek and sparkled brilliantly in the dimly lit room, just like the brightest star in the heavens.

"So," Pete asked again, "is it alright?"

"Yes," she whispered with a tender sigh. "Everything's alright."

Questions:

1) All people will have difficulties that challenge them throughout their lives — this applies to both adults *and* kids. We're already familiar with the kinds of challenges that Rob and his mother have had. What are some of the big challenges you have had in your life? What did you do in response to those challenges? Where is God in these situations? Did you pray for God's help?

2) How does God Comfort us during hard times? Do you think he may bring people into your life during those difficult times to help you? How did Rob help Pete by simply staying for supper that night? How did Pete help his mother while he was talking with Rob?

3) Have you ever tried to comfort and encourage someone else who might be going through a difficult time? How did you do it? Did it help the other person?

4) Why do you think that Pete's mother was so acting in such a troubled manner? Why do you think Pete's mom said that 'everything's alright' at the end of the story? It's a good practice to try to put yourself in someone else's situation and try to see things through their eyes. It may help us to understand why people may behave the way they do, and it may help us to be able to help them through troubles better as well — just like Pete did with his mom in the story.

<u>Bible References Relating to this Story:</u>

Philippians 4:6-7

2 Corinthians 1:3-4

Chapter 13

The Bickering Boys Club

It was an unusually warm spring day near the end of April. Five boys sat in a circle on the floor of the old, wooden garden shed located in Ryan McKenna's backyard. Ryan had told his four friends Pete, Rob, Tony and Gordy that they could use the shed as their new clubhouse.

"Okay, you guys," Pete said with a concerned look on his face. "We've got to come up with a name for our new boys' club that all of us can agree on. It shouldn't have to be this hard."

"Can you read the list of everything we came up with so far?" Gordy asked.

"Sure," Pete began. "We have 'Gordy's Gang', 'Ryan's Raiders', 'Tony's Troopers', and 'Rob's Rangers'. We also have 'The Reckless Revengers', 'The Adventurous Avengers', and 'The Diabolical Dynamos.' Finally — and this is where I think we were getting a little too desperate for names if you ask me — we also have 'The Dirt Bags', 'The Pizza Pirates', 'The Booger Gang', and the 'P, B and J's'."

"The 'P, B and J's'!" Ryan shouted. "That was my idea! Peanut butter and jelly is my favorite kind of sandwich!"

Gordy covered his ears and glared at Ryan who was sitting next to him. "Ow! Why do you have to yell about everything? Do you want us all to go deaf?" he moaned. "What's wrong with you anyways? Do you have a banana stuck in your ear or something? Just speak with a normal voice!"

"I can't help it," Ryan shouted back. "When I get excited about something, I just gotta yell. It's who I am!"

"Come on, you guys!" Tony spoke up. "We got to be able to agree on something. All we seem to do is argue about everything. I don't want to have anything to do with a club that just argues all the time!"

"Well, you argue about stuff just as much as the rest of us!" Gordy responded.

"Not nearly as much as you do, Gordy!" Tony shot back.

"My dad has this old saying, "Ryan interrupted, "It goes like this: 'I would never join a club that would have me as a member'."

"Well, I can agree with *that*!" Gordy said willingly.

"You can?" Ryan asked.

"Sure!" said Gordy. "I wouldn't want to join a club that would have you as a member either!"

"I got an idea," Pete offered. "How about this for a club name: 'The Bickering Boys Club'? It kinda describes us pretty well, don't you think?"

"That's the saddest excuse for a name that I've heard yet!" exclaimed Gordy. "I think I like 'The Booger Gang' better! Come on, Pete! We don't argue all the time!"

"It sure seems like we do," said Rob.

"No we don't!" Gordy retorted.

The boys' discord was interrupted by distant giggling heard outside of the shed.

"Shhh!" whispered Rob loudly to the others. "Listen! What's that sound?"

"It sounds like girls," said Tony. "It's coming from next door."

"That's Meagan Pulaski's house," Ryan said. "She has girl parties over there all the time."

"It sounds like there's a bunch of them," said Rob.

"Hey!" said Gordy with a grin. "I've got a great idea for our club's first order of business! See that water hose coiled up in the corner? Well, even though the weather forecast is calling for sunny skies today, *I* can predict that there will be a chance of showers over in Meagan's back yard!"

The boys grinned with impish excitement.

Tony raised his hand. "All in favor of Gordy's idea to soak the girls with a hose raise your hand!" All the boys raised their hands in unison. "Then it passed! Hey!" he exclaimed. "We finally all agreed on something! Come on! Let's move out, Avengers!"

"No, you meant to say the '*Re*-vengers'," said Gordy correcting him.

"No, it's the 'Rangers'," said Rob.

"'The P, B and J's'!" yelled Ryan.

"Just shut up, everyone, and grab the hose!" growled Tony. "We got work to do!"

The boys' plan did not go as smoothly as they had hoped. They loudly argued about how to attach the hose to the water spigot and the best way to surprise the girls. Twenty minutes later, they were almost ready to put their plan into action.

"Okay," Gordy whispered as the other boys huddled around him. "I think we finally got it! We got the hose hooked up and working, and we got the chair next to the fence. I'll stand on the chair and get their attention while I keep the hose down low so they can't see it. Once they look at me, I'll let 'em have it!"

"I still don't understand why you get to do all the soakin', and we only get to watch," Rob said.

"Like I said, Robby, I've got the most experience doing this kind of covert stuff. Plus, I've got three sisters at home, so I know how the feminine mind works. I'm an expert on women! So, if you want this plan of ours to go right, just let me work my magic!"

"Did anyone happen to notice that it's really quiet next door?" Tony asked. "I wonder if the girls are even still over there. We spent so much time arguing, it took us forever to set this thing up. Maybe they left already."

Pete nodded. "They probably heard all our plans and decided they didn't want to be victims of a practical joke. We were arguing so loud, how could they *not* have overheard us?"

"Well, there's only one way to find out," said Gordy.

Gordy grasped tightly to the end of the hose as he quietly crept over to the chair by the fence. Then he squatted on the chair and carefully peeked over the top of the fence. On the far side of the Pulaski's back yard, he saw Meagan wearing sunglasses and stretched out comfortably on a lounge chair reading a magazine.

"The other girls already left," he whispered. "It's only Meagan now."

"I knew it!" Rob whispered loudly. "We missed them because we took too much time arguin'!"

"Well, Meagan's still there," Tony whispered. "Get her!"

Gordy smiled and gave a "thumbs up" signal to the boys. The rest of the boys grinned deviously and squatted down next to Gordy's chair. Then Gordy stood up straight and addressed Meagan: "Oh! Hello there, Meagan! Fancy meeting you here today!" Gordy said slyly.

Meagan peered over the top of her sunglasses. "Gordy?" she asked. "What are you doing here?"

"Well, I just wanted to warn you that it looks like it might rain, and I didn't want you to get wet or anything."

"Rain?" Meagan said. "There's not a cloud in the sky! Are you sure you're feeling okay?"

"Not only am I feeling okay, but I'm also feeling quite dry," Gordy responded. "But unfortunately for you, things are going to be much different in a second!"

231

"I don't understand," Meagan said shaking her head in confusion. "What are you talking about?"

"Don't say I didn't warn you!" Gordy said as he raised the hose nozzle over the fence top and squeezed the trigger. A small, droopy burst of water shot from the nozzle and immediately turned into a fast dripping trickle. The water didn't even come close to hitting Meagan.

"Oh, I see," Meagan said calmly. "You have a hose, and you're trying to squirt me with it."

"Yeah!" Gordy said as he kept squeezing the trigger. "But what's wrong with it? Why won't this thing work?"

"Well, from where I'm sitting," Meagan said as she lowered her sunglasses further down her nose and squinted at the end of the nozzle, "it looks like the nozzle is clogged with dirt or something."

"Really?" Gordy asked as he turned the nozzle toward his face so he could examine it himself. Suddenly the hose shot out a powerful stream of water directly into Gordy's eyes. Gordy yelled as he fell off the chair and onto Ryan who was squatting down next to him. Ryan screamed as the cold water stream soaked him as well. Gordy dropped the hose. Then the water exiting the nozzle returned to a trickle. The other boys giggled as they saw their two, wet friends struggling to get off each other.

"Ow!" Ryan yelled. "Get off my arm!"

"Stop yelling!" Gordy said angrily. "And by the way, you scream like a girl!"

232

The boys heard someone loudly clear their throat far behind them. They all turned to see Amanda Grant holding a kinked hose in her hands.

"What was that you just said?" she demanded.

"*You*!" Gordy cried pointing an accusing finger at Amanda. "*You* kinked the hose and stopped the water!"

"That's right," Amanda said with a smile.

"But how did you know we were back here?" asked Tony.

"We could hear you guys trying to make plans a mile away," Amanda responded. "You were all shouting and yelling at each other about how you were going to soak us. So we came up with our own plan to soak you guys instead."

"Okay, okay" said Gordy in defeat as he slowly lifted himself off the ground. "So you got us. Ha-ha, very funny. I bet you all think you're so smart! Bet you're all getting a big laugh about this! Come on, guys! Let's make like a tree and 'leave'!"

"But Gordy, you don't understand," said Amanda calmly as she looked past the boys. "We're only getting started. Isn't that right, ladies?" Gordy and the rest of the boys turned around to see Meagan and Sarah Mills standing above them from behind the fence upon their own chairs. They had a water balloon in each hand.

"No party is complete without balloons!" Meagan said cheerfully.

"Where did you get those?" Pete asked nervously.

"We filled up about twenty of them while you guys were arguing. Sarah hid in the bushes with them when you guys finally decided to show up."

"Run!" Gordy yelled as he sprinted toward the back yard. "Quick! Head back to the club house and barricade the door, just like we planned!"

The boys attempted to dodge and outrun water balloons as they frantically ran back to the shed for cover.

Amanda, who now had complete control of the hose, also pursued the boys with a powerful jet of water. She successfully managed to douse both Gordy and Ryan as they tripped and tumbled over each other.

"Get the doors open, Rob!" Tony shouted as a balloon splattered on the back of his neck. Rob and Pete reached the shed doors first and threw them open; they stopped abruptly. Two girls stood in the doorway, each holding a bucket filled with water.

"Becky?" Rob squeaked timidly.

"Yep, it's me," replied Becky Croteau as she and Emma Shultz emptied their buckets over Rob's and Pete's head. "See ya at band practice tomorrow, Robby," Becky said with a wink and a smile as she and Emma walked casually away from the water-logged boys.

The boys finally reassembled in the garden shed after they wrung out their shirts and hung them over the clothesline outside to dry.

Tony cupped his face in his hands and shook his head slowly with despair. "This is so embarrassing!" he lamented. "The girls made us look like a bunch of dorks."

"Well, *this* time they did," Gordy began. "But we all still know that when it comes right down to it, guys are smarter than girls. They just got a lucky break this time around, right?"

The other boys mumbled a somber "yeah".

"Maybe guys are smarter," Pete said, "but the girls are dryer."

"My dad has an old saying," Ryan piped up. "He says 'Women. You can't live with 'em. You can't live without 'em.'"

"What's that supposed to mean?" asked Gordy with annoyance.

"I don't really know," confessed Ryan. "It just sounded like the smart thing to say right now."

"How about this for a saying?" said Gordy. "Girls. Who needs 'em? Who wants 'em?" The other boys looked sheepishly at each other. Some of them blushed, but no one said a word. "Come on, you guys!" said Gordy. "Am I right or what? If you spent just one day with my sisters, you'd know exactly what I'm talkin' about!"

"I don't know," Pete began. "I think Becky Croteau kinda likes Rob."

"What!" Rob exclaimed in disbelief. "If she does, she has a funny way of showing it!"

"Well," said Ryan. "She does call you 'Robby' after all. And there was the 'wink'."

"Would you guys stop it?" Rob yelled as his face and ears turned bright red. "Let's talk about something else!"

"How about the name of our club?" Ryan suggested.

"No, not that again," said Tony. "That's even worse than talking about girls! I'm tired of arguing. That's what got us all wet in the first place."

"Yeah," Rob responded. "If a group of kids can argue as much as we do about the name of a boys' club, I guess I can understand why adults and countries end up fighting with each other all the time. They're all just a bunch of grown-up, arguing kids like us!"

"Well, why don't we all talk about something we have in common for a change," Tony offered.

"Yeah! That's a great idea!" Pete exclaimed.

"Well," Rob began. "We're all boys. We have that in common."

"We all love sports," said Ryan.

"We all like to fish," said Tony.

"We're all wet!" said Gordy. The boys laughed.

"We all go to church," said Pete.

"Leave it to Pete to bring up church," said Gordy rolling his eyes with annoyance.

"Yeah, but he's right," said Tony. "We all go to a church of some sort. Maybe not the same church, but still…"

"Where I go isn't really called a church," said Gordy. "It's called a synagogue. It's a Jewish house of prayer and study."

"How do you like it?" asked Tony.

"It's pretty cool," said Gordy nodding his head with approval. "In two more years, when I'm thirteen, I'll have my Bar Mitzvah, and then I'll be able to lead my family in prayers at home and in the assembly at the temple. I'll invite all of you to

y

236

the celebration, if you want to come." All the boys thanked Gordy for the invitation.

"I went through something like that," Tony began after a brief silence, "I go to a Catholic church, and I went through Confirmation when I was nine. It's part of the sacraments we do. We had a small party with just family, but it was fun."

"Don't you go to a Catholic school too?" Ryan asked.

"Yeah, I do."

"What's it like goin' to a Catholic school?" asked Rob.

"I like it," Tony replied. "I've got lots of friends there, and I'm acing every subject. Straight A's. We have to dress up, though. I don't like that part too much."

"Me, Pete, and Rob all go to the same Congregational church," Ryan began. "My dad told me that our Bible is different than the Catholic Bible. Is that true?"

"Yeah, that's true," said Tony. "Our Bible has more books in it than the Bible you guys use. Other than that, it's about the same. You guys use something called a protestant Bible."

Pete jumped in on the conversation. "Well, Rob, Ryan and I all go to the same church, but even we have different Bibles."

"We do?" asked Ryan with surprise.

"Sure," said Pete. Rob and I use a Bible version called the New Living Translation. You use the New King James Version."

"What's the difference between them?" Ryan asked.

"Well, they're both Protestant Bibles, like Tony said, but my family chose the *New Living Translation* just because we found it was easier to read and understand than the King James Bible which uses old English words like 'thee' and 'thou'. Other than that, they are pretty close in what they say. Each person in our church chooses whatever Bible version they feel the most comfortable with."

"My family uses a Hebrew Bible called the Tanakh," said Gordy. "It has less books in it than either of the Bibles you guys have. It has the Old Testament books, and it's split into three parts. The first part of the Tanakh is called the Torah, which has the writings of Moses from Genesis to Deuteronomy. The second part is called the Nevi'im, which is about the Prophets — well, except for Daniel. And then the third section is called the Ketuvim which has everything else, like Proverbs, the Psalms, Esther, and Daniel."

"Wow," said Pete. "I never knew that! That's pretty cool!" Gordy smiled.

"But doesn't the Hebrew Bible have the New Testament books in it too?" Rob asked. "You know...the books about Jesus and the Apostles?"

"Uh..." Gordy started cautiously. "Well, Rob...Jews do believe in the Mashiach, or what you Christians call the Messiah — y'know, the anointed king. But we just don't believe that the Mashiach was Jesus. We believe that our true king that the prophets predicted would come, well...hasn't come yet."

"What?" exclaimed Rob in disbelief. He turned to Pete. Pete looked back at Rob, shrugged, and remained silent.

"Well, that can't be right!" Rob protested.

"Uh, excuse me?" Gordy replied harshly as he sat up straight. "I believe it *is* right!"

"But no religion is complete without Jesus in it as the Lord of lords and the King of kings!" Rob argued. "A religion without Jesus Christ in it is just plain wrong!"

"Don't you dare tell me what's right and wrong about *my* religion, buddy-boy!" Gordy shot back.

"Well, is there really anybody that *can* say for sure what's actually right and wrong about all this religious stuff anyway?" Ryan asked with sincere curiosity. "I mean, you both can't be right, can you?"

"Just ask the Pope," Tony responded confidently. "He should know the answer."

"What's a pope?" Rob asked.

"You can't be serious!" Tony said shaking his head in disbelief. "You're tellin' me you really never heard about the Pope before? He's in charge of the entire, universal church on earth!" Tony stated proudly. "After all, that's what the word 'catholic' means…universal. So when it comes to religious issues, *everyone* should listen to the Pope!"

"WHAT?" Rob and Gordy shouted in unison.

"Well," Tony continued, "who's gonna argue with the Pope, y'know what I mean? He's, like, in with God. They talk. They're like best buds! Who can argue with that?"

"I can!" responded Gordy. "It was Ha-Shem himself that handed *my* ancestors the Law of Moses and the word of the prophets!"

"Ha-Shem?" Tony asked, looking confused. "Who's that?"

"Is Ha-Shem a Jewish name for God?" Ryan guessed.

"You bet it is!" Gordy responded fiercely. "And it was Ha-Shem himself," he continued, "that calls *us* — the Jewish people — his special people! That outdoes a Pope any day!"

"You're both wrong!" Rob shouted defiantly. "Jesus is the King, and Jesus is the most important part of any religion!"

"My dad has a saying," Ryan chimed in. "He says 'If you want to keep peace in the family, never bring up politics or religion!'"

"You two should convert over to the way we believe!" Rob shouted passionately at Tony and Gordy. "Me, and Pete and Ryan know the right way. You guys are just plain wrong!"

"No," Tony said firmly, "If anyone should convert, it should be you guys! Catholicism is the true religion! I have no doubt that I'm right! So, start converting, boys!"

"I'm in-convertible!" declared Gordy defiantly folding his arms solidly over his chest.

"My dad had an in-convertible once," Ryan stated thoughtfully. "It was a really old Ford T-Bird with a removable roof, except the roof release was broke and we could never get the roof to actually come off. It was a real bummer."

"So, let me get this straight, "Rob began, "We tried to find some stuff to talk about that we all had in common, and we ended up findin' how different our religions are from each other's instead. And here we are arguin' with each other again! We can't all be right, can we? Some of the differences are just …well…too different!"

Tony looked squarely at Pete.

"Hey!" he said, "It was Pete that brought up talking about going to church in the first place. He's like the big religion expert here. So what is it, Pete? What do you say? Who's right?" All eyes focused on Pete.

"Uh…I …uh…," Pete, who had curiously remained very silent throughout this most recent bout of arguments, stammered as he searched desperately for the right words to say as the tempers around him flared. Finally, he lowered his head and desperately blurted out the best thing he could think of at the moment: "My Lord, God almighty! Please help us all!"

Suddenly, the shed door swung open, and a blinding light filled the dimly lit shed. The boys all raised their hands at the same time to shield their eyes from the intense radiance. A figure holding a gleaming, silver disc entered from the brilliance into the open doorway.

"It's an angel sent by God!" Rob cried out fearfully.

"Oh! Thank you, dear!" a soft voice said cheerfully. "What a nice compliment!"

"Oh," said Ryan in a somewhat disappointed manner. "It's no angel. It's just my mom."

"I liked your friend's greeting much better, Ryan," said Mrs. McKenna dryly. "Work on that, won't you dear?"

Ryan's mom was holding a large silver platter loaded with sandwiches.

"I thought you young men might be hungry," she said. "It is past one o'clock, after all." Mrs. McKenna handed out peanut butter and jelly sandwiches to all of the boys.

After each boy had a sandwich, Mrs. McKenna took a small camera from her pocket and instructed the boys to sit closely next to each other. "Squeeze in!" she said. "Now everyone smile!" She took a couple of shots and then placed the camera back into her pocket. "I'll print a picture for each of you. Before you leave, come see me and I'll make sure I get you one."

Mrs. McKenna reviewed the group with a large smile on her face.

"You're such a nice group of boys," she said. "These are the days that you'll remember for the rest of your lives. So much fun. So much excitement! There's nothing stronger than a close group of friends that stick by each other through thick and thin. I hope you're all still good friends with each other when you're my age. You know what your father always says, Ryan. 'Birds of a feather stick together'. You all have so much in common; I don't think you even realize it!" She made a happy sigh.

"Anyway, I should let you get back to playing. You boys have such carefree, uncomplicated lives! I'm sure you have frogs and snakes you want to catch, or space pirates you have to defeat on other planets, or dump trucks that need to move sand in the sandbox, or puppies…"

"Mom," Ryan said with a low, monotone voice. "Can you please…y'know," he said, nodding his head toward the door.

"Oh, right!" said Mrs. McKenna. "If any of you want another sandwich, just come inside. Peanut butter and jelly is my specialty!"

After Mrs. McKenna left, the boys continued their previous conversation in a much calmer manner.

"Okay," Gordy mumbled while chewing his sandwich. "Space pirates and puppies will just have to wait because if you remember just a moment ago, Pete here was going to tell us which religion worldview he thought was the right one.

Protestant versus Catholicism versus Judaism. So, Mr. religious expert," Gordy said with obvious sarcasm, "please grace us with your exquisite pearls of wisdom."

"Yeah, what do you have to say, Pete?" asked Rob.

"Come on, Pete. Tell us," said Tony.

"Wow, this is a great sandwich!" said Ryan.

Pete smiled. He seemed to have more confidence than he had when he was asked the same question just moments ago. Perhaps Mrs. McKenna's timely appearance and insightful words inspired him. Maybe they did have more in common regarding their various religious faiths than they realized.

"Okay, guys," Pete began. "First of all, I'm not a religious expert, but since you asked, this is what I have to say about the whole thing..." Pete took a deep breath. "I can see now that there are definitely some big differences between the Jewish, Catholic and Protestant faiths. But there is one thing we all have in common with our different faiths and it's huge. It's so huge, I can't believe we didn't see it before, and it's something I think we all agree on."

"Really? What's that?" asked Tony.

"We all have faith in the same God," Pete responded. "The God of Abraham, Issac and Jacob. The God of King David and King Solomon. The God of the Prophets Moses, Isaiah, Ezekiel and Elijah. The same God that created the entire universe and everything in it. We might never agree on everything about our different beliefs, but I believe that we all love the same God with all our hearts. We're all trying to follow God in the ways that we personally believe is true and right. From what I read in my Bible, I know that if we seek out God with sincere, humble and repentant hearts, he will be compassionate and merciful toward us even if we don't follow him perfectly or understand him perfectly. I think everyone here will find the same message in their own Bibles."

"And that reminds me of something else we all have in common: God's commands. In Leviticus, God commands us to love our neighbors as ourselves. That's the kind of relationship that God wants us to show to each other regardless of what we believe. I hope you guys consider me your neighbor. I consider you mine!"

"I'm just very thankful that God is patient with all of us when we mess up by fighting and arguing with each other like we've done all day today. I'm not afraid to talk to you guys about our religious differences, but I want to talk about those differences without all of us getting upset and angry. Between the five of us here, we represent some of the biggest religious faiths that are practiced in the world today. I'd like to learn more about them all, wouldn't you? I think that kind of learning would help us to appreciate and understand our faiths and each other better. In Proverbs it says 'Intelligent people are always ready to learn. Their ears are open for knowledge'. Already, before we started arguing about all this stuff, I was beginning to learn things that I never knew about before – like the Hebrew Bible and Catholic confirmation. I know we can all learn from each other without arguing and fighting if we all agree to practice following God's command to love our neighbors as ourselves."

Pete paused for a moment.

"Well," he continued, "now you know my opinion. And I hope you guys don't mind, but every morning I'm going to pray

244

for each of you that you'll stay strong and faithful in your commitment to God and to following God's law about loving each other. I hope you'll pray for me in the same way too."

There was a long silence. The only sound that could be heard was chewing. Finally, Gordy spoke though a mouthful of food.

"You're so preachy, Johnson," he stated matter-of-factly. The rest of the boys nodded in agreement.

"I definitely agree with that," said Tony.

"You really are, Pete," said Rob nodding sympathetically.

"You're kind of wordy and long-winded and redundant," said Ryan patting Pete gently on the shoulder. "People give me a hard time about that too."

"I'm glad you guys all finally agree on something," Pete said hesitantly. "Well, at least I think I'm glad."

"But I'll go along with you on what you just said about praying for each other," Gordy said. "Sounds good to me."

"Yeah, me too," said Tony.

"It's an awesome idea!" Rob said with a big smile.

"Count me in!" exclaimed Ryan.

"Great," said Pete who was very relieved. "Y'know, Ryan," Pete continued," I do think that your mom was sent to us by God today. She reminded me about how much we actually do have in common and how important our friendship with each other should be. Even though we argue sometimes, we really are like a family of brothers, and each of us sees the same God as the head of the family." Ryan smiled and nodded in agreement.

"Anyway," Pete said boldly, "If we can agree on how to talk about a really tricky subject like the differences in our religions, then I'm sure we can agree on a name for our club now!"

245

"Oh yeah!" said Tony. "I almost forgot about that!"

"So what's it gonna be?" asked Gordy.

"Well," Ryan said, "my dad has a saying that could help us out in this situation."

"Oh no!" Gordy said as he closed his eyes and shook his head in despair. "Not again with your dad's sayings! Please!"

"Go ahead, Ryan," said Rob. "What's he say?"

Ryan cleared his throat. "Well, my dad always says that 'you are what you eat'." The boys looked down at the partially eaten peanut butter and jelly sandwiches they were holding.

"So, you think we should be called the 'P, B and J's' because of your dad's old saying?" Tony asked. Ryan smiled and nodded. "Okay," Tony shrugged. "Let's put it to a vote…again. All in favor of calling ourselves the P, B and J's raise your hands." Each boy raised his hand except for Gordy.

"I'll agree to being called the 'P, B and J's' on one condition," Gordy said.

"What's that?" asked Tony.

"I'll go along with you guys if we can go inside and get another sandwich. These really are the best peanut butter and jelly sandwiches I ever had!"

"I knew my mom would make a convert out of you!" exclaimed Ryan with a grin.

"Okay," Tony said. "The motion has passed. We all agree. Come on, P, B and J's! Let's get seconds on some more P, B and J's! Meeting adjourned!"

Questions:

1) How often do you have arguments with other people? What causes these arguments? How do they usually end?

2) If a difference of principle or belief or opinion comes between you and a friend or family member, how do you handle it? How do you think the Lord wants you to handle it?

Bible References Relating to this Story:

Leviticus 19:18

Proverbs 15:1

Proverbs 18:15

Isaiah 26:1-4

Proverbs 15:1

Chapter 14

Kelly

"So, Peter Johnson. What do you want to be when you grow up?" Kelly Spae asked Pete after wiping a dab of hot fudge from her mouth with a napkin.

"Hmm. I don't really know yet," Pete said as she scooped up the last of the melted ice cream sundae from the bottom of his glass dish. "Maybe a pastor or something," he said. He glanced up at his birth mother with whom he had met for the first time just over a month ago.

Pete and Kelly's first encounter occurred through a dinner invitation that Pete and his parents extended to Kelly back in March. Kelly accepted the invitation, and upon leaving that evening after their first, brief encounter, Pete and Kelly decided to spend some additional time together alone to get to know each other better. Pete's parents said it would be fine since they had known Kelly for many years, and they felt comfortable enough to let Pete spend a couple hours alone with her. So when Kelly arrived for their second visit, Pete suggested that they go to the Dairy Bar Ice Cream Parlor that was only a short walk away from his house. They had chosen a corner booth when they arrived at the Dairy Bar so that they could have some privacy as they talked.

"A pastor?" Kelly sounded surprised. "Why do you think you would make a good pastor?"

"Well, I seem to be able to understand the Bible really well," Pete said. "I have memorized a whole bunch of passages from it. My parents think I have memorized at least a quarter of the Bible so far."

"That's amazing!" said Kelly. "It's such a big book."

"Yeah, but sometimes my friends get annoyed with me cause I'm always quoting Bible passages when I try to help them with their problems."

Kelly folded her arms on the tabletop and leaned forward a bit. She studied Pete with her eyes. "You know, Peter, I can see one area where we definitely have the same DNA for sure. Just like you, I have an incredible memory also. As I told you when we first met, I'm a lawyer. A very good lawyer. And one of the reasons I'm so good is that I have memorized volumes and volumes of legal texts that I've studied over the years. So memorizing seems to come pretty easily to me as well. It's certainly comes in handy in my line of work. It seems that you and I share that same quality."

"That's a cool coincidence," Pete said wide eyed.

"It also appears that we share some of the same facial features as well," Kelly said as she scanned Pete's face. "I think we may share the same nose and chin. And then there are those eyes. Yes. Without a doubt, those are my eyes." Pete and Kelly focused on each other's steel, gray eyes for a brief moment.

"Kelly? Would you mind too much if I asked you a question about…well…y'know… my birth father?"

Kelly's smile quickly faded. She unfolded her arms and sat up straight. "Peter, you know your parents preferred that I leave that subject alone so that they can discuss it with you when the time is right."

"Did you promise them that you wouldn't talk about him?" Pete asked.

"Well…no," Kelly replied hesitantly.

"Then please, Kelly!" Pete begged. "I really want to know *something* about my birth father! Who is he? What's his last name? What does he look like? What does he do? I really want to know!"

Kelly looked down at her empty glass dish with a lifeless stare. She let a weak sigh escape through her lips. Finally she looked back at Pete. Her voice was very soft, almost inaudible.

"Honestly, Peter — and I mean very honestly — I don't know anything about your father. I definitely understand how anxious you are to know something about him, but I have no information to give you in that way. I'm sorry."

"But...how's that even possible?" Pete asked with a hint of frustration. "How can you not know about him? You both had me! You gotta know something!"

"Again, Peter, I'm so sorry. I have nothing I can give you. And that's how we're going to have to leave it."

Now it was Pete's turn to gaze lifelessly into the empty glass dish before him.

Kelly finally resumed her relaxed posture and smiled slightly. "So, you want to be a pastor, do you?" she began, changing the subject. "You must have a great passion for choosing that type of profession. If you're like most of the pastors I've met, you certainly wouldn't be interested in that type of job for the money."

"Unfortunately, I have a passion for money too," Pete replied glumly. "I've got a problem with greed, but I'm working on it. I definitely have a passion for following Jesus Christ too, though. He helps me through all my problems — even the ones that seem to take me forever to get over." Kelly nodded.

"What about you?" Pete asked.

"What about me?" Kelly asked with a puzzled look on her face.

"Are you a Christian?" Pete asked.

Kelly laughed out loud. "No, Peter," she replied. "I hope I don't offend you, but I don't believe in Jesus, or God, or heaven, or hell, or any of those things."

Pete thought for a moment. "Well, when you came to dinner, didn't you say it was your college roommate who made a suggestion that you should have me and give me up for adoption instead of...well, you know...the other option?"

252

"Yes, that's right. I followed my roommate's advice to have you."

"And didn't you say that your roommate was a Christian?"

"Yes, she was a Christian, and probably still is. Her name is Kim"

"Well, I thought you also said that you used to go to church with her, right?"

"Yes," Kelly said. "After I had you, I went to church with her for close to a year. I attended church right up until school let out for the summer."

"So, what happened?" Pete asked with a confused expression. "Didn't you believe in Jesus back then?"

"It seems funny to me now," Kelly said, "but at the time I was seriously into the whole Christian thing. I met a lot of diverse and wonderful people at the church. They weren't as stuffy or judgmental as I thought they'd be. And of course I just loved your parents when I first met them. They've both talked to me about Jesus." Kelly sank into the booth's padded backrest. "But despite all that, I found that I also had some big issues with Christianity, and I never went back. Your parents know what those issues are."

"What issues?" Pete asked.

"What issues?" Kelly repeated softly as she stared up at the ceiling with a thoughtful look upon her face. "Well," she began, "here's one issue. Being that I'm a lawyer, I have to deal with hard evidence to win my court cases. It's the tangible facts and evidence that I gather for each case that allows me to convince a jury about the events that my client and I claim happened. If you can observe something directly — to see it, touch it, smell it or

253

hear it — then you know without a doubt that it exists. But I have never observed any so-called 'god' directly; therefore I personally don't believe that there is a god out there somewhere. Please understand, Peter, I'm not trying to change your opinion regarding your Christian faith. I don't want you to think that's what I'm suggesting here. But for me personally, I need proof beyond the shadow of a doubt before I'll believe in something that sounds like a made up fairy-tail or a myth."

"Can I say something about that?" Pete asked cautiously.

Kelly smiled. "I hope you will," she said. "Let's see if we share the same trait of excelling in lawyering skills! Let me hear your rebuttal, counselor."

"Counselor?" Pete asked with a confused look on his face.

"It's just a lawyer term," Kelly said. "Go ahead, Peter. Present your case."

"Well," Pete began, "I *do* think it's reasonable to believe in the God that I read about in my Bible. In my Bible, it says that God is eternal, everlasting and infinite — without a beginning or an end. So it's saying that God always existed. There was never a time when God didn't exist. This makes sense to me because there had to be *something* that always existed or else there wouldn't be anything here now."

"Why do you say that?" Kelly asked.

"Because you can't get something out of nothing," Pete responded. "If you could get something out of nothing, then that would be like a magic trick. It would be like pulling a rabbit out of an empty hat."

"So," Kelly began, "when you say 'you can't get something out of nothing', what do you mean? What's your definition of 'nothing'?"

"When I say the word 'nothing', I'm talking about *absolutely* nothing," Pete replied. "There would be nothing to observe — nothing to see, hear, touch or smell. There wouldn't even be anyone around to do the observing. There wouldn't even be any space or time or energy. Absolutely nothing. So if there was ever a time when there was absolutely nothing, there would be absolutely nothing now because something can't come out of nothing. That's why I say that something must have always existed. And here's the direct proof you're looking for..." Pete picked up his spoon struck it upon his glass dish. The resonant sound that resulted was loud enough to make some of the other customers in the ice cream parlor look in his direction. "The proof," he said confidently, "is that something exists now. Everything from the ice cream dish and spoon to all the stuff in the entire universe. Since something exists now, then something must have always existed because you can't get something from nothing." Kelly smiled and nodded.

"So, this eternal 'something' is what you're calling 'God'?" Kelly asked.

"Yes", said Pete. "In the book of Romans in the Bible it says that 'ever since the world was created, people have seen the earth and the sky. Through everything God made, they can clearly see his invisible qualities — his eternal power and divine nature. So they have no excuse for not knowing God'. Being eternal gives God the divine nature of not having to be created by something

255

or someone else. But *God* is the source of everything else that *does* exists — even space and time itself!"

"What about Jesus?" asked Kelly. "I personally don't doubt that he was a real man who started the Christian faith a couple thousand years ago, but do you really believe Jesus was the Son of God and that he was raised from the dead?"

"I know that Jesus *is* the Son of God, and Jesus *is* alive right now," Pete responded.

"Well, I guess you answered both questions all at once then," Kelly said.

"It says in Colossians," Pete continued, "that 'Christ is the visible image of the invisible God'. And in Philippians it says that 'though he was God, he did not think of equality with God as something to cling to. Instead, he gave up his divine privileges and took the humble position of a slave and was born as a human being. When he appeared in human form, he humbled himself in obedience to God and died a criminal's death on the cross. Therefore, God elevated him to the place of highest honor and gave him the name above all other names'."

"Impressive, Peter!" Kelly said, "You really can quote the Bible word-for-word! You do have a great memory!"

"Thanks!" Pete responded proudly.

"You seem very knowledgeable about God and Christianity," Kelly continued. "But I have to tell you, kiddo, that as far as all of your arguments are concerned regarding God and Jesus, I personally don't accept the Bible as a reliable resource of historically accurate information. Sorry."

"You don't believe in the Bible, Kelly?"

"Nope," Kelly responded confidently. Pete appeared to be stunned for a moment.

"Then why do you say you believe that Jesus was real?"

"Because," Kelly responded, "I've read from a handful of non-Christian resources that lived near the time of Jesus, like Josephus, Tacitus and Seutonius, who mention Jesus and the new Christian sect he started. It's enough to personally convince me that there was a real man named Jesus who started a new religion. But I'm not convinced by those writings that Jesus was a god, or that he was raised from the dead. His followers, who just happened to write the new testament in the Bible and who claimed that Jesus was raised from the dead, could have been involved together in a scheme with the purpose of furthering their own personal agenda."

"Oh," Pete whispered with a confused look upon his face.

"So tell the jury, counselor, what's your proof that Jesus was raised from the dead." Kelly searched Pete's eyes anxiously as she awaited his response.

"Okay," Pete began thoughtfully, "Let me get this straight. If I use any of the testimonies or eye witness accounts out of the Bible, you won't accept it as good evidence?"

"Yes, that's right," Kelly responded. "Convince me without using the Bible."

"Well, nobody has ever found the body of Jesus," Pete offered. "No one in all of history has ever proved to have found a burial site showing it to be the grave or tomb of Jesus Christ.

"I believe that's true," said Kelly. "But the absence of a body doesn't prove the claim that Jesus was actually brought back to life."

257

"Well, I just know it's true that Jesus is the Son of God and that he was raised from the dead," Pete stated confidently. "I don't doubt it for a second!"

"Hmmm...," Kelly said shaking her head doubtfully. "I wish I had your kind of faith, Peter, but I need more assurance than someone simply telling me that they personally know for sure. I'm still just not convinced."

"I don't get it," Pete started. "You went to church and met a lot of Christians who you say were great people, and you didn't see Jesus at work in any of that? Didn't anyone tell you how their faith in Jesus changed their lives?"

"Sure," said Kelly. "Many people did."

"And you didn't believe *any* of them?" Peter asked.

"Christianity seems to be working great for them, Peter. But it's not for everyone. It's certainly not for me. I just can't accept it."

"But why?" Pete asked with a frustrated and confused look on his face. "Is it that you don't believe just because you don't think there's enough proof, or is there something else you've got going on that you're just not telling me about?"

Kelly paused thoughtfully for a moment before replying.

"You know, it may seem that having the ability to remember things as well as you and I would be a great gift, but sometimes I see it more as a curse. Often I think it would be so wonderful if we could just forget certain parts of our past as if they never really happened."

"Like what things?" Pete asked.

"Like things that scare you. Things that hurt you. Things that disappoint you."

"But things like what?" Pete asked again. "Give me some details, and maybe I can help you! I can pray about them."

Kelly smiled weakly and shook her head solemnly.

"Thanks, but you know, I think it's time to change the subject. Tell me some more about this girl you mentioned earlier…Meagan I think you said?"

"Wait a minute," Pete objected. "You won't talk to me about my birth father, and you won't talk to me about what's bugging you from the past either? I thought we got together today to get to know each other better, but you won't tell me any of this important stuff! I told you lots of stuff about me!" Pete's ears and cheeks became bright red with heated emotion.

"Peter, please!" Kelly said sharply. "Let's just talk about something else." Pete looked dejected, but he wasn't going to let the subject go.

"Kelly, listen to me…" Kelly held up her hand and stopped Pete in mid sentence. She looked at her watch briefly.

"Listen, kiddo, I'm afraid the time has come where I should be getting you back home, okay?" She stood up and grabbed her jacket. "I think we had a pretty good talk overall. Maybe we can pick another time to get together again."

"But Kelly," Pete said, "If you won't talk to me about the things that are really bothering you, then at least you can talk about them with Jesus! Like I told you before, Jesus has helped me through a lot of problems! If you just pray to him and trust that…"

"That's enough, Peter," Kelly interrupted curtly. "We're all done with that subject for now. Court is adjourned." She fished for her wallet in her jacket pocket.

"He loves you, y'know!" Pete stated loudly and boldly. "Listen to me, Kelly! Jesus loves you!" Several customers turned toward Pete and Kelly's direction. Kelly stared directly into Pete's eyes with a harsh intensity that Pete had not experienced from her before.

"Listen to me!" she said sternly, "I heard you, okay? Now I'm asking you to please stop bringing it up!"

Several of the customers began mumbling amongst themselves as they eyed Pete and Kelly curiously. Kelly seemed embarrassed and, like Pete, her ears and cheeks also flushed with color. She shook her head sadly and sighed. She put some money down on the table and pocketed her wallet. Then she sat down once again in the booth so that she was eye level with Pete. Pete stared silently down at the tabletop.

"Listen," Kelly began softly, "I know you're just trying to help me, Peter. I appreciate that. Really I do. And I don't expect you to understand where I'm coming from. But if you had lived the kind of life that I have, then maybe you could understand why I'm so skeptical about a God that talks all about loving people, but allows bad things to happen to them. A lot of good people get hurt everyday in this world by bad people — bad people who cause innocent people a lot of pain, and suffering, and fear. The memories of those bad things can last for a very long time for some people. I know this because I'm one of the people who got hurt like that. I personally know how a bad person can get away with a terrible, terrifying thing, and never get caught and punished for doing it. I was living a pretty normal and happy life up until then. But now I think about it every day. I was never even given justice for what happened —

not by God or Jesus or anyone else. The person who hurt me is still out there somewhere. That scares me every day of my life. But I decided that I didn't have to let what happened to me happen to someone else."

"That's why I became an attorney. I focus day and night on being the best attorney I can possibly be. I'm not married, and I have no other children besides you. I stay focused on my mission. I deliver justice to people who deserve it. I put bad people in jail for doing terrible things to others. I don't see God or Jesus doing that." She leaned in closer to Pete and spoke very softly. "My life was turned upside down in a single moment, Peter. If there is a God or a resurrected Jesus, where are they? Where were they? I'm sorry, but I just don't see a real Jesus out there anywhere trying to intervene in my life. Can you see where I'm coming from now?"

Pete continued to look down. He appeared to be mumbling softly to himself.

"Peter?" Kelly said. "Are you listening to me?" There was no response. "Peter?" Kelly repeated. "Hey!" she said as she waived her hand in front of his face several times, trying to get his attention. "Are you ignoring me now?"

Pete finally looked up at Kelly.

"I was praying for you," Pete said. "You finally gave me some stuff to pray about. It probably didn't seem like it, but I heard every word you said. I also asked God to help me with what I should say to you right now."

"You were praying for me just now?" Kelly asked with a frown.

"Yeah," Pete said. "It sounds to me like you've got some pretty serious issues you are trying to deal with, and you need some help. So I did something about it. I prayed that you would get the help you need. I also prayed that you would try talking with Jesus again."

"Peter," Kelly began with an exasperated tone. "You understand where I'm coming from, do you?"

"But I think I do understand," Pete countered. "The day I found out that I was adopted turned my whole world upside down, too. I couldn't understand why you would want to give me away to somebody else. Don't get me wrong. I totally love my parents and my home. I don't want it any other way! But when I heard that you didn't want me and that you gave me up for adoption, well, I thought that maybe you didn't want me because there was something wrong with me. I thought that maybe being born was bad thing for you somehow. That hurt for a little bit, but by praying about it and talking about it with my parents, I got over it pretty much. I had to realize that you didn't even have to have me at all! But now I'm very glad that you *did* give me away! I thank God for that now! It turned out to be alright."

"I'm glad you feel that way now," Kelly said. "I was trying to do what I thought was right at the time. I certainly didn't mean to hurt you in any way."

"Well, we live in an imperfect world filled with imperfect people," Pete said. "People hurt other people all the time; sometimes on purpose, and sometimes not on purpose. But why do you blame Jesus for that? If you wanted him to get rid of all the people that hurt each other in this world, who would be left?

I know that I wouldn't be here right now if that were the case! Isn't it people that have a problem with each other? Jesus isn't the one that's forcing us to hurt each other. Jesus wants us to follow his command to love each other and to treat others the way we would want to be treated ourselves. But we all seem break that command a lot in our lives. We're all guilty of that crime!" Kelly remained silent.

"But, like it says in the book of First Timothy, God wants everyone to be saved, not punished for breaking his law. So God gave us something better than the justice we deserved; he gave us grace and mercy and a chance for a new life through his own Son Jesus! And just like us, Jesus knows personally that life on earth is hard. Sometimes Jesus got sad and cried, and sometimes he got frustrated and upset. And remember, he was treated like a criminal and sentenced to death even though nobody could prove he did anything wrong! Then he was made fun of, and then beaten and crucified to death. God allowed all those bad things to happen to his own Son that he loves more than anything else! That doesn't seem fair, does it?"

"No, it certainly doesn't," Kelly agreed.

"But even though God allowed all that bad stuff to happen to him, Jesus never stopped believing in God's goodness or the promise that God would bring him back to life and make him King of kings and Lord of lords and our Savior," Pete continued. "So God allowed something that seemed really bad at the time to happen in order for something infinitely good to come out of it for all of us."

"You're really persistent, aren't you?" Kelly said shaking her head despairingly. "Believe me, I've heard this all before! And

263

I appreciate you praying for me just now, but I still don't believe in God or Jesus. I don't see them, I don't hear them, and I can't touch them. Period."

"Well, who do you see when you look at me, Kelly?" Pete asked.

"I see a young man named Peter Johnson," Kelly replied dryly.

"That's true," Pete said, "but you told me just a little bit ago that I have your eyes and hair. So you must see part of you in me too, right?"

"Of course," said Kelly somewhat impatiently.

"So what about my father?" he asked. Kelly shifted in her seat nervously, but she remained silent. "Don't you see part of him in me too?"

"Peter, I already told you I don't know anything about your father, and I've asked you not to bring that subject up again."

"I'm not talking about my birth father now. I'm talking about Jesus," Peter replied. "I'm talking about my Father in heaven. Don't you see *him* when you look at me? Jesus sent God's Spirit to live in me. He lives in me right now. That's how I know that Jesus is real. That's how I know that Jesus is alive. Obviously I'm not Jesus himself, and I'm definitely not perfect like Jesus, but I'm part of him and he's part of me." Pete noticed that Kelly was starring at the tabletop looking somewhat weary.

"Look at me, Kelly. Don't you see all three of us in me?" Kelly looked up at Pete. Her eyes scanned his face silently. "When you look at me, do you see the disappointments of your past or do you see the hope of the future?" Kelly opened her mouth slightly as if she was going to say something, but she

264

remained silent. Pete narrowed his eyes. "Kelly, do you see *anything* good here at all?"

"Peter," Kelly finally said, "try to understand. It's just really hard to let go of some things. Maybe in time…"

"Kelly," Pete interrupted, "don't let the bad stuff that someone did to you a long time ago get in the way of the terrific stuff that Jesus wants to do for you right now. I wouldn't be here right now if it wasn't for you. But here I am." Pete reached across the table to grab onto her hand. Kelly, perhaps by a fearful instinct, jerked her hand away a short distance.

"Sorry," she said sheepishly. She looked almost frightened by Pete's gesture, but, in a slightly cautious manner, she reached over and grabbed onto Pete's open hand.

"Listen," Pete said. "Jesus is with us right now. Do you hear him? Do you see him? Can you feel him?" Pete squeezed her hand gently. For several moments, Kelly carefully searched Pete's eyes. After a moment, her frustration seemed to fade, and she laughed nervously.

"Alright, alright! I'll think about it, okay?" she said loudly with mock annoyance. Her cheeks were bright red again with embarrassment. "You are something else, Peter Johnson! I think that this is the third time today you made me blush! So this is how you talk with your friends, huh? My goodness, you don't budge on your convictions, do you? You certainly are a very unique young man. I'd be very happy to have you as my lawyer defending me someday!"

Kelly sighed loudly as she looked at her watch once again. "Okay, it's really getting late now, young man. I've really got to get you back home, and I have an hour drive ahead of me." Pete nodded in agreement.

As Pete was putting on his jacket, Kelly placed her hand on his shoulder. "Peter, this might be a little hard for you to take, but…." she paused.

"But what?" Pete asked wide-eyed.

"Remember you told me that you wanted to become a pastor when you grow up?" Kelly began. "Well, I just think you might want to reconsider what you said. You're simply not being realistic with yourself. I personally don't believe that you'll make a good pastor at all."

Upon hearing these words, Pete's mouth fell open in astonishment, and his entire body seemed to slump with disappointment. Kelly chuckled, and she patted him firmly on the back.

"Mister Peter Johnson," she said with a big smile, "You don't have to wait until you grow up because I think you make a *great* pastor right *now!*"

Pete's expression of horror turned quickly into a large grin.

"Okay," Kelly said, "On our way back to your house, you can finally tell me a little bit more about this girl you seem to really like. What was her name again…Meagan Pulaski?" Now it was Pete's turn to blush.

Questions:

1) How do *you* know that God and Jesus Christ are real and alive? How would you explain that to someone else?

2) Have you ever gone through hard times where you have wondered where God was? Do hard times make move you closer to God, or does it push you away from God? Why?

3) What are some ways you could help someone else that is going through a difficult time?

Bible References Relating to this Story:

1 Peter 3:15-19

Romans 1:20

Philippians 2:5-11

Colossians 1:15

1 Timothy 2:1-4

Psalm 19:1-4

Psalm 23

Chapter 15

Lost Boys!

"We're exploring uncharted territories where no man has ever gone before! There's nothing out here except me, the bears and the coyotes! Oh yeah. Ryan's here too. But other than that, there's not a person as far as the eye can see! You guys could have come with us, but oh-no! You were too afraid that you might get in trouble as usual. So there you are … safe and cuddled up tight in your little tent like a couple of girls! You could be having the adventure of a lifetime with us in the wild! Hey! If we get lost out here or eaten by wild animals, tell my sisters that they're still not allowed in my room! Do you read me base?" The radio crackled and then went silent. Rob and Tony, who were sitting at the far end of their tent, looked at each other and smiled.

"What should I say?" Rob asked.

"Give it to me," Tony said as he grabbed the radio out of Rob's hand. "I got a question for them." Tony pressed the black button on the side of the radio and began speaking. "Uh, base camp to the two crazy boneheads in the woods, we read you loud and clear. Gordy, did you say you and Ryan are exploring uncharted territories?"

"Affirmative!"

"Does that mean that you guys aren't following the trail anymore?"

"That's an affirmative base."

"Just to be clear, when you say 'affirmative', you do mean 'yes' right?"

"Affirmative!" Gordy yelled back.

"You guys are supposed to be following the trail! You're gonna get lost, I just know it!"

"Too Late!" Gordy's voice crackled back over the static. "Ryan and I are out here exploring just like Lewis and Clark did back in the old days!"

"I don't think Lewis and Clark had Walkie-Talkies back then," Rob whispered to Tony.

"Wow!" Gordy's voice chimed out above the radio static. "Hey, base-camp! I can see a big waterfall down there! I gotta go explore it! Who knows what I'll find there!"

"Wait, Gordy!" Tony yelled into the radio. "I want you both to get back to camp right now! You're gonna get us all in big trouble!"

"Uh, I couldn't hear that last thing you said, base camp. I gotta go exploring. Here's Ryan. He wants to say something.

Hold on." There was a brief pause, and then Ryan's deafening, shrill voice exploded inside Rob and Tony's small tent.

"I'm all done exploring!" Ryan yelled frantically. Tony pulled the radio away from his ear quickly. "I want to come back but Gordy doesn't want to. Can you guys come get us? I think we are lost!"

"Wow, Ryan!" Tony yelled back. "You don't have to yell into the radio! Just talk normal!"

"That is normal for him," Rob whispered.

"He's at the waterfall," Ryan continued. There was a slight pause. "He's not listening to me. It's too dangerous, but he won't listen to me and come down. I think he's gonna get real wet!"

Just then, Rob and Tony heard the distant snap of a twig and the sound of footsteps approaching their tent.

"They're back!" Rob whispered loudly.

"What are we going to do?" Tony asked, panic in his voice. "We're in so much trouble! When my Dad finds out that Gordy and Ryan got lost somewhere in the woods, and we let them go... I mean I'm the oldest! I was supposed to be watching everybody!"

The radio suddenly chimed out again with Ryan's explosive voice: "He's gone! Can you hear me? He's gone! I can't see Gordy anymore! Tony! I need help!"

"Quick! Turn it down!" Rob said as he reached for the radio. "Or your Dad will hear us!"

Tony and Rob fumbled the radio controls and finally turned it off and cowered in the corner of the tent. They saw a large, dark shadow pass on the left side of them. Tony and Rob watched the

271

shadow of a hand slowly unzip the front of the tent. Pete popped his head in.

"Sure, you guys make me go back to help carry in the rest of the supplies from the car, and you're both in here taking a nap," he quipped. "Where's Gordy and Ryan?"

Both Tony and Rob motioned for Pete to quickly join them inside the tent.

"What is it? What's going on?" Pete asked, as he made his way inside the tent.

"I made a jigungus mistake!" Tony said. "Gordy and Ryan wanted to go exploring a little ways down the trail, so I let them go."

"What? All by themselves!" Pete cried out in disbelief. "Are you psycho or something? You were supposed to make sure that everyone here stuck together! They could get lost out there!"

"I gave them one of your Dad's radios so we could stay in contact. We were just talking to them."

"I think Gordy might be in some kind of trouble," Rob said. "He was near a waterfall, and then Ryan couldn't see him anymore."

"Well, what's going on with them now?" Pete demanded.

Tony and Rob looked at each other and their eyes grew wide.

"The radio!" they whispered in unison. "We turned it off so that our dads wouldn't hear it."

Tony switched the radio on to a low volume and whispered into it.

"Base to Ryan, do you hear me? What's going on?"

There was a long moment of silence.

"Give it to me!" Pete said as he grabbed the radio from Tony's hand and turned the volume up all the way. "Hey Ryan, this is Pete!" Pete said loudly. "Can you hear me? Say something if you can hear me!"

Nothing. Only the hiss of radio static could be heard.

"Ryan! This is Pete! Answer me if you can hear me! Where are you?" A loud, low voice outside the tent interrupted him.

"What's going on in there?" Tony's Dad asked. "Why is everyone inside on a beautiful day like this? Get out here men!"

Pete put the radio down and looked Tony squarely in the eye.

"Okay, we got to tell our dads what happened, Tony. We don't know what's going on with Gordy and Ryan – they might be in really big trouble."

Tony covered his face with his hands. His head sunk as if he were going to cry. "It's all my fault," he whispered. "They left me in charge and I messed up." He lifted his head and looked at Pete. "Okay," he said with a miserable look upon his face. "I don't care what happens to me. We got to tell them! Gordy and Ryan need our help!"

A half hour later, Pete's Dad, Mr. Johnson, and Ryan's Dad, Mr. McKenna, approached the area from where they believed Gordy and Ryan were last heard. Pete and Rob were allowed to assist in the search for the missing boys, and they followed closely behind the men. Pete called out the boys' names while Rob blew a silver sports whistle. Tony and his father remained at the base camp in case Gordy and Ryan happened to find their way back.

Mr. Johnson and Mr. McKenna stopped to check the trail map with their compass.

"Well, the rise shown on the map is right over there," said Mr. Johnson pointing to a long ridge. "According to the map, we should see the falls once we make it to the top of the ridge."

"How could they have made it so far in such a short time?" Mr. McKenna asked. "We were only gone for thirty minutes!"

"We'll ask them when we find them, Mike," Mr. Johnson said with a reassuring smile. He patted Mr. McKenna on the back to comfort him. "Well, let's keep going. Everyone keep a good lookout and make lots of noise."

They soon made it to the waterfall. The waterfall was about thirty feet tall and twenty feet at its widest. The sides next to the falls were steep and appeared to be slippery in places. The water was fast and strong. It roared loudly as it made its way over the rocks.

"Look!" Rob yelled. He pointed to the shoreline below the falls. "Sneakers!"

Sure enough, there were two pairs of sneakers and socks resting haphazardly near the water's edge, but there was no sign of the boys anywhere in the area.

"They must have waded out into the water!" Mr. McKenna yelled. "But where are they?"

"They might have headed down river," Mr. Johnson yelled back. "Let's follow the brook downstream. Look carefully on the bank for footprints!"

Rob and Pete knelt down at the water's edge to splash some water on their faces to cool off. Rob removed the whistle from around his neck and placed it on top of a large rock on the shore so it wouldn't get wet.

"Come on, guys!" Mr. Johnson shouted. "Let's go! I don't want to lose the both of you, too!"

Pete and Rob jumped up and scrambled over the rocky bank toward Mr. Johnson. The group of searchers then followed the brook downstream about sixty feet when Pete spotted something in a shallow pool near him.

"Oh no!" he mumbled under his breath. A shiver shot through his body and his heart raced.
He reached into the water and pulled out the radio that Gordy and Ryan had been using. "Dad! Look!"

Mr. Johnson saw the radio in Pete's hand and he grimaced. He took the radio from Pete.

"It was left on," he said. Mr. Johnson shook it and dried it with his shirt. Then he adjusted the volume control and pressed the button on the side several times. "Nothing," He said. "It's dead. It's swamped with water."

"So, what are we going to do now?" Mr. McKenna asked anxiously while waving his arms wildly in the air. "I've got a boy missing out here somewhere, and all we've found are his sneakers and a dead radio he was using! What are we going to tell Al and Connie about Gordy? This is terrible!"

"Easy, Mike," Mr. Johnson said calmly. "I know this doesn't look good, but let's just collect our thoughts for a second and think about the best way to proceed."

"We can't even use our cell phones out here to call for help!" Mr. McKenna complained.

"I know, Mike. I know. Just...let's think."

275

There was a brief moment of silence as everyone took a deep breath.

"We don't need a cell phone or radio to call God when we need help!" Rob blurted out. "How about if we pray and ask God to help us find them!" Everyone spun around and looked at Rob with amazement.

"Wow, Rob!" Pete exclaimed. "Why didn't we think of that? That's an awesome idea!"

"We don't have time to pray!" Mr. McKenna said with annoyance. "We need to keep looking! They could be in real trouble right now! We don't have time to waste!"

"I don't mean to speak out of turn, Mr. McKenna" Pete said. "But Rob's right, isn't he dad? In James, it says 'Are any of you suffering hardships? You should pray'. That's what God tells us to do."

"It's so easy to get caught-up in the moment," Mr. Johnson commented. "Our minds get so worried and overwhelmed sometimes, that we totally forget that we have a real, living, bigger- than- life God who cares about us, listens to us, and wants to help us." He patted Rob on the shoulder and smiled at him. "Thanks for reminding us of that truth, Robby." Mr. McKenna was about to protest, but Mr. Johnson stopped him. "Mike," he said, "We've been going to church together a long time. We both agree that faith is an important part about being a Christian. So here's a time where our faith is truly tested, right? Remember the Psalms that says 'God is our refuge and strength, always ready to help in times of trouble. So we will not fear even if earthquakes come and mountains crumble into the sea'.

Mike, do you believe that God keeps his promises to the people that are faithful to him?"

"Well, sure I do, Bill. You know that!" Mr. McKenna said with hurt frustration. "It's just that…well, you know! It's *my* kid that's lost out here somewhere. I'm at my wit's end!"

"I hear ya, Mike," Mr. Johnson replied calmly. "I completely understand. But listen to me for a second. Remember the Psalm? Let's hold God to his promise right now. I don't know how things will work out, but don't be afraid. The king of the entire universe is standing with us right now. He's real and he's listening. So let's take just a moment to pray to him together."

After praying, the men and boys started the search for Gordy and Ryan once again.

"Robby!" Mr. McKenna called out from the opposite bank. "Keep blowing that whistle of yours in case the boys are close by!"

Rob reached down to grab his whistle and realized it was missing.

"Oh no! It's gone! I left it back at the waterfall!" He turned to Mr. Johnson. "It's not that far away! I can get it real quick!"

"Can I go with him, Dad?" Pete asked enthusiastically.

"Go quickly," Mr. Johnson said. "I'll wait for you here where I can keep an eye on you two and on Mr. McKenna. Be careful!"

Pete and Rob sprinted back to the waterfall.

"I can't wait to see what God does to help us find Gordy and Ryan," Pete shouted over the thundering sound of the water.

"Yeah, me too!" Rob yelled back as he scooped up his whistle.

Rob spied a rock nearby that looked almost the same size and shape of a baseball and picked it up. "Whoa!" he said. "Look at this rock! It's almost perfectly round! It's perfect for throwing!"

"Come on!" Pete shouted. "We're on a mission! Get rid of the rock and let's go! They're waiting for us!"

Rob nodded and placed the whistle around his neck. Then he turned to the waterfall and narrowed his eyes, and spit off to the side. Then he did a pitcher's wind-up and threw the rock as hard as he could, aiming for the middle of the falls. The rock cut through the air and then disappeared into the white belly of the falls. Rob smiled.

"That must have gone at least fifty miles an hour!"

"Come on!" Pete shouted again. "Stop playing around! This is serious!"

As Rob turned to leave, he heard a ghastly, high-pitched screech that seemed to echo all around him.

Pete spun around. "Wait! Listen! What was that?" Rob and Pete slowly turned to the waterfall towering above them. Then they heard the screech again — loud and ear piercing. It drifted above the roar of the water and then slowly ebbed away.

"It could be an owl...or maybe an eagle or something," Rob offered.

"But it's coming from the waterfall!" Pete said. "Actually, I think it came from *behind* the waterfall!"

The strange noise rang out again but this time it sounded different.

"It's a word!" Rob called out. "It sounds like 'HELP!'"

"Blow the whistle!" Pete yelled. "Blow it now! We got to get my dad back here! I think we found Gordy and Ryan!"

Rob started blowing the whistle as loud and hard as he could while Pete jumped up and down waving his arms to get his dad's attention. Mr. Johnson called out to Mr. McKenna, and both men ran back to meet Pete and Rob. Mr. Johnson carefully climbed up the side of the waterfall. Mr. McKenna followed close behind. The men found an overhang in the rocks over a large ledge near the middle of the falls which formed a type of shelter from the water. Mr. Johnson crawled on his belly through the narrow opening between the water and rock. He soon saw the mouth of a large pit formed by several large granite slabs near the ledge on which he was crawling. He aimed his flashlight down into the darkness and suddenly a shrill voice cried out.

"Help us! We're stuck down here! It's too slippery to climb out! Don't leave us!"

Mr. Johnson angled his flashlight directly down and saw two, terrified faces staring up at him. Gordy and Ryan were about ten feet below at the bottom of the narrow cave. Mr. Johnson smiled. "We found them! They look okay!"

Mr. McKenna held onto Mr. Johnson's Legs and lowered him into the slimy pit. The men then carefully pulled both boys to safety.

Pete and Rob ran to meet the boys as they climbed down the edge of the falls to safety. Gordy and Ryan were soaking wet and shivering.

"Come on, men," Mr. McKenna said, as he and Mr. Johnson descended the edge of the waterfall. "Let's get back to camp so we can dry off and get warm by a campfire! We can talk about what happened on the way back. Grab your sneakers, and let's go."

On the way back to camp, Ryan explained how he and Gordy ended up stuck in a pit behind the waterfall: "He saw the hole in the rocks," Ryan began, "and Gordy thought he was gonna find gold in it or something, and he fell in."

Gordy shrugged as if it were no big deal. "What?" he asked matter-of-factly. "Everybody knows that there's gold in caves."

"I tried to reach down and pull him out," Ryan continued. "I slipped and dropped the radio by accident and it went into the falls. Then Gordy pulled me down into the hole with him."

"You were supposed to pull me out!" Gordy said with annoyance.

"It was so dark, and cold and scary," Ryan continued, "It felt like we were in there forever. We were so scared that Gordy and I actually started praying to God together for help. And then, all of a sudden, a big rock fell on my foot, and we thought someone was out here looking for us. So I started yelling as loud as I could."

"Tell me about it!" Gordy said rubbing his ears. "You know how he screams! I thought I was going to go deaf!" Gordy looked over at Ryan and grinned slightly. "Actually, Ryan...this time I'm real glad that you have such a loud and annoying voice."

"Thanks, Gordy!" Ryan replied proudly.

"Y'know," Rob began, "that pitch I made was better than any I've ever made in my whole life. I could never have done that without a lot of practice and coaching from my dad. I'm so glad that he's here with us on this camping trip."

"What are you talking about?" Ryan asked with a puzzled expression. "You told us that you didn't even know your dad. So who are you talking about?"

"My Father in heaven who we forgot to say 'thank you' to," Rob replied. He looked up, closed his eyes and yelled out at the top of his lungs, "Thank you, Lord God almighty!" The words could be heard echoing everywhere throughout the woods despite the distant roar of the waterfall. Everyone stopped and stared at Rob with admiration.

"Wow!" Gordy said amazed. "Ryan, you're loud... but I think you've got some real competition here!"

Questions:

1) What was the scariest situation you can remember ever experiencing? Did you pray for God to help you in that situation? Why? What happened?

2) Do you have any experiences where you asked God for help, and you know for sure that God did help you in that situation? Did you remember to say 'thank you' to God afterward?

3) How would memorizing Bible verses help you in your everyday life? Do you think that the Holy Spirit may bring a Bible verse to your mind sometimes to help you figure out what you should do in some situations?

<u>Bible References Relating to this Story:</u>

Psalm 46:1-2

James 5:13

Psalm 31:1-3

Psalm 34:17

Chapter 16

Fame and Fortune

"Happy Birthday, Robby!" Mrs. Johnson called out as she entered her dining room, carrying a single layer cake supporting twelve brightly lit birthday candles. Mr. Johnson jumped out of his chair by the dining room table and quickly switched off the overhead lights.

"Okay, everyone," Mr. Johnson said. "Let's sing!"

Mr. and Mrs. Johnson, Pete, and Rob's mother sang *The Happy Birthday Song* while Rob squirmed uncomfortably in his chair at the head of the dining room table. Mrs. Johnson placed the cake in front of Rob as they finished singing.

"You've got to blow them all out with one breath!" Pete reminded his friend. "If you need some help, I'm always available!"

"I can do it!" Rob replied confidently. "Just watch this!" With one big puff, Rob blew out all twelve candles. Everyone applauded his success.

"You're turning into an old man now, Rob!" Mr. Johnson joked.

"Oh, yes he is!" exclaimed Mrs. Johnson in a playful tone. "Look at his hair. Is he starting to get some gray hairs prematurely?"

"Well, if he is, he's taken after me for sure!" laughed Rob's mother.

Rob shook his head and rolled his eyes with annoyance.

"You guys are all weird!" he said.

"Forget them and let's lick the candles!" Pete said as pulled a candle from the cake. Rob did the same. Both boys stuck the frosted part of the candles into their mouths.

"Mmmm!" Rob said with a smile. "Homemade chocolate frosting! This tastes great, Mrs. J!"

"Your mom helped me make it," said Mrs. Johnson. "She should get half of the credit."

"Wait a minute!" Mr. Johnson protested. "I spread the frosting on the cake! Shouldn't I get something for doing that?"

"Of course you should get something," said Mrs. Johnson. "Here's a knife and a bunch of plates. You have the distinct honor of serving everyone a piece of cake. The birthday boy should get the first piece." Mrs. Johnson handed her husband a knife. Pete and Rob looked at each other and snickered.

"You two think this is funny, don't you?" Mr. Johnson said eyeing the two boys. "But she's right; serving all of you *is* a distinct honor. Do you remember what Jesus told his disciples when they asked him about who gets to be in the place of honor next to Jesus in the Kingdom of heaven?"

"Matthew twenty, verses twenty-six and twenty-seven," Pete replied confidently. "It says, 'Whoever wants to be a leader among you must be your servant, and whoever wants to be first among you must become your slave. For even the Son of Man came not to be served but to serve others and to give his life as a ransom for many.' "

"That's right!" Mr. Johnson said happily. "So in that same spirit, it will be an honor to serve all of you!"

After everyone had finished their cake, Rob opened the gifts that the Johnson's and his mother placed before him. His mother bought him five new baseballs, and the Johnson's bought him a new, leather baseball glove that fit his right hand perfectly (since Rob is left-handed) and a new wooden baseball bat.

"Sorry I couldn't get you more, Robby," Rob's mother said. "Maybe someday I'll be able to do somethin' more, but right now...well...you know what it's like."

"Yeah, It's okay mom," Rob said softly. "I ain't worried about it."

Out of the corner of his eye, Rob spied an unopened gift that was almost a foot long and thin, wrapped in brightly festive paper. It was on top of the dining room table near the cake. "Hey," he said, "how did I miss that present?" Rob was about to take the gift when Pete quickly grabbed it away.

"Oh, Man!" Pete exclaimed. "Sorry about that, Rob! This is for another party later this week over at Meagan Pulaski's. How did this end up here?" he asked his parents.

"Oops!" Mrs. Johnson said apologetically. "That was my fault. I saw it lying on the kitchen counter next to the tape. I just assumed it was for Robby's birthday."

Rob looked at Pete with a painful expression on his face.

"Meagan's havin' another party?" he asked.

"Yeah," Pete responded with a concerned look. "Didn't you get an invitation?"

"What are ya talkin' about?" Rob asked glumly. "When do I ever get an invitation to her parties? Why would things change now?"

"Because I asked her not to forget you this time," Pete said.

"You did?" Rob's expression brightened.

"Yeah," Pete said. "I think she gave your invitation to Becky Croteau so that Becky could give it to you this week sometime when you start *Summer Band Days* at the school."

"Whoa!" Rob exclaimed with excitement. "I can't believe it!"

"He's more excited about being invited to Meagan's party than his new baseball equipment!" said Mrs. Johnson with a grin.

"So, who's the party for, anyways?" Rob asked.

Pete furrowed his brow as if he were trying hard to remember.

"Hmmm, good question," Pete said scratching his head thoughtfully. "Well, I can tell you this: he's a new friend of Meagan's, and he doesn't live too far away from her house. Oh yeah! I just remembered that he's going to *Summer Band Days* too. His name is on the invitation along with the time, date, gift ideas and all that stuff. I'm sure everyone will get to know more about him at the party."

"What instrument does he play?" Rob asked excitedly.

"Uh…some sort of…musical thingy," Pete responded with a shrug.

"That's a lot of help!" Rob replied sarcastically. "Well, it don't matter anyways. Him and I already have one thing in common already: this will be my first year at *Summer Band Days* too! Maybe he's gonna be a good guy to hang out with and do stuff with." Pete nodded, and then he picked up the baseball bat.

"Speaking of doing stuff…baseball anybody? There's still enough light outside to play!" Pete said.

"Let's go!" Rob shouted. He scooped up the baseballs into the baseball mitt and headed toward the door. "This has been one awesome party!" he exclaimed. "I'm goin' to *Summer Band Days,* and I'm finally invited to one of Meagan's parties, and I got all this cool baseball stuff! And the cake was good too! Life is good!"

The following Monday was the first day of the two week session of *Summer Band Days* which was taking place at Rob's school. Band members from the school and from several of the other surrounding school systems met in the large gymnasium. Rob saw Becky Croteau from a distance and waved to her, but Becky didn't seem to see him.

"I wish Pete was here," Rob mumbled under his breath. "I don't know half of these kids! Everyone else has someone to talk to except me. I wish I was more popular in school so I didn't have to feel like such a loser all the time."

The organizers of the event separated the students into smaller groups based on the instruments that they played. Rob was placed into a team with five other drum students. Rob and the others on his team were directed to a corner classroom on the first floor of the school.

When Rob entered the classroom, he noticed two fully assembled drum sets side-by-side. One of the two sets looked dull and worn in many places. A large label attached to the bass drum indicated that this well used drum set belonged to the school. The other drum set, however, appeared to be brand-new, and it glimmered with brilliance and youthful energy that made the school's set seem old and tired in comparison.

Shortly after the students took their seats, a young man ambled casually into the classroom. He appeared to be in his young twenties. He was dressed in long, baggy jeans, bright, multicolored sneakers and a tie-dyed tee shirt. A set of drumsticks stuck out of his back pocket. His hair was long, blonde and tied neatly into a pony tail. He had long, light colored sideburns, and his eyes shined with an intense blue hue. It appeared that he was trying to grow a goatee, as there was some very light and very hard to see hairs left to grow from his chin. Otherwise, his face was smooth and clean. Almost immediately after this young man entered the room, the two girls in the class began whispering and giggling amongst themselves. The young man was chewing bubble gum. He skillfully maneuvered the gum within his mouth and blew a huge bubble. After it popped, he spit the gum in the garbage pail and grinned at the class with a set of very white, perfectly straight teeth.

"Dudes and Dudettes!" he began. "My name is Tim, but everyone calls me 'Cap'. I'll be your drum instructor for the next two weeks, 'kay?" The students remained still and silent. "We're here to make music and have fun," Cap continued. "I'm not big into rules, so I'm not going to give you a big list of 'do's' and 'don'ts', except for one." He walked over to the new drum set and placed his hand on top of it gently. "This beautiful little darlin' you see right here is mine. No one here gets to shake hands with my baby except for me, 'kay? You guys will be using the school's kit and the drum pads to practice on. Everyone cool with that? If everyone's cool with that, give me a big 'yippee-ki-yay'!" Some of the students quietly mumbled the phrase back while others simply remained silent.

"That all you guys got?" Cap said throwing his hands up in the air in disbelief. "You're about to play the drums, and that's all you guys can give me? Where's the excitement? Where's the passion?" There were a couple of giggles, but the classroom remained relatively quiet. "Okay, okay!" Cap said as he shut his eyes and shook his hands in the air. "Let me show you what you guys look like to me right now, 'kay? This is you..." Cap stuck out his bottom lip as if he was pouting, and he allowed his shoulders to slouch. His arms dangled down lifelessly at his sides. His transformation gave him the appearance of a hopeless, miserable wretch. He slowly shuffled his feet over to the drum set and lazily flopped down onto the stool behind the bass drum. Several of the students snickered.

"I'm one of Cap's students," Cap mumbled in a mournful, monotone voice. "I'm here to play the drums for you." He pulled the drumsticks out of his back pocket and began to slowly

289

and softly tap the tom-tom's and the snare drum with a simple, repetitive rhythm. He pretended to fall asleep, snoring loudly with his eyes closed as his head tilted back. He faked almost falling off his stool in the midst of his "nap", and then suddenly awoke with a violent jerk and a comical, wide-eyed expression of surprise upon his face. There was now loud laughter coming from most of the students, including Rob. Cap finished his act by half-heartedly trying to hit the crash symbol but completely missed it three times before actually making contact. At this, every student in the classroom was laughing hysterically.

"Now that's you guys!" Cap shouted as he straightened up and returned to his original character. "Pathetic, isn't it? Now let me show you what you *could* be, 'kay?" Cap held both of his drumsticks above his head shut his eyes, and tilted his head back. "'YIPPEE-KI-YAYYYYY!'" he shouted at the top of his lungs. He was so loud, that some of his students were startled to the point that they jumped in their seats. Cap beat his drumsticks together loudly as he danced rhythmically around the room. The only sound heard was that of the tapping sticks. When he returned to the drum set he very slowly sat down on the stool and paused for a moment with his head down. The room was silent. Suddenly, Cap's arms raced into a blur of rhythmic beating upon the drums that was almost too fast to see. For the next minute and a half, Cap demonstrated his varied skills on the drums as the students sat in wide-eyed awe of their new teacher's impressive performance. When he stopped playing, Cap shot up off the stool and leaped onto the teacher's desk on the other side of the room. He raised one fist in the air. "Now let me hear it!"

he shouted to the class. "Give me a drummer's YIPPEE-KI-YAY!"

This time the entire class shouted the phrase. Cap had them repeat the phrase several more times, each time trying to get the students to shout louder than the previous time.

"That's what I want to hear, and that's how I want to hear it!" Cap shouted. "Drummers are exciting people! They want the world to stop and listen to what they've got to play. And drummers want to hear the world say back to them 'Hey, dude! That was, like, totally awesome! Play some more!' 'Kay? You guys got it now? Let me hear an 'Aye, aye, Cap!'" This time the students shouted the phrase back in unison both loudly and clearly. "Awesome!" Cap replied. "Now I think you're ready to start learning something about drumming!"

At break time, Rob saw Becky Croteau in the hallway stooped over a drinking fountain.

"Good!" Rob said to himself. "She's alone! Maybe she brought Meagan's invitation for me today!" Becky stepped away from the drinking fountain and wiped her lips as she turned to leave.

"Becky!" Rob called out. "Wait up!"

Becky turned toward the voice and smiled.

"Hi, Robby!" Becky said cheerfully. "How do you like your class so far?"

"It's awesome!" Rob replied. "We have this really cool teacher! Everyone in class really likes him. He says I have what it takes to be a professional drummer!"

"That's great!" said Becky. "Our bass guitar teacher is pretty good too."

"So…," Rob began hesitantly, "Are you going to any…parties anytime soon?" Before Becky could say anything, another voice called out from the distance.

"Hey, Becca!" shouted a boy from down the hall who was making his way through the crowd toward them. When Becky saw the boy she looked slightly flustered. She turned to Rob and placed her finger over her lips as if to silence Rob.

"No more talk about parties right now, okay?" Becky whispered as the boy quickly approached.

"Becca, it's almost time to get back to class," the boy said. "Come on. Let's go."

"Sure…in just a second. I was just talking to my friend, Rob, here. He and I are in the junior church band together. He plays the drums."

"Drums. Cool. That's almost like being a musician," the boy quipped as he stared unblinking into Rob's eyes. Rob gave Becky an unsure glance. "Just kidding, man," the boy laughed. "My name's Paul. I play the bass. I just moved to town two months ago from Michigan. I'll be going to school here this fall."

"Paul doesn't live too far from Meagan's house," Becky added giving a slight wink to Rob.

"I don't live too far from Meagan's either," Rob said. "I'm three streets away from her. Maybe we'll end up walkin' home from school together sometime."

"Maybe," Paul said cautiously. "What street do you live on?"

"Pine street," Rob replied.

Paul wrinkled his nose with disdain.

"Sorry, man," he said with mock sympathy.

"Why do you say that?" Rob asked.

"I live in the total opposite direction."

"Oh," Rob said somewhat disappointed.

"And from what I've heard," Paul continued, "Pine street's pretty run down, and most of the people that live there are bad news." Rob looked at Becky with a confused expression as if he were asking Becky to translate Paul's meaning.

"Uh...well," Becky began apologetically in defense of Rob, "I know Rob pretty well. I can tell you that he's a great guy and lives in an awesome house!"

"On Pine Street?" Paul replied doubtfully. He grimaced and shook his head in a pitiful fashion. "Anyway, we better go Becca," he said. "or we'll be late." Paul walked a couple of steps away.

"Okay," Becky replied softly after a pause. She looked at Rob. "New kid!" she said nervously with a shrug and a thin smile. "What are ya gonna do? Anyway, I hope to see you soon, Robby!"

"Later," Paul said curtly as the couple turned toward their classroom and left Rob behind alone in the hallway.

Later that evening, Rob walked over to Pete's house to play with the new baseball equipment he received for his birthday.

"So, how do you like your class?" Pete asked as he threw a ball to Rob. The ball hit Rob's new leather glove with a loud smack.

"I like my class. And I really, really like my new teacher! Everyone likes him. He's real popular. Today, he heard me play and then held me after class after everyone else left. Usually that means that I'm gonna get detention again. But he told me — just me — that I've got a special talent for playin' the drums. 'I'm gifted' is what he said!"

"That's what Mr. Croteau said about you too, back in December," Pete remarked.

"Yeah, that's right!" Rob said. "Mr. Croteau said I got drummer's blood in me!"

"So did you meet any new kids today?" Pete asked.

"Yeah," Rob said glumly.

"Who?"

"A kid named Paul," Rob replied. "He just moved here from somewhere else. He lives near Meagan's house now." Rob threw the ball back to Pete. Pete caught the ball and then looked up to the sky as if he were trying to remember something.

"Wait a minute," Pete said slowly. "That name sounds familiar."

"Yeah, it should," Rob said with a downcast expression. "That's the guy who the party's for at Meagan's, isn't it? You know...the kid whose name you couldn't remember the other day?"

"What makes you so sure it's him?" Pete asked.

"Cause Becky told me not to talk about parties around him before she introduced him to me," Rob said. "Then she said that he lives near Meagan's house an' she gives me this wink." Rob attempted to recreate Becky's wink for Pete.

"Maybe she winked at you because she likes you...*Robby*!" Pete sang out Rob's name with mock sweetness and a sly grin.

"Give me a break!" Rob retorted hotly. "She don't like me. Remember? The last time she winked at me, she dumped a bucket of cold water over my head!"

"Oh, I know that!" Pete said with a nod. "I was standing right next to you — soaking wet just like you!"

"Besides," Rob continued, "She don't like me as much as she likes that new kid, Paul. It's like they went together with each other everywhere today! I think they're...well, stuck on each other! Becky don't have time for me with that new Paul kid around!"

"Sounds like you don't like Paul too much," Pete guessed.

"I think Paul's a jerk!" Rob said after he spit on the ground. "I'm not even sure I wanna go to a party if it's gonna be for him — even if it *is* at Meagan's house! That guy's stuck on himself, if you ask me! I bet he thinks he's the greatest guy in the world!"

"You don't even really know him that well, Rob. You just met him today. Why don't you give him more of a chance before you judge him?"

"Hmmm. Maybe I should," Rob replied with a doubtful expression. "But I still think the kid's a jerk!"

"Sounds to me," Pete started with a large smile, "that you're jealous about him and Becky!"

"Oh, just zip your lip and throw the ball!" Rob responded sharply. "Let's talk about somethin' else – like me being a famous, professional drummer someday!"

"Wow!" Pete exclaimed. "And you think that *Paul* is stuck on himself?"

"Just throw the ball, Bible boy!" Rob said with annoyance.

"Okay, Lefty McGwyn!" Pete nodded. "Try to catch my famous curve ball!" And with that challenge, the boys returned to playing catch.

At lunchtime the next day, Rob remained in his classroom while the rest of the drum students left to eat outside at the picnic tables. Rob cautiously approached Cap's drum set in the corner. Although he knew he wasn't allowed to touch it, Rob couldn't help but to run his hand gently over the top of the bass drum.

"You like that kit, dude?" a voice behind him asked. Rob jumped and spun around. Cap had just walked through the door.

"Yeah," Rob replied with a frightened look upon his face.

"I bought it last year brand new," Cap said with a sparkle in his eye. "This girl really sings, doesn't she?" Rob nodded.

"I wish I had a kit like this at home to practice on," Rob said looking at the drum set with great admiration. "All I got are a pair of beat-up old drum sticks I'm borrowing from the church band. That's what I use to practice on at home — along with some plastic buckets that I'm using for drums."

"Plastic buckets is a cool way to start off, but a guy with your talent really should have an actual drum set to practice on," Cap said. "I'd be glad to talk with your parents about starter kits and prices if you want."

Rob shook his head. "Naw, that's okay" he said. "We can't afford to buy anything. We can hardly pay the electric bill at home. It's just me and my mom, and she don't work."

"Bummer, dude!" Cap said shaking his head. "Feel free to play the school's set during breaks, 'kay? Get in as much practice as you can on a real kit."

"Thanks!" Rob said enthusiastically.

"What do you got cookin' for lunch?" Cap asked.

"I got a smooshed PB & J, and a cold Toasty Pop," Rob answered.

"You wanna slice of cold cheese pizza?" Cap fished through his backpack. "I've got two slices here, but I'm only eating one."

"Uh…Okay," Rob replied hesitantly. "Thanks."

"You like cars?" Cap asked as he took a bite of his pizza.

"Sure," Rob responded.

"You want to see something over-the-top awesome?"

"What?" Rob asked.

"Parking lot. Let's go, dude," Cap said bluntly as he headed to the classroom door.

As Rob and Cap walked across the school parking lot, Rob asked Cap how he attained the title of "Cap".

"Were you a captain in the army or somethin'?" Rob asked.

Cap laughed.

"No way, little dude!" Cap replied. "The military has too many rules. You would never find me there. I only play by my own rules, and that's the only way anyone can truly be free!"

"So, how did you get the name 'Cap'?" Rob inquired again.

"All the kids in my high school marching band voted for me to be the drum major. Now that's a huge honor to be in charge of the whole marching band! But I felt that all those new responsibilities as drum major would take me away from what I really wanted to be doing in the band, which was simply playing the drums with the rest of the guys in the drum section. So I told them 'thanks, but no thanks'. Then we had to elect another drum major instead. But throughout the year, all the kids – including the new drum major – were asking for my opinion and advice on things. It was like I was the second in command to the drum major, so they gave me the new, made-up title of 'drum captain'. After a while the kids in the band just started calling me 'Cap'." Cap smiled boldly. "You're hanging with a pretty popular guy right now, Robby-dude! Soak up the vibes!"

They stopped in front of a brilliant white car gleaming with bright chrome trim.

"Well, here she is!" Cap said with enthusiastic pride as he gently patted the hood with his hand.

Rob's mouth fell open with awe. "Whoa!" he exclaimed. "This is like a fancy sports car!"

"It's a 1994 Camaro convertible with a V8 engine and manual transmission," Cap said proudly. "It's an oldie, but a goodie. There's still plenty of fire in this little rocket. You want to hear it?"

"Sure!" Rob said eagerly.

Cap hopped into the driver side and started the engine. He revved it loudly several times, which attracted the attention of all the students eating lunch at the picnic area across the parking lot.

"Can I sit in it?" Rob yelled out.

"Sure. Hop in," Cap said as he put on a pair of sunglasses.

Rob jumped into the passenger seat and put his seat belt on.

"This is amazing!" Rob said. "I can't believe I'm in a car that has no roof! This is so sweet! We don't even have a car at home! My mom don't drive."

"Driving is freedom, little dude," Cap said. "If you can't live free, then you're not really living at all. That's my motto. You control life. Don't let life control you."

Rob looked over at the picnic tables and saw Becky, Paul and some of Becky's girl friends eating lunch at one of the tables.

"Look!" Rob shouted. "I see my friend Becky over there!" he said pointing. "She's eating with that new guy that she likes. I think the guy's a dork, myself. He spends all his time with her! I don't even get to talk with her anymore! But, man…if she could just see me now! She would be so impressed with…"

Suddenly, Cap threw the car into gear and floored the gas pedal as he quickly let off the clutch. The tires screeched and the car quickly lurched forward. Cap did a couple of 360-degree spins in the middle of the parking lot. At first, Rob looked horrified as he tightly gripped the armrest as the car spun around and around. Then he looked at Cap, who had a confident and reassuring smile upon his face. Rob eased up, and in the excitement shouted out "YIPPEE-KI-YAY!" at the top of his lungs. Cap nodded with approval.

Next, they sped toward the picnic area by the school. Cap slowed the car down to a crawl as they drove past the students. Most of the students were cheering and applauding the thrilling maneuver that Cap had just accomplished with his vehicle. The car slowly approached Becky who looked bewildered.

"Robby?" Becky called out. "Is that you in there?"

"Don't say anything," said Cap calmly. "Just wave to her as we go by. Just smile and wave."

Rob obeyed. Becky's eyes were wide with surprise. She didn't appear to be as impressed as Rob had imagined. Instead, she looked rather shocked. Rob noticed that the new kid, Paul, was gapping at him also. But unlike most of the other students who seemed generally impressed with Cap's wild stunt, Paul had a sour look upon his face — like someone had just force-fed him an ice-cold, slimy spinach and sauerkraut sundae with a Brussels sprout on top. Rob grinned with delight. He gave Becky a quick salute and a wink. Cap hit the gas again, and the car squealed away to a parking spot near the school exit. Rob shrieked with joy.

"That was so awesome!" he cheered.

"I just made you famous, dude!" Cap said with a grin.

"I know!" Rob replied. "Everyone looked at me like I was the most awesome kid on the planet! I can't believe this is really happening to me!"

"So, you got a thing for Becky, huh?" Cap asked, bluntly changing the subject.

"Maybe," Rob said hesitantly.

"Maybe?" Cap repeated with a frown. "There's no maybe! It's either 'yes' or 'no', dude!"

"Yes?" Rob squeaked with uncertainty as his cheeks flushed with embarrassment.

"Look, dude," Cap said with an authoritative tone, "you shouldn't have to even think about it. Deep down inside, you know what you want. And if you want something, then go for it. If you wait around second-guessing yourself by saying half-baked things like 'maybe', then life's gonna pass you by along with Becky. So if you like this girl, then go for it, 'kay? Don't waste your time thinking about it. That's my advice to you."

As Rob fidgeted nervously in his seat, he hit something on the floor with his foot. He looked down and saw an empty brown bottle vibrating on the floor mat. Cap noticed Rob staring curiously at the bottle.

"That must have rolled out from under the seat when I spun out back there," Cap said. "Just kick it back behind the seat with the others."

Rob pushed the bottle back with his foot and heard it "clink" several other empty glass bottles under his seat. Rob looked over at Cap with a concerned and inquisitive stare.

"What?" Cap asked defensively. "Come on, dude! Don't look at me like that! You never had a drink before? Not even a beer?"

"No!" Rob said with an offended tone.

"Well, don't judge me, dude!" Cap said with an equally offended tone.

"But…I didn't say anything about…"

"You didn't have to," Cap said as he glanced at Rob with an accusing stare. "Your face says it all! So before you judge me, dude, try to see things my way, 'kay? Y'know, most people start their morning with coffee. Coffee has caffeine in it, which is a drug, right? So what if I start the day with a little fermented barely and hops? You got to do whatever it takes to get you going in the mornings, right?"

"I just have chocolate frosted Toasty Pops in the morning," Rob replied innocently.

"See?" Cap said defensively. "Everybody knows that's junk food. Each morning you're putting a ton of sugar and fat and artificial garbage into your body. At least beer and whiskey are all natural! So, should I jump all over you because you chose to eat a Toasty Pop before you came to school today?"

"Well...I guess not," Rob said apprehensively.

"Straight up, dude! There's nothin' illegal about it! It's a free country, after all. So, be free! Be free! Am I right?" Cap glanced at Rob. Rob nodded cautiously. Cap smiled. "Glad you see things my way!"

Cap peered at Rob over the top of his sunglasses. He stared directly into Rob's eyes with a serious expression which caused Rob to turn timidly away. "But as a big favor to me, Robby dude...let's just keep my particular breakfast of choice our little secret, 'kay? This is just between you and me. It's not for the teachers, it's not for your ma, and it's not even for your friends. Look... if you stand by me, I'll let you rock out on the school kit after class each day for a half hour or so. I'll give you your own private lessons for free for the next week. I usually charge twenty bucks an hour, but for you, free. What do you say? You watch my back, and I'll watch yours, 'kay?"

Rob was silent for a moment before he finally nodded his head.

"Dude! You don't look convinced to me," Cap said as he playfully pushed Rob's shoulder with his hand and smiled. "Have we got a deal, or what? You watch my back, and I'll take good care of you, 'kay?"

"Kay," Rob finally replied with a weak smile.

"Dude!" Cap said again with a big grin. "You're in!"

"Well...there's just one more thing," Rob began shyly.

"What's that? Name it."

"Well...when I practice...well...can I play...your drum set?"

Cap hesitated for a moment.

"Sure. Go for it. Knock yourself out. Treat her with respect. And don't let anyone else play her, 'kay?"

"Kay!" This time, Rob replied with sincere enthusiasm.

"Listen, man, I gotta hit the convenience store before lunch is over, so if you'll pardon me..." Cap motioned to Rob's door with his index finger.

Rob smiled and nodded vigorously. "Sure, Cap! Whatever you say!"

Rob jumped out of the car and headed back to the school to play Cap's drum set. He heard Cap's tires squeal against the pavement, and he turned to watch as his teacher raced boldly through the parking lot's exit without even pausing at the stop sign.

Many of the kids eating lunch cheered wildly for Rob as he approached the picnic area. Rob grinned with pride.

"Robby!" Becky called out. "What did you think you were doing? Are you crazy or something? Paul and I were just about to go over there and get you out of that car!"

Rob stopped abruptly. It sounded like Becky was scolding him.

"Whoa!" Rob said as he raised his palms toward Becky as if he were trying to keep her at a distance. "What's wrong?"

"What's wrong is that you got into a car with someone who's basically a stranger! He did dangerous stunts in the parking lot with you in the car with him! You could have been hurt — or worse!"

"I was wearing my seat belt!" Rob quickly replied. Paul stood up next to Becky.

"You don't get it, do you, man?" Paul said with contempt. "You shouldn't get in a car with a stranger. It's bad news. Not cool. Everyone knows that."

"But I do know him!" Rob argued. "He's my teacher!"

"Doesn't matter, man," Paul replied coolly. "Your parents never said it was okay to do that, did they? Really dumb move if you ask me. It's a good way to turn up missing."

"Paul's right!" Becky said with a concerned expression on her face. "Your teacher was irresponsible — and so were you!"

Rob shot an angry look at Becky. "Well, if it's such a bad thing to do, then why are all the other guys out here cheering for me? They think I'm awesome!"

"Well, they're all irresponsible too!" Becky shouted as she looked angrily around the picnic area. "They don't know you like I do, and they obviously don't care about you like I do!" Becky suddenly stopped herself and her cheeks flushed bright pink. "Uh...what I meant is that they don't care for you like Paul and I do. Isn't that right, Paul?"

"Yeah. Right," Paul said sarcastically as he rolled his eyes with insincerity.

"Well," Rob said with an angry stare, "why don't you and your new 'friend' finish lunch together. I got more important stuff to do. Right now I got a date with a drum set!" Rob set off toward the school entrance with a huff.

"Wait, Robby!" Becky called after him apologetically. "Don't go away mad!"

"Yeah, just go away — loser!" Paul mumbled quietly under his breath.

Early Friday evening, Rob and Pete walked into the classroom where Rob had been taking his drum classes.

"Hey! Where is he?" Rob exclaimed with disappointment. "Where's Cap? I really wanted you to meet him, Pete."

"You said he was going to stay late tonight, right?" Pete asked.

"Yeah!"

"Well, I hope he shows up soon," Pete said looking at the clock. "We don't have much time before the party at Meagan's begins."

Rob's eyes grew wide. "Meagan's party!" he shouted. "I totally forgot about it!"

"You were so excited about it before," Pete said. "How could you forget about something like that?"

"I've been spendin' so much time with Cap, I haven't had time to think about it. We've had lunch together every day this week, and I stay late to practice on his drum kit. I practice even during the breaks."

"It sounds like maybe you're a little too attached to this new teacher," Pete remarked.

"He's made me real famous!" Rob responded. "I got to ride in his cool car, and I'm the only one he'll let on his own, personal drum set. Cap even picks me every time to do the demo's during class time. I'm so popular, everyone is, like, real jealous of me!"

"Yeah, but jealousy doesn't make you popular in a good way," Pete replied. "It usually makes you really *un*popular with people. Oh...and Becky did tell me about the famous car ride you took with your teacher. I have to say that neither one of us are very impressed with *that* kind of fame. That really wasn't a very smart thing to do."

"Oh yeah...Becky," Rob said thoughtfully. "We got into a little fight about that whole thing. I never tried to see her this week to see if she had an invitation for me." Rob was silent for a moment, and then he shrugged indifferently. "But, hey! She didn't try to find me either! You know what, Pete? I'm not too worried about the party. I always thought that only the popular kids got invited to parties at Meagan's, but now I know that isn't true! I finally made it – now *I'm* popular! And I don't feel like I have to go to another popular person's house like Meagan's to try to prove it to myself. Like Cap says...I just gotta be free! I gotta do my own thing."

"Well, whatever you decide to do, just remember that I *did* get an invitation, and I'm still going," Pete said boldly. "At least walk over to Meagan's house with me. Maybe when we get there, you'll change your mind."

"First, listen to me play the drums!" Rob said excitedly as he dashed behind the drum set while grabbing his old drum sticks from his back pocket. "You can see how good I am now after a week of totally awesome lessons with Cap!"

"Well...," Pete said with uncertainty as he gazed up at the clock again.

"Please, please, please!" Rob begged. "Just give me a couple of minutes!"

"Well…okay," Pete said reluctantly. "But I'm sitting in the opposite corner way over there so you don't blow me away when you get going on that thing. I know what you're like! My ears can only take so much!"

Pete took a seat across the room, and Rob began a loud drumming routine. A minute later, Cap raced into the room.

"Robby! Stop for a minute, dude!" Cap said frantically as he grabbed the ends of Rob's drum sticks to silence them.

"Cap!" Rob smiled. "You made it! I got…"

"Listen, Robby! This is really important!" Cap whispered loudly, failing to see Pete sitting in the far corner. "I got in a little trouble this morning. I almost hit a little girl with my car when I came into the school's parking lot. I was going a little fast, I guess. Her ma reported me to the superintendent. She might try to sue the school! And a teacher said he saw me drinking out of a flask in the men's room this afternoon. He reported me too. So now the super, the principal and the teacher are on their way down here to ask you some questions about me."

"How do they know I'm here?" Rob asked in bewilderment.

"Think about it, dude!" Cap said tapping his head with his index finger. "You were just playing the drums! I was waiting outside the principal's office while they were inside discussing all these allegations against me. Then we heard you all the way down the hall playing my drums. They know you hang out with me a lot, and I overheard them talking about coming down here to ask you some questions to find out if you had seen anything

307

suspicious about me this past week. So I ran down here to as fast as I could to remind you about the deal we had made together before the big guys show up." Cap placed his hands on Rob's shoulders and stared intently into his eyes. He spoke very quickly. "I've done a lot for you this week, now it's your turn to make good on your promise. This is where you come through for me, 'kay? Put a good word in for me or something! Tell them what a great teacher I am! Tell them that I'm responsible and trustworthy! But whatever you do, *please* don't tell them the truth about what you saw! I could get fired and lose my driver's license over this thing, dude! And I don't need them snooping around my car right now either. That would be *very* bad for me! So, don't say a word about those empty beer bottles you saw floating around in my car, 'kay?"

"Whoa!" Pete exclaimed from the back corner. "Hold on a second here! Rob, what's he talking about?" Cap spun around with a look of horror upon his face.

"Who are you? Where did you come from?" Cap demanded rudely.

"I'm Rob's friend, Pete!" Pete said as he stood up. "What's this you're talking about having a bunch of empty beer bottles in your car?"

Cap placed his index finger to his lips to motion that Pete should silence himself. He shook his head dolefully. "Perfect!" Cap mumbled eyeing Rob. "It's your Christian friend you keep talking about, isn't it? This is just what I need right now!"

"Rob's not gonna lie for you," Pete said confidently. "Isn't that right, Rob?"

"Well...I...," Rob seemed frightened and confused. "But he's my teacher, Pete. And I made a promise."

"But Jesus is your Savior, Rob. Remember your promise to him. Remember his promise to you. Hold onto your faith in God! Remember to trust him now! You have a choice to make, and you already know exactly what God wants you to do! Listen to him!"

Distant footsteps and low voices were heard approaching from the hallway. Cap turned back to Rob in desperation.

"The drum set's yours," Cap blurted out.

"What?" Rob asked in wide-eyed disbelief.

"You heard me, dude," Cap whispered hoarsely. "My drum set. You know you want it, so take it! Just don't rat me out, and you can take home the entire kit after next week! I'll give you everything! It's yours! Think about *that* promise when you're talking to these guys!"

Three well-dressed men entered the classroom.

"Mr. Baker," Principal Baraedo said looking directly at Cap, "What's going on? Was there an important reason for your abrupt departure from the waiting room?" The Principal eyed Rob and Pete.

"I just wanted to see who was playing my kit, that's all," Cap replied with forced calm. "I'm pretty protective of it. It's very expensive, you see. Very valuable. It's a perfectly, fine tuned instrument with perfect pitch. I don't let just anyone play with it." Cap turned to Rob and nodded his head slightly.

Mr. Baraedo eyed Rob for a moment and then turned his attention again to Cap.

"Mr. Baker, you told us initially that you would be happy to help us with our investigation, wasn't that correct?"

Cap nodded silently.

"Good," Principal Baraedo said coolly. "Then we would appreciate it if you wouldn't run out on us like that again without some kind of notice. Please stay put until we get to the bottom of this." He looked over to Rob again. "Rob, I'd like you to answer some questions about Mr. Baker here. Can you join us in the hallway for a moment?"

Rob remained silent. He stood up and looked back and forth between Pete and Cap. His gaze drifted over to Cap's drum set for a moment before he slowly walked out into the hallway.

"Uh, Mr. Johnson," Principal Baraedo said pointing to Pete. "Would you be able to stay for a moment also? We may want to ask you some questions as well. It shouldn't take long."

"Okay," Pete replied. The three men exited the room and closed the door behind them.

Cap looked over to Pete. "So," he whispered. "What do you want?"

"What are you talking about?" Pete asked.

"You know," Cap said. "You overhead what I said to Rob. You know the truth about what's going on. What do you want that will keep you from ratting me out?"

"There's nothing you have that I could possibly want!" Pete replied folding his arms over his chest defiantly.

"Dude," Cap continued, "every man has a price."

Cap looked up at the small rectangular window in the classroom's door. No one from the hall was standing in front of it at the moment. Cap grabbed his wallet out of his pocket and thumbed through its interior. He withdrew a single bill. "This is the best I've got right now, 'kay? Do we have an understanding, dude?"

"Stop calling me 'dude'!" Pete said angrily.

"Sure, sure," Cap said apologetically. "Whatever you say, Pete." Cap checked the door again to make sure that no one was peering in, and then he presented the money to Pete. "Think of all the totally awesome things you could do with this. You would be the richest kid in school." Cap sat down and held the money so that the desk at which he was sitting hid the bill from the door's view. He unfolded the bill so that Pete could examine it better. At first, Pete tried not to look at the money, but eventually he gave the money a quick sideways glance. His eyes grew wide in awe. He unfolded his arms and leaned closer to the bill, eyeing it intensely.

"A fifty dollar bill," Pete whispered.

"That's right, Pete. It's a lot of money for such a young guy like yourself. Just think of all the cool things you'll be free to do with this little jewel. It's like a little piece of freedom in the palm of my hand!"

"Can I hold it for a second?" Pete asked with great interest.

"Go for it," Cap said as he handed the bill to Pete.

Pete brought the fifty-dollar bill close to his face.

"Wow!" he said. "This is amazing!" He looked up at Cap. "You said this is mine, and I can do whatever I want with it?"

"On one condition," Cap whispered. "It's yours as long as you don't tell the big guys out there anything about the conversation I had with Rob about those beer bottles in my car, 'kay? Deal?"

"Deal!" said Pete happily. "*This* fifty-dollar bill definitely came from God! I really think this was part of his plan! He wanted me to get this one!"

Cap breathed a sigh of relief. "See," he said, "Every man has his price. Christian or no Christian, when you get right down to it, we're all the same. I mean, look at the news…the folks that call themselves Christians are no better than the rest of us. They're always getting into trouble. We're all in the same boat. We're all sinners, isn't that right, Pete?"

"That's true," said Pete who could not take his eyes off of the money. "We're all sinners."

"So," Cap began as he leaned back comfortably in his chair, "do you have plans for that cash?"

"Yep," Pete said confidently. "I know exactly what I'm going to do with this." Pete held up the bill so that Cap could see the front of it clearly. "Do you see that mark right next to President Grant's head?" Pete asked.

"Yeah," Cap said squinting a little. "What is that? Like, some kind of fingerprint?"

"It's more like a thumbprint — a chocolate thumbprint," Pete said as he placed his outward, extended thumb next to the thumbprint on the bill. "You see, Cap, I don't want this money so I can spend it. I want this particular fifty-dollar bill to prove something to myself right now."

"Wait a minute!" Cap said as his eyes darted back and forth between Pete's thumb and the mark on the bill. "That kinda looks like…*your* thumb print!"

"That's because it is," Pete said. "Almost a year ago, I found this fifty-dollar bill in a box of baseball cards. This money didn't belong to me, so I hid it from my parents. I hid it because I really wanted it, so I just decided to take it, even though it belonged to someone else. I wanted to keep it because, unfortunately, I really, really like money. It's like I'm addicted to it. It's a problem I have, and I know it. I even got into a big fistfight with my best friend, Rob, over money. It tempts me and tries to control me." Pete paused for a moment. "It sounds like you might have the same kind of problem with alcohol." It appeared as if Cap was going to say something, but he simply snickered with contempt instead. "Anyways," Pete continued, "I've been practicing for this kinda thing for a long time now with the help of my dad and the help of the Word of God. I have a poster in my room that my dad and I made together. It says 'No one can serve two masters. For you will hate one and love the other; you will be devoted to one and despise the other. You cannot serve both God and money'. That verse popped into my head after I saw my thumbprint on this fifty dollar bill. This stain on this fifty dollar bill reminds me how I've been a slave to money. But I'm proving to myself right now that money doesn't control me like it used to. Today I'm gonna set myself free!"

Pete ripped the fifty-dollar bill in half, and then ripped the two resulting pieces in half again.

"What the ...?" Cap said bewildered. "You're crazy, man! What are you doing? That's my fifty dollars!"

"No, it was mine," Pete said. "And like you said, I could do anything I wanted with it." Pete walked over to the garbage pail and threw the pieces into it.

Cap scowled at Pete. "You're really wacked-out, little man! You're way out there somewhere!" he said. "But don't forget you still made a promise to me! You took the money, and you promised not to rat me out! You said you're a Christian, and Christians aren't supposed to break their promises or lie, right?"

"That's funny!" Pete said with a wry grin. "Didn't you just say that Christians are sinners just like everybody else? Are you saying that now I'm supposed to be perfect because I'm a Christian?"

"But you...," Cap began, pointing an accusing finger at Pete.

"Don't worry," Pete interrupted. "As far as the promise I made to you...I *will* keep it! *I'm* not gonna rat you out."

"You're confusing me, man!" Cap said with a worried expression.

Just then, the classroom door opened. Rob entered the doorway first, his head hung low. He peeked up sheepishly, first at Pete and then at Cap, and then looked down again. Principal Baraedo followed Rob into the room. The Principal looked over to Pete.

"Pete...," he began. Pete raised his hand and interrupted the principal.

"Excuse me, sir," Pete said. "May I just say something first?"

"Hmm?" Principal Baraedo said with surprise. "Yeah, sure. Go ahead."

"Well," Pete began, "I just want you to know that I'm not going to say anything about Cap one way or the other."

"Okay," the Principal said slowly with a hint of suspicion.

"Sir, remember that you told me once that I'm a real good student, and that I have good judgment?"

"Yes, I did say that," Principal Baraedo agreed. "You have demonstrated to me many times that you are hard working, wise, and a good judge of character."

"Well then," Pete continued, "all I want to say is that I agree with everything that Rob just told you out in the hallway. Everything he said was the truth." Rob's whole body shook with surprise, and he looked over to Pete with an astonished expression. Cap fussed nervously in his chair.

"Is that right, Pete?" Principal Baraedo asked as he thoughtfully stroked his chin with his index finger and thumb. Pete responded with a confident nod. "Fair enough," said Principal Baraedo. "We will certainly consider your advice as we make our decision about Mr. Baker's future. You must have a great deal of confidence in your new friend here," he said motioning to Rob. "However, I need to tell you that I wasn't going to ask you anything. I was simply going to tell you that you were free to go. You too, Mr. McGwyn. You're free. Enjoy the weekend. Mr. Baker, will you kindly return with me to my office?"

Cap stood up slowly and looked at Rob. Rob quickly looked down again.

"I had to tell the truth," Rob said softly.

Now it was Cap's turn to hang his head low. His body slumped and he shuffled sadly and slowly toward the doorway. As he passed by Rob, Rob reached out and touched his arm to stop him.

"Don't give up, Cap!" Rob said quietly. "You can fight your problems and win. I know it! I got problems, and I've been fightin' them over the last year with the help of God and Pete! I used to lie to people all the time, and I was ready to lie for you to get the drum set just now. But I can't be free if I'm livin' a lie. And you can't really be free if you got all this bad stuff hangin' over you that you keep hidin' away from everybody. Your drinkin' is controllin' you instead of you controllin' it. From everything you've been tellin' me over the past week, I know how much you want to be free for real. So fight for it! Like Jesus says in the Bible, 'the truth will set you free'." Cap snickered and shook his head doubtfully. "Cap, you almost ran over a little girl today! You've got a problem! So get some help! People will be there ready to help you if you want them to. You don't have to go through this alone! To start with, I'm gonna pray for you if you don't mind. It will help… trust me. Do you mind if I pray for you, Cap?"

Cap turned to Pete for a second. Pete nodded his head with reassurance. Then Cap turned back to Rob. He briefly smiled and nodded. "'Kay, Robby," he said softly. "Go ahead and pray. I think I'll need all the help I can get at this point. Thanks, man." He gently patted Rob's shoulder several times and exited the doorway. Pete and Rob were left alone in the classroom.

"Wow!" Rob said to Pete. "You really took a big chance on me! You didn't even get to hear a word I said out there. What made you think that I wouldn't lie to get the drum set?"

"Because you've come a long way in just a year," Pete replied. "Actually, we *both* have. We've been practicing and getting better at doing what Jesus wants us to do. We're both becoming stronger, more mature followers of Christ. Like it says in Hebrews five, verse fourteen, 'Solid food is for those

316

who are mature, who have trained themselves to recognize the difference between right and wrong and then do what is right'."

Rob shook his head in agreement. "Y'know, this last year has been like a big adventure that we've been on together with God," Rob said. "I wonder what we're gonna get to go through next year?"

"God knows!" Pete said with a smile. "But as for you and me...we just have to stay tuned!"

"So," Rob began, "do you mind if we pray for Cap now? Y'know...the both of us?"

"That's an awesome idea! Let's do it!" said Pete.

After praying for Cap, Rob walked over to Cap's drum set. He ran his hand over the top of the bass drum. "This really is a beautiful kit," he said. "But y'know, I don't really need a drum set right now, anyway," he said. "I guess this just isn't the time to..."

"THE TIME!" Pete shouted. Rob jumped.

"You scared me half to death!" Rob yelled back. "What did I say?"

"Look at the time!" Pete said frantically. "If I stay here any longer, I'm gonna be late for the party, and it's supposed to be a surprise party too!"

"I forgot too!" Rob said.

"Let's wrap this up, Rob!" Pete shouted. "We're all done here, so let me get my backpack. You turn out the lights. It's time for us to get going!" Pete grabbed his backpack and raced for the door.

Just before he turned off the lights, Rob turned around to look at the drum set in the corner one last time. "Bye, Cap," he whispered. "I hope Pete and I get to see you again sometime." Rob turned out the light and chased after Pete as they both hurried off for one last adventure before the day's end.

Questions:

1) Has anyone ever asked you to keep a secret? Some secrets are good to keep and some are bad to keep. What are some examples of good and bad secrets, and what makes them good or bad?

2) In this story, why was it a bad idea for Rob to get into a car with his teacher? What could have happened? How can you tell if an adults intentions toward you are good or bad? What should you do if an adult (even if they are a teacher, coach, church leader, relative, etc.) shows that he or she has bad intentions for you? Who should you tell?

3) This story shows how Christians need to rely not only on Christ, but also on other Christians around them to help them be strong in their faith and to help them faithfully practice Christ's commands each day. Who do you have in your life to help you follow Christ each day?

4) How did memorizing Bible verses help Pete in this situation? Have you memorized any Bible verses? If you have, have they helped you out in any situations yet?

5) If you are a Christian, do you think you are getting better at following Jesus as you get older? Why? What are some ways that can help you improve following Jesus?

Bible References Relating to this Story:

John 8:31-32

Luke 11:27-28

Philippians 4:8-9

Hebrews 5:14

Hebrews 10:23-25

James 1:12-15

Chapter 17

The Big Surprise!

"Wow! What a day this has been!" Pete said to Rob as they quickly left the school building. "It's almost seven O'clock! I don't want to be late for this party at Meagan's house! It's a good thing I packed the present in my backpack this morning; otherwise, I would have to go all the way back to my house to get it." Rob was quiet. "What's wrong, Rob? Still thinking about what just happened with Cap?"

"Yeah. That, and I'm not sure if I'm really invited to another one of Meagan's parties. I never got an official invitation, remember?"

Pete stopped in his tracks and spun around to face Rob.

"Rob, do you want to go to this party or not?"

321

"Well...," Rob began thoughtfully. "Yeah, I guess so. Even if it's for that Paul kid, I guess it beats all the other stuff I had planned for tonight."

"What other stuff did you have planned for tonight?" Pete asked suspiciously.

"Nothin'," Rob replied flatly.

"So, 'yes' or 'no', do you want to go or not?" Pete asked again.

"Yes," Rob replied shyly.

"Good!" said Pete enthusiastically. "I'm pretty sure that they put you down on the list this time anyway. Just stick with me. I'm sure Meagan will let you in when we get there. She usually has plenty of everything. Don't worry about it."

"But what if she really didn't invite me?" Rob asked. "I don't want to look like a loser begging to get into her party."

"Just trust me," said Pete. "I've been to her parties before. I know what I'm talking about. But we better hurry...It's gonna start in about seven minutes. It's a surprise party, and we got to get into our places. Come on! We're gonna have to run!"

The two boys crossed the road and ran with all their might. They turned down a short, dead-end street and stopped at a large, yellow house.

"Here it is!" Pete said gasping for air. "Right next to Ryan's house. I hope they didn't start yet!"

Becky Croteau appeared from behind a corner of the house. She motioned to the two boys.

"Am I late?" Pete asked.

"Shhh!" Becky whispered loudly as she looked past the boys. She strained her eyes to look down the street. "Keep your voice down! What took you so long?"

"It's a long story," said Pete.

"Well, you're lucky, Pete!" Becky replied. "He just happens to be late too." She glanced over at Rob briefly. "But you both better get down into the basement and hide quickly! I'm on the lookout for the party boy so I can lead him down to the basement when he gets here. Everyone else is already down there, so hurry up! Go down the hill and get into the basement with everybody else."

"You want me to go down too?" Rob whispered anxiously. "Am I really invited?"

Becky nodded. "Of course you are," she said softly. "You didn't come to see me this past week to get your invitation, did you?"

Rob hung his head low. "I guess I got...well...a little messed up this week," he replied. "I'm sorry for the way I acted, Becky. I..."

"Well, you can tell me about how sorry you are later," Becky whispered impatiently as she looked past Rob with wide eyes. "He's here right now! Get lost, the both of you! Hurry! Go, go, go!"

She pushed them down the hill toward the basement door at the back of the house as Rob tried unsuccessfully to turn around to see the birthday boy's approach.

"But, I have no gift to bring!" Rob said with panic in his voice.

"Don't worry about that now," whispered Pete. "Let's just get inside!"

Pete slid the basement's sliding glass door open and he quickly entered into the shadowy room. Rob followed quickly behind.

"Shut the door!" Pete whispered.

As Rob slid the door shut behind him, he noticed that the glass on the sliding door was entirely covered with what looked to be shiny gift wrapping paper which blocked the low light of the evening sun. When rob turned around, he could barely see a thing.

"Everyone must already be hiding down here somewhere, Rob," Pete whispered loudly to Rob. "I don't see anyone."

"Well," Rob whispered back, "I guess we should hide too, and wait for Paul to come in."

"Wait for who?" Pete asked.

"I thought you were supposed to have a good memory!" Rob said with annoyance. "You know...Paul. Becky's new friend that she's all ga-ga about! Paul's the guy this party is for, remember?"

"Hold on a second," Pete said. "This party isn't a guy named Paul."

"Well, who is it for then?" Rob asked.

"The party is for Robert T. McGwyn," Pete said somewhat loudly.

Rob stared curiously into the darkness for a moment as if he were trying to remember a boy he might have met with the name of Robert T. McGwyn.

"Wait a minute!" Rob said with confusion. "Who did you just say the party was for?"

"You!" Pete stated in a voice even louder than before. "The party is for you, Robert T. McGwyn!"

"Me?" Rob asked. He looked around into the still shadows of the dark basement. "Are you sure?"

"YES!" Pete shouted. "THE...PARTY...IS...FOR...YOU, ROBERT...T...MCGWYN!" Pete emphasized each word very slowly, clearly and loudly.

"That's your cue, you dork!" came a voice from the dark, back corner of the basement. "Can't you hear him, or do you have a banana stuck in your ear or something?"

"Gordy?" Rob called out into the darkness. "Is that you?"

"Can someone turn on a light so I can find the light switch I'm supposed to turn on?" screamed out another voice.

"Ryan? Are you in here too?" asked Rob.

"Come on you goober heads! You rehearsed this!" shouted a female voice from the other side of the basement.

"Meagan?" Rob seemed to be surrounded by familiar voices, but could see no one.

"We're not the 'Goober Heads', Meagan! We're the 'P, B and J's'!" Ryan's voice called out defiantly.

"You're gonna be called 'The *Toasted* PB and J's' when I get a hold of you guys!" Meagan's voice shot back angrily.

"Ow!" Ryan screamed. "Tony, get off my thumb!"

"What are you doing on the floor anyways?" Tony's voice rang out.

"I tripped over something!" Ryan yelled.

"That something happens to be me!" Gordy yelled back.

Suddenly there was loud whispering and snickering breaking out all over the basement. Then there was the sound of some metal objects crashing to the floor in the back corner.

"I think I got a bucket stuck on my head!" a muffled voice cried out.

"This is a really strange surprise party," said Rob. "Is this what's supposed to happen? I've never been to one before."

In the dim light, Rob could see Pete shaking his head back and forth slowly. His eyes were closed and his hand was clasping onto his forehead. "Oh, brother!" he mumbled with a tone of disappointment. "Sometimes the best plans just seem to…"

"Wait a minute!" Rob interrupted as the commotion in the darkness grew louder. "Usually there's a light switch next to a door."

Rob reached back and found some switches near the side of the sliding glass door. He flipped them all up. Suddenly the basement was flooded with light which revealed a large room filled with a crowd of people who instantly froze in place in whatever awkward position they happened to be in at the time. In one corner, Tony, Gordy and Ryan were as still as statues despite the fact that they were all jumbled upon each other on the floor. It appeared that there was a bucket over Gordy's head. On the other side of the basement, Meagan Pulaski, Amanda Grant, Sarah Mills, and Heather Shultz were crouched down upon their haunches like lionesses ready to pounce upon an unsuspecting antelope. Some parents were present also, including Pete's parents and Kelly Spae. Mr. Croteau, Rob's music teacher, was there along with some of the kids from the church band. Each of the band members held their musical instruments in a manner as if they were just about ready to start a song. Despite this vast array of variable and somewhat comical postures, there were at least two common features that everyone in the crowd displayed: first, each person had a very surprised look upon their face, and, second, each person was staring directly at Rob. The entire basement was completely silent.

"Surprise?" Rob croaked out weakly as if he were trying to guess the crowd's intentions. But it was Rob's simple utterance that released the crowd from their inanimate stupor.

"SURPRISE!" everyone replied loudly in unison. The basement instantly transformed into a whirlwind of motion and sound which seemed to implode upon Rob. Mr. Croteau directed the band to play *The Happy Birthday Song*. Everyone else gathered around Rob and shook his hand and patted him on the head as they all sang 'Happy Birthday!' to him.

"Welcome to party central, Robby!" Meagan called out.

Pete's parents congratulated Rob.

"Happy birthday *again*!" Mr. Johnson said as he gave Rob a huge bear hug that lifted him off the floor. "Two birthday parties in one year, and you don't get any older! Now that's the way life should be!" Rob smiled up at him. After Mr. Johnson returned Rob to the floor, Mrs. Johnson took Rob by the hand.

"Happy birthday, Robby!" said Mrs. Johnson. "You've had quite an adventurous year, and we're glad you spent so much of it with us. Now just remember…you're one of the family now, so we expect to see even more of you before your next birthday!" Mrs. Johnson hugged him gently. "I hope you don't

327

expect me to lift you off the ground like my husband just did!" she said. Rob giggled.

"Happy birthday, Robby!" said Kelly Spae, Pete's birth mother. She shook Rob's hand firmly. "You have quite a following here I see. This is such a big crowd of friends and family – everyone should be so fortunate to have such a large fan club. I'm glad I could be here to be part of it!"

"Thanks!" Rob replied as he looked slowly around the room. He seemed to be taken aback by the crowd that had gathered together to celebrate because of him. As he studied the joyous scene, he spied Tony, Gordy and Ryan walking toward him.

"Hey! Happy birthday, man!" Tony said as he raised a hand to give Rob a high five. They smacked their palms in the air. "Welcome to twelve!" Tony said. "Take it from me, twelve is an awesome age!"

"Thanks!" said Rob.

"Y'know," Tony continued, "In a couple more months, I'm gonna leave you in the dust! I'm gonna be a teenager! Can you believe that?"

"That's kinda scary to think about," Rob replied. "I think I like being just a kid. I'm not in any hurry to be a teenager!"

Gordy pushed Tony aside.

"Hey, bro," he said in a very reserved manner. "Happy birthday, yada, yada, yada!" He gave Rob a firm handshake and then suddenly pulled Rob close. "Hope you don't mind," Gordy whispered into Rob's ear, "but I had to bring my three sisters to this shindig! Sorry about that, bro!" Rob shrugged.

"That's okay," he replied cheerfully. "I don't mind."

"Robby!" Ryan shouted. "This was supposed to be a surprise party for you, but I couldn't find the light switch. But I know where it is now – you know – for the next time we surprise you! Just let me know when you're gonna show up, and I promise I'll surprise you better!" Rob laughed.

"That's all right Ryan!" Rob said with a smile as he playfully mussed up Ryan's hair with his hand. "I was still surprised! *Way* surprised!" Rob was finally looking comfortable in the party atmosphere that surrounded him.

"Hey, Robby!" said a cheerful voice directly behind Rob. He turned around to see Becky Croteau standing behind him next to the sliding glass door. "I just happened to have that 'invitation' that I was supposed to give you. Here it is!" Becky handed Rob an envelope. Rob opened it and found an invitation tucked inside of a birthday card. The card was signed by everyone in the room.

"Hey! This is a birthday card!"

Becky simply smiled and winked at him in response.

"There goes that wink again!" Ryan observed. "She did that to you before, remember Robby?" he shouted. "I think that means that she really... *mmffpp mmffppf!*" Gordy had quickly covered Ryan's mouth with his hand before Ryan could finish his sentence.

"Wow! I've wanted to do this for the longest time!" Gordy said as he struggled to hold his hand over Ryan's mouth. Tony helped Gordy drag Ryan to the back of the crowd before Ryan could say anything else. Rob laughed.

"Hey! Happy birthday, big guy!"

Rob looked up to see his two Sunday school teachers, Ben and Jill, approach him with bright smiles on their youthful faces.

"So, Rob," Ben began as he placed his arm affectionately around Jill, "I see that after all this time, you're still bringing people together!" Ben and Jill smiled tenderly at each other.

"Oh, yeah! That's right!" Rob exclaimed. "I guess it kinda was me who got you guys thinkin' about dating in the first place, wasn't I?"

"Don't forget me!" Mrs. Johnson chimed in. "I helped too!" Everyone laughed.

Ben glanced around the basement nodding his head in approval. "Great food! Great music! Great friends! Great party!" he said. He turned to Rob. "Y'know, all these people are here because of you, buddy!"

"I know!" Rob replied in disbelief. "I can't believe it! I can't believe this is actually happening to someone like me!"

Jill gave Rob a warm hug which made his ears turn bright red with embarrassment.

"We knew there was more to you than just being able to do an armpit fart!" Jill whispered slyly into his ear.

"Oh, yeah!" Rob said, "I almost forgot! I did that the first time I went to Sunday school!"

"Well, we never forgot about it!" Jill chuckled. "It still makes me laugh when I think about it! You're a very memorable guy, Robert T. McGwyn. You've really grown spiritually over the past year, and it's been a great blessing for us to be able to witness that transformation. I'm glad Ben and I could be a little part of that." Rob smiled. "I also wanted to thank you for helping both Ben and me to grow, too."

Rob looked shocked. "I helped *you* two grow?"

"Sure you did," Jill replied. "You might not have realized it, but you really challenged Ben and me in many different ways this past year."

"Yes!" Ben agreed nodding his head vigorously. "You've been a HUGE challenge for us, that's for sure!"

Jill grunted at Ben and playfully shoved him away a short distance.

"Well, it's the truth!" Ben said looking Rob with a wily smile.

Jill continued: "But that experience just helped make us better teachers all around, and we're very grateful to you for that, Rob. Thanks!"

"Well, I think *I* was the lucky one," Rob said with a genuinely grateful look upon his face. "I always thought that you were both great teachers right from the very beginning, and, besides…neither one of you ever threw me into detention!"

After Ben and Jill left, Rob turned to Pete.

"Was it you that got all these people together and planned this whole thing out?" he asked.

Pete shook his head. "Nope," he said. "It wasn't me. But the person who came up with this party idea is standing in this very room right now!" Rob looked over to Pete's parents.

"Was it either of you guys?" he asked.

"No, it wasn't us either, Robby," said Mrs. Johnson with a smile. "But the person who's the brains behind this party is actually pretty shy and is trying to hide from you right now. But I think that with a little coaxing, I'll be able to get her to come out from behind me."

"It's a 'her'?" Rob asked with surprise. Mrs. Johnson turned around and guided a small figure to the front of the crowd.

"Oh, I'm so embarrassed at these things!" said a familiar voice. Rob's eyes grew wide.

"Mom?" he said in disbelief.

"Happy birthday, Robby!" said Rob's mother with a huge smile and trembling lips. She held out her arms. Rob slowly approached her and gave her a long hug.

"Thanks, mom," he whispered into her ear. Rob's mother began to cry.

"You never had a real birthday party till now," she sobbed. "All these people helped me. I've wanted to do something like this for so long, but I just didn't know how. But all these people here, they helped me, y'see. We've been talkin' about it for months now! I'm so glad I got to see this, Robby! It makes me feel good for the both of us!" She pushed away from Rob and covered her face. "Oh, I'm so embarrassed for cryin'! I need to get away for just a little bit, that's all. Just for a little bit." Mrs. Johnson put her arm around Rob's mother and led her to a chair near the back wall. Pete noticed that Rob's eyes looked a little misty.

"So are you ready for your present?" he asked.

"A present?" Rob quickly snapped back into party mode.

"Sure," said Pete as he unzipped his backpack. "What's a birthday party without a present?" Pete removed a long, thin gift wrapped in colorful, festive paper from his backpack. "Remember this?" he asked Rob. "You almost opened it at your birthday party at my house last week!"

"That was for me?" Rob asked. "You told me it was for someone else!"

"No," said Pete. "I said it was for *another* party this week which just happens to be your *second* birthday party that we're having right now! We left this present out on the table on purpose so I could tell you about Meagan's 'surprise' party. It was all part of the plan! Becky and I really had you going this past week. Since Monday, you thought this was gonna be a party for that new kid, Paul!" Pete said with a sly grin. Rob laughed.

"Yeah," Rob agreed, "You guys really got me good!"

Pete raised the gift above his head. "Present time!" he shouted. The room became quiet. "Rob," Pete began. "This gift is from me. I've known for a long time how much you wanted these, so I'm real happy to give them to you now. So here you go...to my best friend!" Pete handed the gift to Rob.

"Wow! Thanks!" Rob said with a smile. "What could it be?"

"There's only one way to find out!" Pete said.

Rob ripped away the wrapping paper to reveal pair of brand-new, hickory drum sticks. "Wow! My very own drum sticks!" he exclaimed. "Now I don't have to borrow those old, beat-up sticks from the church anymore! Thanks, Pete!"

Mr. Croteau, who was standing near the back of the basement, cleared his throat loudly. "May I have your attention, ladies and gentlemen!" he announced. The crowd shifted their attention to Mr. Croteau. "As you may or may not know, I am Rob's music teacher. I have had the distinct pleasure to have known Rob for eight months now. When I first met him one evening last December, just before the Christmas concert, I

333

heard him tapping a couple of pencils along to the songs that the band was practicing, and I said to myself, 'Gee, this kid seems to have some musical talent'. Little did I realize just how much talent and potential he actually has! Rob, you have come such a long way in such a short time that it really makes my head spin! We have discovered that you have quite a gift from God. I hope you will use it to serve him faithfully. I just have to tell everyone here, though, that in eight months, Rob has surpassed my own drum playing abilities, and I have been practicing for well over eight years now!" There was a low rumble of laughter. "And so, without further ado, I'd like to present my daughter, who's the bass player of our little church band here, to present to you, Robert T. McGwyn, your final present for your twelfth birthday." Mr. Croteau stepped aside as Becky took center stage.

"Robby," Becky began, "it's been awesome getting to know you and playing in the band with you over this past year. So here's a present for you that everyone here chipped in for. We think you'll really like it, and we all hope you'll show us how it works once you see what it is!" The crowd laughed. "Okay guys," Becky said as she stepped to the side, "Take away the sheet!"

A couple of the band members pulled away a blue sheet that was covering a large object. When Rob saw what was under sheet, his mouth hung wide open, and his eyebrows shot up. He fell to his knees. He was speechless. In front of him stood a brand new drum kit with all of the accessories. There was a large bass drum supporting two, smaller tom drums above it. These were surrounded by a snare drum, a crash symbol, a high-hat cymbal, and a stool. The drum casings were colored in a sparkling candy-apple red, accented beautifully with dazzling chrome trim.

"Rob! Are you alright?" Pete laughed.

"Now this *is* a real surprise!" Rob whispered hoarsely.

"Go ahead!" Pete said as he helped his friend off of his knees. "Let's hear what you've got to play!" Everyone cheered and applauded as Rob made his way to the stool that sat behind the drums. Rob didn't take his eyes off of the drums for a second. He ran his hands over each part of the kit slowly and very gently.

"You're treating it way too kind!" Gordy shouted. "Aren't you supposed to beat that thing or something?" Everyone laughed, including Rob.

"Speech! Speech! Speech!" Tony called out. Everyone else in the room soon joined Tony in reciting the chant. Rob finally changed his focus from the drums to the friends and family that surrounded him. He held up his hands. The crowd settled down once again.

"Wow!" Rob started. "I never thought that any of this could ever happen to somebody like me. All this...it's so amazing!" Rob paused for a moment thoughtfully before continuing. "A year ago, I just thought of myself as a loser — someone who hung out by himself a lot and always seemed to get into lots of trouble. If someone told me a year ago that I'd have, like, this big party on my next birthday at Meagan's house with a whole bunch of people who actually liked me, I'd think that they were crazy! But a lot has changed in this last year! And the biggest thing to change for me personally was becoming a Christian. It's probably the biggest change for me in my whole life, now that I think about it!"

"I found out that being a Christian has a lot to do with doin' things with other people. I don't think I could be a Christian and still be a loner! I know that Jesus wants me to be doin' things with other people that show that I care about them and love them, just like all you guys are doin' for me right now! So I want to say 'thanks' to all of you all for all of this! The party, the drums, the friends and family — everything! Thanks!" Everyone clapped.

"I want to especially thank my mom for planning this party for me. Thanks, mom!" Rob's mother smiled and waved from her chair near the back wall as the others in the room clapped for her. "And I also want to especially thank the Johnson family too. Mr. and Mrs. Johnson were the ones that first told me about Jesus. They showed me Jesus' love from all the stuff that they done for me *and* my mom this last year. And I want to especially, *especially* thank my best friend, Pete, because it was Pete that helped me almost every day in the real world to live my life the way Jesus asks us to. He never gave up on me, even when I started going back to my old ways!" Pete blushed. "But Jesus must truly live in him," Rob continued, "because no one else has done for me the kinda stuff that he's done for me. He's followin' Jesus for real. Pete's the real deal. So thanks, Pete, for helpin' to get me together with Jesus, and thanks for helpin' me to change my life." Pete, who was still blushing, nodded to Rob in appreciation. Everyone applauded, cheered and whistled for Pete which only made him blush more.

"Don't forget how much you helped me, Rob," Pete spoke up, "Remember, you helped me to practice what I preached, so the 'thanks' goes both ways!" Rob nodded to Pete with a smile.

"I got just one more 'thank you' to give," Rob continued. "And after that, then me, and Becky, and the rest of the band can play for everyone, and then you guys can dance and eat cake and all that fun stuff. I just want to thank God for everything. All of this was possible because of God's love that shows up in all of you. Uh...but I'm still not really good at prayin' out loud in front of a bunch of people, and I don't quite know how to put the feeling of thanks that I'm feelin' for God into a prayer right now. So, I was wonderin'...Pete? Could you...y'know ...do a prayer for all of us?"

"Hmmm," said Pete thoughtfully. "Well, I do know a Psalm from the Bible that may be just the right kind of prayer for this kind of party. It's the last Psalm, number one hundred and fifty. Sometimes when you don't have the exact words to express your thanks and praise to God, you can do it in other ways that we can all appreciate! Even musically!" Rob smiled at him. "Okay," said Pete. "Here it goes..." Pete cleared his throat and bowed his head.

"'Praise the Lord! Praise God in his sanctuary; praise him in his mighty heaven! Praise him for his mighty works; praise his unequaled greatness! Praise him with a blast of the ram's horn; praise him with the lyre and harp! Praise him with the tambourine and dancing; praise him with strings and flutes! Praise him with a clash of cymbals; Praise him with loud clanging cymbals.'"

337

"I'll be happy to do that in just a second!" Rob interrupted lightheartedly. Laughter exploded from the crowd and then drifted off quickly.

"Finish it, Pete!" Mr. Johnson called out.

So Pete finished it: "'Let everything that breathes sing praises to the Lord! Praise the Lord.' **Amen**."

Question:

1) What's *your* real life story about your own adventures with God?

Made in the USA
Charleston, SC
20 November 2015